Measuring Up

Measuring Up

What

Educational

Testing

Really

Tells Us

DANIEL KORETZ

HARVARD UNIVERSITY PRESS

Cambridge, Massachusetts

London, England

2008

Library of Congress Cataloging-in-Publication Data

Koretz, Daniel M.
  Measuring up : what educational testing really tells us / Daniel Koretz.
    p.   cm.
  Includes bibliographical references and index.
  ISBN 978-0-674-02805-0 (cloth : alk. paper)   1. Educational tests and measure-
ments—United States.   2. Test bias—United States.   I. Title.
  LB3051.K667 2008
  371.26—dc22   2007045473

Contents

Measuring Up

Prologue

EDUCATIONAL TESTING is ubiquitous in America, and its importance is hard to overstate. Testing has an enormous impact on the practice of education, and it looms large in the minds of countless families as they decide where to live and whether to use public schools. Tests also have a powerful influence on public debate about many other social concerns, such as economic competitiveness, immigration, and racial and ethnic inequalities. And achievement testing seems reassuringly straightforward and commonsensical: we give students tasks to perform, see how they do on them, and thereby judge how successful they or their schools are.

This apparent simplicity, however, is misleading. Achievement testing is a very complex enterprise, and as a result, test scores are widely misunderstood and misused. And precisely because of the importance given to test scores in our society, those mistakes can have serious consequences. The goal of this book is to help readers understand the complexities inherent in testing, avoid the common mistakes, and be able to interpret test scores reasonably and use tests productively.

Testing has become the subject of intense controversy, and quite a number of polemics have been published in recent years, both pro-testing and anti-testing. This book is not among them. There are ample references to political controversies over testing throughout the book, and I don't shrink from explaining the positions I consider best supported by the evidence. For example, research to date is consistent in showing that high-stakes testing—holding people accountable for improving scores—can produce egregious inflation of scores, and I describe some of that evidence in a later chapter. My goal, however, is not to be an apologist for one position or another. Rather, I want to clarify both the strengths and the limitations of achievement testing. Although scores used without regard for their limitations can badly mislead, scores used carefully can provide valuable information that is unavailable from other sources. To extract the good while avoiding the bad requires knowing something about the complexities of testing, just as using a powerful medication while avoiding harmful side effects requires knowledge and caution. More then a decade ago, Don Stewart, then the president of the College Board—an organization that sponsors the SAT, one of the most widely used and best-known tests in the United States—put it well: he said that in using tests, we need to strike a balance between enthusiasm, on the one hand, and realism and respect for evidence, on the other.

Some of the complexities of achievement testing can seem daunting, even incomprehensible to most users of test scores. The hapless parent or school principal who downloads the technical report for her state's testing program can be excused for being nonplussed when reading, for example, that the results were scaled using a three-parameter logistic item response theory model.

The good news is that these intimidating technical details, while critically important to the construction of tests and the operation of testing programs, are not necessary for understanding the most important principles of testing and the controversies that current testing engenders. At the Harvard Graduate School of Education, we enroll a large number of master's students every year who need to know the basics of educational testing—they need to become informed consumers of test scores and careful users of tests—but don't have the mathematical training, the time, or the need for a traditional mathematical introduction to measurement. Some years ago I prepared a course specifically for these students, designed to give them an understanding of the core principles of measurement and of the current controversies in the field, such as high-stakes testing and the testing of students with disabilities. The course requires no prior mathematical training and includes very little mathematics. That course led to this book.

This book, even more than the course that spawned it, avoids mathematical presentations. It includes no equations and only a few graphs. It does not, however, avoid using technical concepts, such as reliability and measurement error, because one needs to have a grasp of them to understand and make informed judgments about some of the issues that arise in testing. So readers will find some didactic sections scattered throughout the book, sometimes as separate chapters and sometimes not. I have tried to arrange things so that readers so inclined could skim those parts, but I did so reluctantly because that material is important, and I hope every reader will take the time to digest it.

The reader also may find it helpful to know a few conventions I followed in writing this book. Academics pepper their text with citations to support their assertions and to give proper credit to others, but lay readers can find these an annoying distraction. Some citations, however, are necessary, both as a matter of ethics—to give credit to others for their work—and for the occasional reader who wants more detail. Therefore I provide a modest number of citations to give credit or to provide references to sources, but I have made them endnotes to get them out of sight. In contrast, readers may *want* to see the occasional explanatory note, so these are presented as footnotes at the bottom of the relevant page. Technical terms are explained when first introduced.

Chapter 1

If Only It Were So Simple

SEVERAL YEARS AGO, I received a phone call from a total stranger who was about to move into my school district and wanted me to help her identify good schools. She assumed that because of what I do for a living, I ought to know this. I took her question more seriously than she wanted and told her briefly what I would look for, not only as an expert in testing and educational research but also as a parent of two children in school and a former elementary and middle-school teacher. As a first step, I suggested, she should gather as much descriptive information as she could readily obtain to get a notion of which schools she might want to consider. Test scores would be high on my list of descriptive information, but many other things might be important as well, depending on the child: the strength of the school's music or athletic programs, some special curricular emphasis, school size, social heterogeneity, and so on. Then, once she had narrowed down her list far enough (this was a very large district), I said she should visit a few schools that looked promising. A visit would allow her to get a glimpse of the characteristics of the schools, including those that might help account for their test scores. I explained some of the things that I had looked for when I had checked out schools and classrooms for my own children—for example, a high level of student engagement, clear explanations from teachers before students undertook tasks, a level of enthusiastic activity when it was appropriate, and spirited discussion among the students. With both the observations and descriptive information in hand, she would be better able to identify schools that would be a good match for her children.

She was not pleased. She clearly wanted an answer that was uncomplicated and that would entail less work, or at least less ambiguity and complexity. A simple answer is reassuring, especially when both your children's education and a very large amount of money are at stake. (This was in Bethesda, Maryland, where housing prices were outrageously high.)

A few weeks later, I mentioned this conversation to a friend who at the time ran a large testing program. He replied that he received calls of that sort all the time and that few callers wanted his answers either. They wanted something simpler: the names of the schools with the highest test scores, which the callers considered enough to identify the best schools. He told me that in one conversation, he had finally lost his patience when the caller resisted a more reasonable explanation and had told her, "If all you want is high average test scores, tell your realtor that you want to buy into the highest-income neighborhood you can manage. That will buy you the highest average score you can afford."

The home buyer's phone call reflected two misunderstandings of achievement testing: that scores on a single test tell us all we need to know about student achievement, and that this information tells us all we need to know about school quality. Later chapters will explain why neither of these common assumptions is warranted. A third common misconception is that testing is simple and straightforward. Early in his first term as president,

George W. Bush, one of whose signature programs, No Child Left Behind, is built around testing, declared, "A reading comprehension test is a reading comprehension test. And a math test in the fourth grade—there's not many ways you can foul up a test . . . It's pretty easy to 'norm' the results."[1] Whatever one thinks of No Child Left Behind—and there are good arguments both for and against various aspects of it—this claim was entirely wrong: it is all too easy to foul up the design of a test, and it is even easy to foul up in interpreting test scores. And Bush is hardly alone in this mistaken view. A few years ago, a representative of a prominent business group addressed a meeting of the Board on Testing and Assessment of the National Research Council, of which I was then a member. She complained that her bosses—some of the most prominent CEOs in America engaged in education reform—were exasperated because we in the measurement profession kept giving them far more complicated answers than they wanted. I responded that we gave them complex answers because the answers are in fact complex. One of her bosses had been the CEO of a computer company in which I then owned some stock, and I pointed out that my retirement savings would have taken a beating if that particular CEO had been foolish enough to demand only simple answers when his staff confronted him with problems of chip architecture or software design. She did not appear persuaded.

Perhaps testing seems so misleadingly simple because for those of us raised and educated in the United States, standardized testing has been ubiquitous, just a fact of life. We were administered achievement tests in elementary and secondary school. Most of us took tests for admission to postsecondary education, many of us repeatedly. We take pencil-and-paper or computerized tests to obtain our driver's license. Many take licensure examinations for entrance to a trade or a profession. Testing has become a routine part of our vocabulary and our public discourse. For many years,

Parade magazine has featured a regular column by Marilyn vos Savant, who is declared by the magazine to have the highest IQ in the country. Rather than simply saying that Ms. vos Savant is one damned smart person, if indeed she is, the editors use the everyday vocabulary of "IQ"—just one type of a score on one type of standardized test—instead of plain English. The editors of *Parade* have been justifiably confident that their reference to IQ makes their point, even though very few readers have any idea what an IQ test contains or any familiarity with the arguments about what IQ tests actually measure.

The labeling of Ms. vos Savant points to another issue: the rhetorical power of testing. Referencing her IQ score doesn't really add information for the typical reader; it is just another way of saying that she is smart. But it does seem to give the assertion more weight, a patina of scientific credibility. (In this particular case, that patina is ill deserved: the assertion that any one person has the highest intelligence in the country, or the highest achievement as measured by some other test, is absurd for any number of reasons, but that is another story.) We are supposed to believe that her intelligence is not just the opinion of the editors but rather something that science has validated.

Careful testing can in fact give us tremendously valuable information about student achievement that we would otherwise lack—otherwise, why would we do it?—and it does rest on several generations of accumulated scientific research and development. But that is no reason to be uncritical in using information from tests. One need not be a psychometrician to understand the key issues raised by achievement testing and to be an informed user of the information tests provide.

So what are some of the complications that make testing and the interpretation of scores so much less straightforward than most people believe? At first, they may seem discouragingly numerous. About three weeks into the first class I taught at Harvard, a student raised her hand and blurted out, "I am so damned frustrated!" I was taken aback; the course was new and unconventional, and I had no idea how well it would work out. And this student was initially one of the most enthusiastic; if even she was becoming discouraged, I saw trouble in the horizon. I asked her why she was so frustrated, and she answered, "Every day we come here, a few additional simple answers go down the drain. When do we get something to replace them?" Voicing an optimism that I did not yet feel, I told her that over the course of the semester she would cobble together a new understanding of tests, one that would be more complex but much more reasonable and useful. Fortunately, she and her fellow students did. Learning about testing, numerous other students have told me, is a bit like learning a foreign language: daunting at first, but increasingly easy with practice.

Of the many complexities entailed by educational testing, the most fundamental, and the one that is ultimately the root of so many misunderstandings of test scores, is that test scores usually do not provide a direct and complete measure of educational achievement. Rather, they are incomplete measures, proxies for the more comprehensive measures that we would ideally use but that are generally unavailable to us. There are two reasons for the incompleteness of achievement tests. One, stressed by careful developers of standardized tests for more than half a century, is that these tests can measure only a subset of the goals of education. The second is that even in assessing the goals that can be measured well, tests are generally very small samples of behavior that we use to make estimates of students' mastery of very large domains of knowledge and skill. As explained in the following chapters, an achievement test is in many ways like a political poll, in which the opinions of a small number of voters are used to predict the later votes of many, many more people. These facts generate most of the complexities that are explained in this book. At the end of the book, I will offer a variety of suggestions for sensible and productive uses of tests and test scores, many of which ultimately rest on a single principle: don't treat "her score on the test" as a synonym for "what she has learned." A test score is just one indicator of what a student has learned—an exceptionally useful one in many ways, but nonetheless one that is unavoidably incomplete and somewhat error prone.

One sometimes disquieting consequence of the incompleteness of tests is that different tests often provide somewhat inconsistent results. For example, for more than three decades the federal government has funded a large-scale assessment of students nationwide called the National Assessment of Educational Progress, often simply labeled NAEP (pronounced "nape"), which is widely considered the best single barometer of the achievement of the nation's youth. There are actually two NAEP assessments, one (the main NAEP) designed for detailed reporting in any given year, and a second designed to provide the most consistent estimates of long-term trends. Both show that mathematics achievement has been improving in both grade four and grade eight—particularly in the fourth grade, where the increase has been among the most rapid nationwide changes in performance, up or down, ever recorded. But the upward trend in the main NAEP has been markedly faster than the improvement in the long-term-trend NAEP. Why? Because the tests measure mathematics somewhat differently, taking somewhat different samples of behavior from the large domain of mathematics achievement, and the improvement in student performance has varied from one component of mathematics to another. Such discrepancies are commonplace. They need not indicate that anything is "wrong" with either test (although they may); they can arise simply because different tests measure somewhat different samples of knowledge and skills. And these disparities are not a reason to put test scores aside. Rather, they indicate the need to use scores cautiously—for example, by looking at multiple sources of information about performance and by paying little heed to modest differences in scores.

However, there are cases in which a discrepancy between two tests can signal that something is wrong, and in today's world, a particularly important instance can arise in the case of high-stakes testing—that is, when educators, students, or both are held accountable for test scores. When scores have serious consequences, scores on the test that matters often go up far faster than scores on other tests. The experience in Texas during George Bush's tenure as governor provides a good illustration. At that time, the state used the Texas Assessment of Academic Skills (TAAS) to evaluate schools, and high-school students were required to pass this test in order to receive a diploma. Texas students showed dramatically more progress on the TAAS than they did on the National Assessment of Educational Progress.[2] This is not a problem specific to Texas; similar discrepancies have been found in several other states and localities as well. In these cases, the obvious question—addressed in some detail late in this book—is whether scores on the high-stakes test have become an inflated and therefore misleading indicator of what students actually have learned. This question is logically unavoidable, but in practice it is widely ignored even by many people who ought to know better, simply because the problem of score inflation is at best inconvenient and at worse threatening. (The latter is one reason that there are so few studies of this problem. Imagine a researcher approaching a commissioner of education or a state testing director and explaining, "I would like access to your test data to explore whether the score increases you have been reporting to the press and the public are inflated." This is not an appealing prospect.)

Even a single test can provide varying results. Just as polls have a margin of error, so do achievement tests. Students who take more than one form of a test typically obtain different scores.

For example, when students take the SAT college-admissions test more than once, fluctuations in their verbal or math scores of 20 or 30 points from occasion to occasion are common. These arise partly because the test forms, while designed to be equivalent, have different content, and the student may luck out one time or the next. Fluctuations also occur because students have good and bad days: perhaps the student was too nervous to sleep well before the first test or had a stomach ache during the second. Therefore, it makes no sense to place much faith in small differences in scores, and the College Board, the sponsor of the SAT, urges users not to. Small differences in scores are simply not robust enough to be trustworthy. Some state and local testing programs provide information about this margin of error to parents, giving them a report—which I suspect many find perplexing—showing that their child's level of achievement actually lies somewhere in a range around the score she received.

Then there is the problem of figuring out how to report performance on a test. Most of us grew up in a school system with some simple but arbitrary rules for grading tests, such as "90 percent correct gets you an A." But replace a few hard questions with easier ones, or vice versa—and variations of this sort occur even when people try to avoid them—and "90 percent correct" no longer signifies the level of mastery it did before. And in any event, what is an "A"? We know that to obtain a grade of "A" can require much more in one class than in another. Psychometricians therefore have had to create scales for reporting performance on tests. These scales are of many different types. Most readers will have encountered arbitrary numerical scales (for example, the SAT scale, which runs from 200 to 800); norm-referenced scales that compare a student to a distribution of students, perhaps a national distribution (for example, grade equivalents and percentile ranks); and the currently dominant performance standards, which break the entire distribution of performance into just a few bins, based on judgments of what students should be able to do. These various scales have different relationships to raw performance on the test, and therefore they often provide differing views of performance.

Further, sometimes a test does not function as it should. A test may be biased, producing systematically incorrect estimates of the performance of a particular group of students. For example, a mathematics test that requires reading complex text and writing long answers may be biased against immigrant students who are competent in mathematics but have not yet achieved fluency in English. These cases of bias must be distinguished from simple differences in performance that accurately represent achievement. For instance, if poor students in a given city attend inferior schools, a completely unbiased test is likely to give them lower scores because the inferior teaching they received impeded their learning.

These complications do not always have simple, unambiguous resolutions. Years ago, a prominent and very thoughtful education reformer came to a meeting of the National Research Council Board on Testing and Assessment, the same group visited by the disgruntled representative of the business community I mentioned earlier. He requested that the board sponsor a study panel that would generate the optimal design for an assessment program. To his evident annoyance, I responded that this would not be a sensible undertaking because there is no optimal design. Rather, designing a testing program is an exercise in trade-offs and compromise, and a judgment about which compromise is best will depend on specifics, such as the particular uses to which scores will be put. For example, the assessment designs that are best for providing descriptive information about the performance of groups (such as schools, districts, states, or even entire nations) are not suitable for systems in which the performance of individual students must be compared. Adding large, complex, demanding tasks to an assessment may extend the range of skills you can assess, but at the cost of making information about individual students less trustworthy. Any design that offers you gains on one front is likely to impose costs on another, and the task of sensible design entails carefully weighing the inevitable trade-offs.

But few people are involved in constructing or choosing among tests. Most of those who are interested in testing—parents, politicians, citizens concerned about the quality of our schools or the preparation of our workforce—simply want to make sensible use of scores. To what extent is it really necessary for them to confront this welter of complications?

Testing is by its nature a highly technical enterprise that rests on a foundation of complex mathematics, much of which is not generally understood even by quantitative social scientists in other fields. Many of the technical reports posted on the Web by state departments of education and other organizations that sponsor tests confront readers with bewildering technical terms and, in some cases, the even more intimidating mathematics that formalizes them. This creates the unfortunate misapprehension that the principles of testing are beyond the reach of most people. The mathematics is essential for the proper design and operation of testing programs, but one does not need it to understand the fundamental principles that underlie the sensible uses of tests and the reasonable interpretation of test scores.

But the core principals and concepts are truly essential. Without an understanding of validity, reliability, bias, scaling, and standard setting, for example, one cannot fully make sense of the information yielded by tests or find sensible resolutions to the currently bitter controversies about testing in American education. Many people simply dismiss these complexities, treating them as unimportant precisely because they seem technical and esoteric. I suspect this was part of the issue for the delegate from the business group I mentioned earlier. This proclivity to associate the arcane with the unimportant is both ludicrous and pernicious. When we are ill, most of us rely on medical treatments that reflect complex, esoteric knowledge of all manner of physiological and biochemical processes that very few of us understand well, if at all. Yet few of us would tell our doctors that their knowledge, or that of the biomedical researchers who designed the drugs we take, can't possibly be important because, to our uninformed ears, it is arcane. Nor would we dismiss the arcane engineering that goes into modern aircraft control systems or, for that matter, the computers that control our cars. Ignoring the complexities of educational testing leads people to major misunderstandings about the performance of students, schools, and school systems. And while the consequences of these misunderstandings may not seem as dire as airplanes falling from the sky, they are serious enough for children, for their teachers, and for the nation, which relies for its welfare on a well-educated citizenry.

Chapter 2

What *Is* a Test?

ON SEPTEMBER 10, 2004, a Zogby International poll of 1,018 likely voters showed George W. Bush with a 4-percentage-point lead over John Kerry in the presidential election campaign. These results were a reasonably good prediction: Bush's margin when he won two months later was about 2.5 percent.

Polls of this sort are so routine that few people encountering them give much thought to anything but their final results. Occasionally, the polls are substantially wrong—the classic example is Truman versus Dewey in 1948, but a more recent and more dramatic example is the unexpected victory of Hamas in the Palestinian elections of 2005—and these events often generate some discussion about how polls are actually conducted and how it could be that the polls in question were so far off the mark. More often, however, the average newspaper reader pays the workings of polls no heed.

The basic principles underlying polling, however, are fundamental to social science, and they provide a handy way to explain the workings of achievement tests.

Would you have any reason to care how those 1,018 partici-
pants in the Zogby poll voted? In rare cases—in Florida in 2000,
for example—one might indeed worry about the votes of such a
small number of people. In most cases, however, the people sampled for a poll are far too few to affect the outcome of the actual
election. The total number of votes cast in the 2004 election exceeded 121 million, and Bush's margin was more than 3 million
votes. Had all 1,018 of the likely voters polled by Zogby voted for
just one of the two candidates, the change in the final count—
only about 500 votes—would have been too small to notice.

So why should we care about these 1,018 people? Because together they represent the 121 million people we *do* care about,
and the 1,018 allow us to predict—in this case, serviceably well—
the behavior of the larger group. We cannot measure directly the
voting intentions of roughly 121,000,000 people because it would
be prohibitively expensive and time consuming to do so. And
we are not so much interested in the voting intentions of those
121,000,000; we are interested in knowing how they will actually
vote, and no amount of money or effort will tell us that with certainty before Election Day rolls around. Faced with the infea-
sibility of directly measuring what we really care about, we rely
on a more practical proxy measure: we poll a small number of
people about their intentions and use their responses to predict
the unobtainable information that we really want about the entire
population of voters.

Our ability to make this prediction from the results of the poll
depends on several things. It depends on the design of the sample,
which must be carefully chosen to represent the larger population
of likely voters. If Zogby had sampled only individuals in Utah
or, conversely, Massachusetts, the sample would not have been a
good representation of the nation's voters and would have yielded
a misleading prediction. (When I lived in the Washington metropolitan area, we had our own variant of the saying, "As goes Ohio,

so goes the nation." Ours was, "As goes the District of Columbia, so goes Massachusetts.") Pollsters would not make such an obvious mistake, but more subtle errors of sample design, some of which may be unanticipated, can badly bias the results. Accuracy also depends on the way in which survey questions are worded; there is abundant evidence that even seemingly minor changes in the wording of questions can have substantial effects on respondents' answers. For example, one study compared responses to the following pair of questions:

Original question: "What is the average number of days each
  week you have butter?"
Revised question: "The next question is just about butter. Not
  including margarine, what is the average number of
  days each week you have *butter?*"

The questions were given to equivalent groups of respondents. One might think that the clarification in the second question would be unnecessary, but the responses indicated otherwise. Of those asked the original question, 33 percent answered zero days and 23 percent answered seven days. Of the equivalent sample given the revised question, 55 percent answered zero days, and only 9 percent answered seven days.[1]

Finally, accuracy depends on the ability or willingness of respondents to provide the requested information. The sampled individuals may be willing to respond but lack the information requested—as when students are asked about parental income, for example. They may refuse to respond, as I do routinely when market research firms call me at dinnertime. They may respond but provide inaccurate information. Survey researchers worry about what they call "social desirability bias": a tendency for some respondents to provide socially acceptable but inaccurate answers. One might expect this to happen if one asks about undesirable behaviors or attitudes—say, racial bias—but one also finds over-reporting of socially desirable behaviors, attitudes, and status. That this bias can be severe has been well documented for more than half a century. For example, a study published in 1950 documented substantial overreporting of several different types of socially desirable behavior. Thirty-four percent of respondents reported that they had contributed to a specific local charity when they had not, and 13 to 28 percent of respondents claimed to have voted in various elections in which they had not.[2] But when all goes well, the results from a tiny sample provide a reasonable estimate of the findings one would have obtained from the population as a whole. That was true of the Zogby poll.

Educational achievement tests are in many ways analogous to this Zogby poll in that they are a proxy for a better and more comprehensive measure that we cannot obtain. In most cases, the consumer of test scores—a parent learning about the performance of a child, a superintendent looking for strong and weak areas of performance in schools, a politician who wants to criticize schools or bask in the glow of their improvement—wants to draw conclusions about students' mastery of a large range of knowledge and skills. In the case of an end-of-course test, this might be something like mastery of the concepts and skills of basic algebra. In other cases, the range of knowledge might be far broader yet. For example, many states administer mathematics tests that are designed to provide information about the cumulative mastery of mathematics over many grades.

The full range of skills or knowledge about which the test provides an estimate—analogous to the votes of the entire population of voters in the Zogby survey—is generally called the *domain* by those in the trade. Just as it is not feasible for the pollster to obtain information from the entire population, it is not feasible for a test to measure an entire domain exhaustively, because the domains are generally too large. Instead we create an achievement test, which covers a small sample from the domain, just as the pollster selects a small sample from the population. And as in the case of a poll, small size is not the only limitation of the sample we measure. Just as a pollster cannot directly measure later voting behavior, there are some aspects of the goals of education that achievement tests are unable to measure.

The analogy between the Zogby political poll and an achievement test fails in one respect: this particular poll was used to predict something that lay in the future and was therefore necessarily unknowable, while achievement tests are usually (but not always) used to measure what students already know. This difference, however, is more apparent than real. In both cases, a small sample is used to estimate a much larger set: in one case, the behavior of a larger group of people, and in the other, a larger set of knowledge and skills. And in both cases—although for somewhat different reasons—the larger set cannot be directly and comprehensively measured.

The results of an achievement test—the behavior of students in answering a small sample of questions—is used to estimate how students would perform across the entire domain if we were able to measure it directly. In the case of the Zogby poll, we were concerned that the poll results give us an accurate estimate of the later votes of the entire population, but we did not really care about the final votes cast by the few people in the sample. Achievement testing is analogous. We should not be terribly concerned about the performance of students on a specific item on the test (these are called *items* because they need not be written in the form of questions), just as we should not worry about the later voting of a single Zogby respondent. The importance of the test item, like the importance of the survey respondent, lies in the larger set of knowledge and skills that it represents.

The accuracy of the estimates based on a test depends on several factors. Just as the accuracy of a poll depends on careful sampling of individuals, so the accuracy of a test depends on careful sampling of content and skills. For example, if we want to measure the mathematics proficiency of eighth-graders, we need to specify what knowledge and skills we mean by "eighth-grade mathematics." We might decide that this subsumes skills in arithmetic, measurement, plane geometry, basic algebra, and data analysis and statistics, but then we would have to decide *which aspects* of algebra and plane geometry matter and how much weight should be given to each component. Do students need to know the quadratic formula? Eventually, we end up with a detailed map of what the test should include, often called "test specifications" or a "test blueprint," and the developer writes test items that sample from it.

But that is just the beginning. In the same way that the accuracy of a poll depends on often seemingly arcane details about the wording of survey questions, the accuracy of a test score depends on a host of often arcane details about the wording of items, the wording of "distractors" (wrong answers to multiple-choice items), the difficulty of the items, the rubric (criteria and rules) used to score students' work, and so on. And just as the accuracy of a poll depends on respondents' willingness to answer frankly, the accuracy of a test score depends on the attitudes of the test takers—for example, their motivation to perform well. It also depends, as we shall see later, on the behavior of others—in particular, the behavior of teachers. If there are problems with any of these aspects of testing, the results from the small sample of behavior that constitute the test will provide misleading estimates of students' mastery of the larger domain. We will walk away believing that Dewey will beat Truman after all. Or, to be precise, we will believe that Dewey did beat Truman already.

This might be called the *sampling principle* of testing: test scores reflect a small sample of behavior and are valuable only insofar as they support conclusions about the larger domains of interest.

This is perhaps the most fundamental principle of achievement testing. A failure to grasp this principle is at the root of widespread misunderstandings of test scores. It has often led policymakers astray in their efforts to design productive testing and accountability systems. And it has also resulted in uncountable instances of bad test preparation by teachers and others, in which instruction is focused on the small sample actually tested rather than the broader set of skills the mastery of which the test is supposed to signal. Many other key principles of testing, as well as more than a few of the most heated current debates—in particular, the debate about holding teachers accountable for test scores—stem directly from this fact of sampling.

Constructing a hypothetical test will help make this principle, and several other essential principles of testing, concrete. Suppose that you publish a magazine and have decided to hire a few college students as interns to help out. You receive a large number of applicants and have decided that one basis for selecting from among them is the strength of their vocabulary.

How are you going to determine which applicants have particularly strong vocabularies? If you knew the applicants well, you would have some knowledge of their vocabularies based on accumulated experience over many discussions in many contexts. However, if you don't know the applicants, you have little to go on. You might give each a brief interview, but this would likely yield information that is both sparse and inconsistent from one applicant to the next. Your conversations with applicants could go in very different directions, affording some applicants more of an opportunity than others to demonstrate a strong vocabulary. You would not want to pass up a strong applicant because your conversation with her happened to end up focusing on the Red Sox rather than the balance of trade.

One obvious option is to give the applicants a vocabulary test to supplement what you learn about them from other sources, such as your interview. This has several obvious advantages. The test, unlike your interviews, would be designed specifically to elicit information about each applicant's vocabulary. It would also be consistent from applicant to applicant. Each applicant would face the same tasks, and their performance would therefore not be subject to the vagaries of conversation. An applicant who ended up discussing the Sox would take the same test as the applicant who discussed the trade deficit.

This is the reason for *standardization*. People incorrectly use the term *standardized test*—often with opprobrium—to mean all sorts of things: multiple-choice tests, tests designed by commercial firms, and so on. In fact, it means only that the test is uniform. Specifically, it means only that all examinees face the same tasks, administered in the same manner and scored in the same way. The motivation for standardization is simple: to avoid irrelevant factors that might distort comparisons among individuals. If you were to give your applicants tasks that were not standardized, you might mistakenly conclude that those given easier words to define (or whose tests were scored using more lenient standards) had stronger vocabularies. There are disadvantages to standardization as well, particularly for some students with disabilities or limited proficiency in the language of testing, but for the most part, standardized assessments are more likely to provide comparable information than unstandardized ones.

So let's assume that you choose to administer a standardized test of vocabulary and therefore need to construct one. You would then confront a serious difficulty: although many parents may find this fact remarkable in the light of their own experience, the typical adolescent has a huge working vocabulary. One well-regarded recent estimate is that the typical high-school graduate has a working vocabulary of about 11,000 root words, and the typical college graduate about 17,000 root words.[3] Clearly, you are not going to sit the applicants down and ask them about 11,000 or

17,000 words. It isn't even practical to ask them about the subset of these many thousands of words that they may actually need in their work at your magazine. That subset is also too large.

What you would have to do is select a sample of those thousands of words to put into your test. In practice, you can get a reasonably good estimate of the relative strengths of applicants' vocabularies by testing them on a small sample of words, if those words are chosen carefully. Assume in this case you will use forty words, which would not be an unusual number in an actual vocabulary test.

The first key to obtaining useful information from the test then becomes selecting the words to include in the test. Figure 2.1 gives the first three words from each of three word lists from which you might select in constructing your test. The additional words on each of the three lists that are not shown in Figure 2.1 are similar to the three shown in terms of difficulty and frequency of use. Which list would you use? Clearly not list A, which comprises specialized, very rarely used words that few if any of your applicants would know. (Truth be told, I constructed list A by leafing through my unabridged dictionary for words that I did not recollect ever having encountered before. For the curious, *siliculose* is a botanical term that refers to plants that have two-valved seed capsules, such as mustard plants; to *vilipend* is an archaic term meaning to disparage; and the *epimysium* is the outer membrane encasing a muscle.) Because virtually none of your applicants would know the words in list A, the test would be too hard for them. Everyone would receive a score of zero or nearly zero, and that would make the test useless: you would gain no useful information about the relative strengths of their vocabularies.

List B is no better. The odds are high that all of your applicants would know the definitions of *bath*, *travel*, and *carpet*. Everyone would obtain a perfect or nearly perfect score. Once again,

A	B	C
siliculose	bath	feckless
vilipend	travel	disparage
epimysium	carpet	minuscule

FIG. 2.1.   Three words from each of three hypothetical word lists.

you would learn nothing, in this case because the test would be too easy.

Therefore you would construct your test from list C, which comprises words that some applicants would know and others not. You may say that some of these words are not the right difficulty—perhaps *minuscule* is too easy for college students—but that is an empirical question that a careful test author would answer by trying out possible items in a pilot test. You want to end up with a list of words that some applicants but not all can define correctly. There are technical reasons for choosing the specific difficulty range of test items, but for present purposes it is enough to see that you want items of moderate difficulty that some of the students will answer correctly and others incorrectly.

In this example, the sampling principle of testing is clear. You are interested in the applicants' mastery of a large number of words—the domain—but the evidence you have is their mastery of only the small sample included in the test. In this case, the sample is the 40 words on your test, and the domain that sample represents is applicants' working vocabularies, comprising thousands of words. You would have tested perhaps 1 word for each 300 or 400 that the applicants know. It is apparent why performance on the individual items included in this test should not be a focus of concern: the specific 40 words tested don't much matter, because they are a drop in the bucket. What matters is only the estimate they provide of mastery of the larger domain of from which they are sampled.

But is sampling always as serious a problem as it is in this contrived example? There are instances in which it is not. In fact, there are rare cases in which one can test an entire domain, with no sampling at all. For example, I have had students interested in assessing emergent literacy skills in young students. One such skill in alphabetic languages is letter recognition, and there are not a whole lot of letters to learn, so one can easily test students' knowledge of all of them. In this case, the tested content is the domain, not a sample from it.

For the most part, however, the tests that are of interest to policymakers, the press, and the public at large entail substantial sampling because they are designed to measure sizable domains, ranging from knowledge acquired over a year of study in a subject to cumulative mastery of material studied over several years. The Massachusetts Comprehensive Assessment System (MCAS) tests can serve as an example. Students in Massachusetts must attain a passing grade on the tenth-grade mathematics and English language arts tests in order to receive a high school diploma. The tenth-grade mathematics test covers five areas of mathematical knowledge studied over several years of schooling: number sense and operations (which includes arithmetic); numbers, relations, and algebra; geometry; measurement; and data analysis, statistics, and probability. In the spring of 2005, students' scores in mathematics were based on forty-two test items, an average of fewer than nine items for each of the five areas of mathematics. (Additional items contributed to scores for schools but not for students.)[4]

This is obviously a severe degree of sampling, but if certain conditions are met, forty-two items is a large enough sample to provide a good deal of useful information. One requirement is obvious: the items have to be chosen carefully to represent appropriate content, just as Zogby's 1,018 survey respondents had to be selected carefully to represent likely voters. If trigonometry is not included in the mathematics curriculum through the tenth grade, for example, trigonometry items should not be in the tested sample. And two other considerations have already been noted: the importance of standardization and an appropriate level of difficulty.

The question of difficulty requires more discussion because it is at the root of several serious misunderstandings in today's debates about testing. For your vocabulary test, you chose vocabulary words at a moderate level of difficulty because you needed items that *discriminated* between students with large vocabularies and those with small vocabularies. In this context, the term *discriminate* has no negative connotations; it does not imply being unfair to a person or a group. Items and tests that discriminate are simply those that differentiate between students with more of whatever knowledge and skills one wants to measure and those with less. In this case, you want items that are more likely to be answered correctly by students with stronger vocabularies. Items that are too hard or too easy can't discriminate—virtually no applicants will know the meaning of *vilipend*—but items with moderate difficulty may also fail to discriminate if they measure something other than the proficiency the test is designed to assess. Without discriminating items, you would have no basis for using performance on the test to rank applicants in terms of your estimates of their actual vocabularies.

In public debate, psychometricians are often lambasted for searching for discriminating items. One will sometimes hear claims that the use of discriminating items "creates winners and losers" and that designers of certain types of tests have this, rather than accurate measurement, as their goal. However, there is nothing pernicious about choosing discriminating items. Discriminating items are simply needed if one wants to draw inferences about *relative* proficiency. This was clear in the vocabulary example: you chose discriminating items in order to be able to gauge the relative vocabularies of applicants. You did not *create* differences in vocabulary among your applicants by making this choice; you simply made it possible for the test to *reveal* the differences that already existed.

There are other uses for which nondiscriminating items are fine. For example, a teacher may want to know whether her class has mastered a list of spelling words presented in the past week, and in this case she might be happy indeed if the items on her quiz did not discriminate at all—that is, if most students got most of them right. The key is the particular inference the teacher wants to base on test scores. She would have no basis for an inference about relative proficiency if she used nondiscriminating items, but she would have a basis for an inference about mastery of that specific material.

Figuring out when discriminating items are needed is a bit trickier in practice than it may seem at first glance, and a misunderstanding about this point is widespread in the world of educational policy. Many current testing programs are designed in part to determine whether students have reached a set performance standard, such as the "proficient" standard mandated by No Child Left Behind (NCLB). Many politicians and educators argue—incorrectly—that this is analogous to a test of the week's spelling words, in that they are interested only in whether students have mastered what it takes to reach the proficient standard. If they don't want to differentiate among kids beyond distinguishing between those who are or are not proficient, why would they need discriminating items? But even if one were interested only in the binary distinction between proficient and not proficient—which in my experience few people actually are—the complication is that

A	B	C
siliculose	bath	~~feckless~~/parsimonious
vilipend	travel	disparage
epimysium	carpet	minuscule

FIG. 2.2.   Substituting words in a hypothetical word list.

"proficient" is merely an arbitrary point on a continuum of performance; it does not indicate mastery of all of a discrete set of skills. To get reliable information about which kids really have reached proficient status, one needs test items that discriminate well among kids whose mastery is near that level of proficiency. (An even larger issue is deciding where to put the cut score that divides the failures from the "proficient" successes. This is discussed in Chapter 8).

Returning to the vocabulary test: what would have happened if you had chosen words differently, while keeping them at the same level of difficulty and discrimination? Figure 2.1 showed only the first three words in each of three word lists. Those lists, however, could contain hundreds of words of roughly comparable difficulty and frequency of use. You might choose one set of forty from list C, and I might choose another forty from list C. Should we care?

To make this concrete, assume that you selected all three of the words shown in the figure, so your test included *parsimonious, disparage,* and *minuscule.* I happened also to choose the latter two, but I did not choose *parsimonious,* selecting *feckless* instead. This is shown in Figure 2.2. For the sake of discussion, assume that these two words are equally difficult. That is, if we gave items about these two words to a large number of students, the same proportion would answer both items correctly.

What would be the impact of administering my test rather than yours? Over a large enough number of applicants, the average score would not be affected at all, because the two words in question are equally difficult. However, the scores of some individual students *would* be affected. Even among students with comparable vocabularies, some would know *feckless* but not *parsimonious,* and vice versa.

This illustrates *measurement error,* which refers to inconsistency in scores from one measurement to the next. To some degree, the ranking of your student applicants will depend on which words you select from column C, and if you tested applicants repeatedly using different versions of your test, the rankings would vary a little. Almost anyone who has taken college admissions tests or has children or students who have done so is familiar with this. Many students take the SAT or ACT college admissions test more than once, and their scores almost always vary somewhat, even though the tests are constructed carefully to be comparable from one form to the next. One source of this inconsistency in scores is that the authors of the tests select different items for each form, and one form may be slightly more advantageous or disadvantageous than the next for a particular student, even if the forms are equally difficult for all tested students averaged together. Another source of inconsistency is the fluctuation over time that would occur even if the items were the same. Students have good and bad days. For example, a student might sleep well before one test date but be too anxious to sleep well another time. Or the examination room may be overheated one time but not the next. Yet another source of measurement error is inconsistencies in the scoring of students' responses.

This is what is meant by *reliability.* Reliable scores show little inconsistency from one measurement to the next—that is, they contain relatively little measurement error. *Reliability* is often incorrectly used to mean "accurate" or "valid," but it properly refers only to the *consistency* of measurement. A measure can be reliable but inaccurate—such as a scale that consistently reads too high. We are accustomed to highly reliable measurements in many aspects of our lives: for example, when we measure body temperature or the length of a table we are considering buying. Unfortunately, scores on educational tests tend to be much less reliable than these measurements.

So when all is said and done, how justified would you be in drawing conclusions about vocabulary from your small tested sample of words? This is the question of *validity*, which is the single most important criterion for evaluating achievement testing. In public debate, and sometimes in statutes and regulations as well, we find reference to "valid tests," but tests themselves are not valid or invalid. Rather, it is an inference based on test scores that is valid or not. A given test might provide good support for one inference but weak support for another. For example, a well-designed end-of-course exam in statistics might provide good support for inferences about students' mastery of basic statistics but very weak support for conclusions about mastery of mathematics more broadly. Validity is also a continuum: inferences are rarely perfectly valid. The question to ask is *how well supported* the conclusion is. It is hard to contrive an example of an important conclusion about student performance that would be perfectly supported by performance on a test, although it is not hard to come up with some that are not supported at all. Many of the more specific issues addressed in later chapters, such as reliability and test bias, are pieces of the validity puzzle.*

None of the preceding is particularly controversial. The final

---

* Specialists in measurement often use the term *validity* to refer to the effects of a testing program as well as the quality of the inference based on scores, often labeling these effects "consequential validity." While I can only laud the focus on the impact of testing—I have spent more of my career on that issue than most of my peers—I have found that labeling them in this way generally confuses people who are not immersed in the field's jargon. Therefore, as I explain further in Chapter 10, I never use the term *validity* in this book to refer to the impact of testing.

step in the example, however, is contentious indeed. Suppose you are kind enough to share with me your final list of forty words. Or perhaps, to be more realistic, you don't share them but I either see them or somehow figure many of them out. And suppose I intercept every single applicant en route to taking your test, and I give each one a short lesson on the meaning of every word on your test. What would happen to the validity of inferences you might want to base on your test scores?

Clearly, your conclusions about which applicants have stronger vocabularies would now be wrong. Most students would get perfect or nearly perfect scores, regardless of their actual vocabularies. Students who paid attention during my mini-lesson would outscore those who did not, even if their actual vocabularies were weaker. Mastery of the small sample of forty words would no longer represent variations in the students' actual working vocabularies.

But suppose you are not interested in ranking your applicants in terms of the relative strength of their vocabularies but only in knowing whether their vocabularies reach a level that you consider adequate. You will not hire anyone whose vocabulary fails to reach that "adequate" level, and you are unconcerned about differences in vocabulary among those who reach or exceed that level. Inferences of this latter sort are called *absolute* inferences in the trade: you are comparing a student's performance not to the performance of others but rather to an absolute standard. Many of the most important results from current K–12 testing programs, including those used for accountability under No Child Left Behind, are absolute rather than relative inferences. For example, a recent article in the *Washington Post* reported that "in Virginia, fourth-graders made slight gains in both math and reading . . . 39 percent of children are considered proficient in math, compared with 35 percent in 2003."[5] Moreover, NCLB mandates that schools be rewarded and punished on the basis of changes in the percentages of students who reach that one level of performance. How much worse or better than "proficient" one scores, or which of the proficient students have the highest levels of mastery, does not matter for purposes of accountability and in some cases is not even reported.

These absolute inferences are undermined as well by my teaching the applicants your forty words. As a result of my little lesson, the forty words no longer represent the domain of vocabulary. In theory, a student could know no words at all other than the forty and still get a perfect score. In principle, one could teach the forty words, and nothing else, to Koko the gorilla (albeit in sign language), and she could then demonstrate a strong vocabulary on the test. So again, mastery of the little sample would not, under these conditions—in the presence of my lesson to applicants—tell you anything useful about the strength of the applicants' vocabularies, that is, whether they had reached the "adequate" threshold.

Try yet another inference, also very important in current testing programs—this time, that the students' vocabularies have improved as a result of my lesson. In actual practice, inferences of this sort are currently a common defense of spending instructional time on test preparation: people argue that while students may not be learning all of what you want them to learn, at least they are learning something of value. In the case of our example, this too would be clutching at straws. You started by choosing words that are moderate in difficulty. So let's assume that the average applicant knew about half of the words on your test. When I got done with them, they knew all forty, at least for a few days, until they forgot some of them. So as a rough estimate, their vocabularies would have increased by twenty words, from, say, 11,000 words to 11,020, or from 17,000 to 17,020. An improvement, perhaps, but hardly enough to merit comment. There may be cases in which learning what is specifically on the test constitutes substantial improvement, but the general conclusion remains that even inferences about improvement are undermined by certain types of test preparation that focus on the specific sample included in the test.

This last step in the example—teaching students the specific content of the test, or material close enough to it to undermine the representativeness of the test—illustrates the contentious issue of *score inflation,* which refers to increases in scores that do not signal a commensurate increase in proficiency in the domain of interest. My test preparation would have undermined the validity of all of the different inferences about vocabulary one might base on your hypothetical test, except for the essentially useless inference about mastery of the forty words actually included. Inflation of scores in this case did not require any flaw in the test, and it did not require that the test focus on unimportant material. The forty words were fine. My response to those forty words—my form of test preparation—was not. What matters is the inference from the tested sample to proficiency in the domain, and any form of test preparation that weakens that link undermines the validity of conclusions based on scores. In real-world testing programs, issues of score inflation and test preparation are far more complex than this example suggests, and I will return to them in a later chapter to show how severe the problem can be and explain some of the mechanisms that underlie it.

Chapter 3

What We Measure: Just How Good Is the Sample?

IN THE PREVIOUS CHAPTER, I made a passing reference to one important limitation of achievement tests: "Just as a pollster cannot directly measure later voting behavior, there are some aspects of the goals of education that achievement tests are unable to measure." This assertion sets the teeth of many education critics on edge and often earns whoever utters it the label "anti-testing" or "anti-accountability." Tests measure what is important, their argument goes, and those who focus on other "goals" are softies.

These critics are not entirely wrong. Some people who make this claim about the limitations of testing are in fact opponents of standardized testing, and many oppose externally imposed accountability for schools. But this is a red herring. One does not need to be an opponent of either testing or educational accountability—I am not—to recognize this limitation of testing, and ignoring it is a recipe for trouble.

When Richard Nixon made overtures to China, pundits were nearly unanimous in saying that he was politically able to do so only because of his record as a foreign-policy conservative. By a similar logic, a good vantage point from which to examine this limitation of testing is a currently obscure paper published more than half a century ago by E. F. Lindquist of the University of Iowa, unappealingly entitled "Preliminary Considerations in Objective Test Construction."[1] Whatever one might say of Lindquist, no one could ever accuse him of being anti-testing. In fact, it would be hard to think of anyone who did more to foster the development and use of standardized achievement tests than he. Lindquist spent his entire, prolific career in the field and was truly one of the progenitors of American achievement testing. While few outside of the profession recognize his name, some of the products of his work are household terms. He was one of the developers of the Iowa Tests of Basic Skills (ITBS), one of the oldest standardized achievement tests for the elementary and secondary grades; the Iowa Tests of Educational Development, a much less commonly used high-school achievement test battery; the ACT college admissions test; the GED high-school graduation equivalency test; and the original National Merit Scholarship Qualifying Test. In addition, he and his colleagues invented the first optical scanner for scoring tests—an innovation that greatly speeded the scoring of tests and thereby contributed to an enormous expansion of standardized testing in the 1950s and 1960s. All of which is to say that we can safely lay the distracting anti-testing label aside in considering Lindquist's arguments.

Lindquist's paper is a good starting point for other reasons as well. In it, he offers one of the best explanations of standardized testing extant, and he was remarkably prescient in anticipating controversies that engulfed the world of educational policy decades after he wrote. In fact, to those newly immersed in testing, encountering Lindquist's paper can be a tad disconcerting for this reason. One student of mine, a former teacher who had thought deeply about testing for years before starting his graduate study, read Lindquist's paper at the end of my class and then sent me an e-mail in which he wrote: "(1) Why haven't I read this before? (2) I don't know whether to be cheered or disheartened by this. (3) This was written 20 years before I was born. Is there anything left for me to do? (4) Didn't anybody read this? I find it hard to believe that we've really made any progress in these areas that he writes about." His wife added that Lindquist needed a blog.

Lindquist made precisely the argument with which I started this chapter—that the goals of education are diverse, and that only some of these goals are amenable to standardized testing. First, he said that while we can easily test to find out whether a student has learned some types of knowledge and certain particular skills, some other types of skills are far more difficult to test. A currently important example might be the ability to design and implement a scientific experiment. Yet more difficult to measure are some of the dispositions and abilities that many of us would want schools to foster, such as an interest in learning (students will need to continue to learn throughout their lives), an ability to apply knowledge gained in school productively in later work, and so on.

This does not imply, as some critics of testing would have you believe, that standardized tests can measure only relatively unimportant things. The evidence shows unambiguously that standardized tests can measure a great deal that is of value, and clearly Lindquist believed this. But Lindquist was warning us that however valuable the information from an achievement test, it remains necessarily incomplete, and some of what it omits is very important. This warning has been repeated many times over the intervening half century by others in the field. For example, a recent ITBS manual advises school administrators explicitly to treat test scores as specialized information that is a supplement to, not a replacement for, other information about students' performance. And for the same reason, it warns that it is inappropriate to use a score from a single test, without additional information, to assign students to special education, to hold students back, to screen students for first-time enrollment, to evaluate the effectiveness of an entire educational system, or to identify the "best" teachers or schools.[2] And, again, this is not the position of anti-testing advocates; it is the advice of the authors of one of the best-known achievement tests in America. Unfortunately, the warning that test scores, however useful, provide limited information has been widely ignored—as we shall see, even more so in recent years, as test scores have increasingly come to stand alone as a summary measure of the achievement of students and the performance of schools.

Second, Lindquist argued that even many of the goals of schooling that are amenable to standardized testing can be assessed only in a less direct fashion than we would like. Many of the objectives that are the focus of daily attention for teachers and students are just proxies for the ultimate goals of education because those ultimate goals are too general and too remote from the decisions that have to be made continually in a classroom. For example, why do we teach students algebra? One reason, at least in my view, is to teach students how to reason algebraically so that they can apply this reasoning to the vast array of circumstances outside of school to which it is relevant. This sort of very general goal, however, is remote from decisions about the algebra content to be taught in a given middle school this Thursday morning. Once it has been decided that students should study algebra, curriculum designers and teachers must make a large number of specific decisions about what algebra to teach. For example, do students learn to factor quadratic equations? Many considerations shape these decisions, not just a subject's possible utility in a wide range of work-related and other contexts years later.

An anecdote may clarify the difference between learning content specified in a curriculum and later application of that knowledge. Many years ago, I had Sunday brunch in Manhattan with three New Yorkers. All were highly educated, and all had taken at least one or two semesters of mathematics beyond high school. In my experience, New York natives make their way about town in part by drawing on a prodigious knowledge of the location of various landmarks, such as the original Barnes and Noble store on Fifth Avenue. That Sunday morning, I found to my surprise that none of the three New Yorkers could figure out the location of the restaurant where we were to have brunch. It was on one of the main avenues, and they knew the address, but they could not figure out the cross street. I suggested that the problem might turn out to be a very simple one. I asked if they knew where the addresses on the avenues in that part of Manhattan reached zero and, if so, whether they reached zero at the same street. They quickly agreed that they did and gave me the name of the cross street. I then asked if the addresses increased at the same rate on these avenues, and if so, at what rate. That is, how many numbers did the addresses increase with each cross street? They were quite certain that the rate was the same, but it took a little more work to figure out what it was. Using a few landmarks they knew (including the original Barnes and Noble store), they figured out the rate for a couple of avenues. The rates were the same. At that point, they had the answer, although they had not yet realized it. The problem was a simple linear equation in one variable, like the ones they had studied in middle school—that is, $y = a + bx$, and they had figured out both a, the intercept (the cross street where addresses reached zero), and b (the slope, the rate at which the addresses increased). As you might imagine, they were a bit taken aback when I explained this and gave them the solution. All three were competent in dealing with algebra much more complex than this, but they had not developed the habit of thinking of real-world problems in terms of the mathematics they had learned in the classroom.

Now, it is hard to argue that being able to use algebra to locate a restaurant for Sunday brunch is the kind of educational outcome over which we ought to lose sleep, but both the ability and the inclination to apply the knowledge and skills learned in school to later endeavors certainly is an important goal. We don't put students in school simply to do well while they are there. We put them in school because we think it benefits both them and society as a whole—to make them more successful in advanced study, more successful in the world of work, and better citizens, and to enable them to manifest their own potential and lead fuller lives.

Therefore, Lindquist argued, in the ideal world we would assess achievement by measuring the ultimate goals of education. He wrote: "The only perfectly valid measure of the attainment of an educational objective would be one based on direct observation of the natural behavior of . . . individuals. . . . Direct measurement is that based on a sample from the natural, or criterion, behavior . . . for each individual."[3] Thus, for example, if we wanted to know whether schools successfully imparted the skills and dispositions needed to use algebra successfully in later work, we would go observe students later in life to see whether they used algebra when appropriate and whether they were successful in their applications of it.

But this sort of measurement is clearly impractical, Lindquist maintained, for many reasons. The criterion is delayed, for one. We really can't afford to wait a decade or two to find out whether this year's eighth-graders can use algebra in their adult work. Even if we were to wait a decade or two, the criterion behaviors—in this case, applying algebra successfully when appropriate—are often infrequent. I use algebra often; most of you probably don't, so an observer would have to watch you for a long time to learn whether you had acquired these skills and dispositions. And even if we were willing to wait for these outcomes to arise, it would be too costly in both time and effort to measure achievement this way. Moreover, some of the criteria—some dispositions, for example—are not directly observable.

These reasons may seem obvious, but Lindquist added two others that are less apparent, both of which have profound implications for testing and led directly to the particular form that the ITBS and most other standardized achievement tests of that era took. First, he pointed out that naturally occurring samples of behavior are not comparable. For example, suppose that I used a bit of algebra this morning, while a friend of mine, who is the dean of a law school, did not. Does that indicate that I successfully acquired more of this set of dispositions and skills than the dean did? That's not an unreasonable guess; after all, people who are uncomfortable with mathematics or not particularly successful at it are much less likely to pick psychometrics than, say, law as a profession. But while this may seem like a sensible guess it is not a safe one, and in this particular case, it is entirely wrong: the dean was a mathematics major through his four undergraduate years at a particularly demanding college. So how do we explain the hypothetical fact that I used algebra and the dean did not? He and I face different demands at work: I often need to deal with algebra, and he rarely does. From simply observing of the two of us at work, you would not be certain which of several explanations is correct—that is, whether the dean uses algebra less because he is not inclined to, because he does not do it well, or because his work simply does not call for it. In Lindquist's terms, our work environments are not comparable, and therefore our behavior—whether or not we use algebra—does not necessarily mean the same thing about achievement for both of us.

Second, Lindquist noted that some criterion behaviors are complex, requiring a variety of skills and knowledge. In such cases, if a person performed poorly on one of these criterion behaviors, one would not know why. Of the several things one needs to know to perform the task well, which does the unsuccessful person not understand? Of the several necessary skills, which does the person lack? And, critically important for Lindquist's view of the role of achievement testing: if one cannot identify the reason for poor performance, how can one improve instruction in response?

Lindquist then spelled out several implications of this reasoning for achievement testing. First, a test author usually has to focus on the proximate goals of educators, even if these are only proxies for the ultimate social goals of education. In Lindquist's view, this means focusing primarily on the curriculum. In the current jargon, this translates as "aligning the test with standards," but the basic idea is the same. Second, since we cannot wait around for years to see if a behavior occurs, we have to do something to elicit that behavior now. That something is the test. Third, to avoid the problem of confusing differences in knowledge and skills with differences in the people's environments (mine and that of my friend, the dean of a law school), we have to put all test-takers in the same environment when we elicit the behaviors that we will measure. This means that we have to *standardize* the test, making it the same for all students.

This much is relatively uncontroversial. True, *standardized test* is a term often used disparagingly in current debate, but as I explained in the previous chapter, that often reflects a misunderstanding of the term rather than an objection to standardization. Almost all large-scale achievement tests are standardized, no matter what they include and what form they take, and most teachers even attempt to standardize their own classroom assessments for their own students.

Two other implications of Lindquist's reasoning, however, are controversial and have if anything become more so in recent decades. First, to help guide instruction, Lindquist wanted as much as practical to isolate specific knowledge and skills. In his view, this required designing tests to include tasks that focus narrowly on these specifics. For example, Lindquist would have argued that if you want to determine whether third-grade students can manage subtraction with carrying, you give them problems that require subtraction with carrying but that entail as few ancillary skills as possible. You would not embed that skill in complex text, because then a student might fail to solve the problem either for want of these arithmetic skills or because of poor reading, and it would be hard to know which. This principle is still reflected in the design of some tests, but in other cases, reformers and test developers have deliberately moved in the opposite direction, attempting to create test items that present complex, "authentic" tasks more similar to those students might encounter out of school. Both sides in this argument are both right and wrong: there are advantages and disadvantages to both ways of designing tests. This is one of the many cases in which the designing of tests entails compromises, trade-offs between competing goals.

Finally, Lindquist argued that the interpretation of performance on tests should reflect their necessary and systematic incompleteness. That is, one should see a test score as a measure of how students can do on one particular and important but limited slice of the outcomes we want schools to produce. Therefore, one should ideally use test scores as complements to other information about students' achievement. That other information will have strengths and weaknesses different from those of the test scores. One such source of information is that gleaned by teachers in the course of their own instruction and classroom testing. An astute teacher can observe many things that are difficult to test, but her judgments lack the standardization that test scores offer and are therefore much less comparable from one setting to another. For example, we know that teachers' grading is on average much more lenient in high-poverty schools than in low-poverty schools. By assembling information from several sources that have

different strengths and weaknesses, we can obtain a more complete view of what students know and can do.

Lindquist's views on this last issue are still reflected in the ad-
monitions of some current experts in measurement. Here again,
the ITBS manual noted earlier serves as an example: it warns administrators not to use the scores alone as a summary evaluation
of a school or program.[4]

Is Lindquist's advice actually followed in practice? In some
quarters, yes. This is precisely what college admissions officers are
doing when they conduct a "holistic" review of applicants, considering not only SAT or ACT scores but also grades, personal statements, persistence in extracurricular activities, and so on. Colleges
tend to be quite secretive about their admissions process; one
long-time admissions director from a highly selective college (no,
not Harvard) once told me that his policy was to reveal to each
constituency precisely as little as they needed to know about what
his office did. I can tell you, however, that our selection of applicants at the Harvard Graduate School of Education is consistent
with Lindquist's advice. Members of the admissions committees
on which I have sat treat any single measure, including Graduate
Record Examination (GRE) scores, as far from complete or sufficient. The committees have tried to assemble an overall view
from all the data at hand, often debating how to interpret inconsistencies among them (such as markedly higher grades than
scores, or vice versa).

Unfortunately, this is more the exception than the rule, and
in much of the testing that now dominates K–12 education,
Lindquist's advice that test scores must be seen as incomplete
measures is widely ignored. The more important tests have become as a means of monitoring schools and holding them
accountable, the farther we have strayed from Lindquist's advice.
Scores on a single test are now routinely used as if they were a

comprehensive summary of what students know or what schools produce. It is ironic and unfortunate that as testing has become more central to American education, we have strayed ever farther from the astute advice given so long ago by one of the nation's most important and effective proponents of standardized testing.

Chapter 4

The Evolution of
American Testing

DURING THE LATE 1990S, children of families that moved a few miles in either direction across the Potomac River were confronted with dramatically different testing programs in their schools. The Maryland program in effect at that time, the Maryland School Performance Assessment Program (MSPAP), comprised only large performance tasks, all of which required students to write out their answers, and some of which entailed group activities, hands-on manipulation of apparatus, and work carried out over a period of several days. On the other side of the river, the Virginia schools used multiple-choice tests. The explanations of what these tests were designed to measure—called standards of learning (SOLs) in Virginia and learning outcomes in Maryland—were also strikingly different: Virginia's SOLs tended to be far more detailed and specific than Maryland's learning outcomes. The contrast between Maryland and Virginia was particularly extreme, but the pattern was not: the details of testing programs vary markedly from state to state and even, to a lesser degree, from locality to locality within some states.

This diversity notwithstanding, most large-scale testing programs in the United States share several fundamental characteristics. Almost all are "external" tests, that is, tests mandated by agencies outside of the school. Almost all state education agencies now impose tests on public schools, and many local districts add additional ones. Virtually all of the programs use standardized tests, which means that the content, administration, and scoring of the tests are, at least in the ideal, uniform from one child or school to another. Many tests are intended to monitor the performance of entire schools and states, and in particular to measure change in their performance over time. Most have high stakes—substantial consequences—for educators, students, or both. These characteristics of testing programs have become so commonplace that few of us pay them much heed.

But the nature of educational testing has undergone dramatic changes in recent decades, and many of the features we take for granted now are really quite new. Most important, there has been a fundamental change in the primary functions of large-scale achievement testing, with accountability gradually superseding diagnosis of the strengths and weaknesses of individual students' learning. This shift in how tests are used has been accompanied by changes in the types of conclusions test scores are used to support. Inferences about individual students remain important—indeed, in many states and localities, these conclusions have much more serious consequences than they did three or four decades ago—but in many cases, conclusions about the performance of groups, in particular the performance of schools and districts, are far more consequential. Conclusions about achievement at any given time have given way to inferences about changes in performance over time, particularly changes in the aggregate performance of schools and districts. To a substantial degree, traditional methods for reporting performance on tests, many of which compared a student's performance with the performance of other students, have given way to methods that compare students' results with expectations set by policymakers or others. The format of large-scale tests has also changed, with less reliance on traditional multiple-choice items.

Large-scale group achievement tests date back to at least the 1840s in the United States, and at least one current testing program, the New York State Regents Examination program, dates back to the latter half of the nineteenth century. For our purposes, however, it is sufficient to look back roughly half a century, to the 1950s.

Readers as old as I will remember the 1950s as an era of low-stakes testing—that is, testing that rarely had serious consequences. Few states imposed testing programs, but many school districts purchased achievement tests from commercial publishers and administered them annually. The district in which I attended school, Syracuse, New York, administered the Iowa Tests of Basic Skills, which was one of five commercially published tests that dominated achievement testing in that era. These five tests were standardized. They were largely or entirely multiple choice, which permitted testing of a substantial amount of content within a short time, kept costs down, and allowed for perfectly consistent scoring by machine.

The ITBS and other similar tests that dominated achievement testing in my youth—and that are still widely used today, albeit with much more competition from newer tests that have since become popular—were originally designed primarily for diagnostic purposes, to help teachers and administrators identify relative strengths and weaknesses in their students' achievement. They were also intended to identify areas of strength and weakness within schools and school districts, in order to facilitate improved instruction. However, they were not intended to provide summary evaluations of the performance of schools, districts, states, or nations, or to hold educators accountable.

These tests were not treated as trivial, but in most instances students and teachers did not stand to suffer any dire consequences or reap any great rewards as a result of the scores. There were, however, some exceptions. For students intending to compete for admission to selective colleges and universities, admissions tests such as the SAT (then the Scholastic Aptitude Test, briefly the Scholastic Assessment Test, and now just the SAT) were relatively high-stakes tests, although the pervasive frenzy of preparation courses for these tests that engulfed my children's entire cohort decades later had yet to appear. Achievement and other tests, including IQ tests in some jurisdictions, were also high-stakes propositions for students on the cusp of assignment to special education or other special placements. For most of us, however, and for most of our teachers, the achievement testing we encountered before college-admissions testing was not cause for any great anxiety.

Typically, these tests broke achievement into many small pieces, and their current editions still do. For example, a recent edition of the ITBS for middle-school students broke operations with fractions, decimals, and percents into four different categories of test items, including "compare and order" and "apply ratio and proportion in problem solving."[1] This fragmentation of performance has more recently been disparaged by some critics who argue for embedding skills in larger, more realistic tasks, but the purpose of breaking down performance into discrete skills was straightforward. It was Lindquist's argument, explained in the previous chapter: if one breaks skills and knowledge into small pieces, one can more easily ascertain which specific skills contribute to students' weaknesses and thus help educators improve their teaching. For example, if we can pinpoint the specific missing skills that cause students to perform poorly on problems with fractions, a teacher or a school administrator may be able to improve the teaching of those particular skills.

The tests most widely used in the 1950s were *norm-referenced tests* (often labeled NRTs). A norm-referenced test is simply one on which performance is reported by comparison with a distribution of scores in some reference group. The standards for comparison are called *norms,* and the group in which the norms are obtained is generally called a "norm group" or "standardization sample." For example, the parent of a student administered an NRT might receive a report such as this: "Mark's score in reading placed him at the 60th percentile rank nationally," which means that 60 percent of students in a nationally representative sample of students scored lower than Mark.

The word *norms* often causes confusion because it is used with precisely the opposite meaning in economics. In that field, "normative economics" refers to studies that entail evaluative judgments, while value-free studies are labeled "positive economics." In contrast, in measurement, norms have nothing whatever to do with values. Norms are simply a distribution of performance used as a standard of comparison to give meaning to scores. Indeed, the fact that norm-referenced reporting is value-free and purely descriptive led to its falling into disfavor among many educators and policymakers in recent years. I return to this in discussing the alternative, performance standards, in Chapter 8.

While the norm group is often a national sample of students, it can be any useful comparison group. For example, the average for a school can be compared with a national distribution of school averages, and performance in a particular type of school—say, Catholic schools or schools serving low-income students—can be compared to the distribution of performance in similar schools. Norm groups can even comprise states or countries, and norm-referenced reporting can be used with any tests that show variations in performance. For example, the periodic international comparisons of student performance that are covered extensively by the press, such as the Trends in International Mathematics and Science Study (TIMSS), use country norms: the level of each nation's performance is clarified by comparing it with the distribution of performance in other participating countries. In the absence of these norms, it is hard to know what to make of the U.S. average score of 504 in eighth-grade mathematics. Knowing that the average scores were similar in Australia, New Zealand, Scotland, and Sweden, but far higher in Korea, Taiwan, and Singapore, helps us make sense of the U.S. results.[2] (A few key findings of the international studies are described in the following chapter.)

We use norm-referenced reporting routinely, often without giving it any thought, to make sense of all manner of information in our lives. How do I know whether my car, which gets about thirty-two miles per gallon on the highway, is efficient? By comparison with my neighbor's SUV, which gets about half that, and a good friend's Prius, which gets about half again as much—or by comparison with the more extensive norms one can get from *Consumer Reports* or the EPA's estimates. How do we know whether a high-school student who runs a mile in a bit over four minutes is a star? Norms again. How do we know to commiserate when a colleague announces that her trip from DC to Chicago took her eight hours door to door? Because as bad as air travel has become, we know that eight hours is unusually long. Why do newspaper writers always get space from their editors for stories about international assessments, such as TIMSS? Because country norms—in particular, how we stack up against the highest-performing countries, such as Singapore and Japan—give readers a way to judge the relative adequacy of American performance that they would be hard-pressed to evaluate otherwise. (Why it seems newsworthy that we scored lower than Singapore but not newsworthy that we matched Australia, Sweden, and England and outscored Norway—in this case, all results from the 2003 iteration of TIMSS—is an interesting question about which I can claim no expertise.) In each case, we use norms to make sense of quantitative information that otherwise would be hard to interpret.

Nonetheless, in many quarters, norm-referenced reporting of performance on tests has an undeservedly bad name. There seem to be three reasons for this. The first is simple lack of knowledge. Many people erroneously believe that "norm-referenced" refers to something other than the way in which results are reported—for example, something about the content of the test or the format (multiple choice). If they dislike one of these other things—for example, if they find multiple-choice testing objectionable—they mistakenly criticize norm-referenced testing instead.

The second basis for criticism of NRTs is a notion that norm-referenced reporting, rather than providing a clear statement of whether performance lives up to someone's expectations, predisposes people to accept the status quo. "Above average" sounds good, the argument goes, but if the average performance is well below expectations, some performance that is above the average may nonetheless be unacceptable. This is an oversimplification. It is true that norm-referenced reporting does not necessarily provide information about whether performance has reached reasonable expectations, but as the examples above show, it is often useful—indeed sometimes essential—for precisely that purpose. Moreover, norm-referenced reporting can be paired with other forms of reporting that directly compare performance with expectations, such as standards-based reporting (discussed below). Almost all states now report student performance in comparison with expectations. For example, public reports typically show the percentage of students in a school who reach a performance standard labeled "proficient." But because they are so useful, norm-referenced results are sometimes reported alongside them: for instance, the percentage reaching "proficient" in a given school will be compared with the percentage statewide, so that parents and the press can see whether that school's performance is atypically high or low.

A third argument against NRTs reflects a widespread misunderstanding: that norm-referenced testing actually contributes to variations in student performance. It is not always clear whether the critics mean to imply that NRTs create an illusion of variation or exaggerate variation that is really there. During a *Talk of the Nation* segment broadcast on National Public Radio from the Harvard Graduate School of Education in March 2002, Jeff Howard, a social psychologist who is a prominent advocate for higher educational standards, made the following assertion: "Norm-reference testing, which a lot of us in the audience grew up on, create[s] winners and losers. You got the top decile, you got your bottom decile, you got your average and above-average. They are designed to designate winners and losers."[3] This is one of the most fundamental misconceptions in the current debate about testing. Tests may "designate" winners and losers, but they don't *create* them. There simply *are* winners and losers. Anywhere you look in the world, even in much more equitable societies, there is enormous variation in how well students perform. For example, if you look at tests of eighth-grade mathematics, you find that the total variation in student achievement in the United States is similar to that in Japan—a more socially homogenous society in which there is no tracking by ability through the eighth grade.[4] If you choose not to measure that variation then you won't see it, but it is there regardless. We have seen this already in Chapter 2: the vocabulary test did not *cause* some students to know fewer words than others. It simply helped ascertain who knew more, and who less. For other purposes, you might choose not to rank students, and you might therefore not give them a test designed to display all variations in performance, but those variations would be there nonetheless. The tree really does make noise when it falls, even if no one is there to hear it.

Similarly, when critics use "standardized test" as a term of opprobrium—as they frequently do—it is not always clear what they are actually complaining about. The term is misused to denote all manner of things: norm-referenced tests; tests comprising specific types of tasks (in particular, multiple-choice tests); external tests imposed on schools by outside agencies; and tests developed by commercial publishers or others for a national audience, rather than by individual states or districts. These uses of the term are red herrings, one and all. One can certainly find standardized tests with these attributes; for example, the ITBS remains a norm-referenced, multiple-choice, external test developed by a university research group and marketed nationally by a major publisher. However, a test can be standardized without having any of these attributes. A test that requires students to perform hands-on science experiments can be standardized, as can an assessment that is reported in terms of expectations for performance rather than norms, so long as the tasks, administration, and scoring are uniform. In fact, almost all large-scale achievement and admissions testing programs used in the United States over the past half century have been standardized tests. An exception, rare in large-scale testing programs, are so-called portfolio assessments, in which students compile for later evaluation a collection of products generated in the course of regular classroom work. A few states, for example, Vermont and Kentucky, have implemented portfolio assessments in recent decades. In these programs, neither the tasks nor the administrative conditions under which the work was produced were standardized, although the scoring was.

The common regime of low-stakes, diagnostic, norm-referenced achievement testing began to change, initially very slowly, in the 1960s. Until then, the use of test scores to monitor the performance of education systems was for the most part limited to local districts that chose to monitor the performance of their own schools. In the 1960s, two actions by the federal government began to change this. In 1965 Congress enacted the Elementary and Secondary Education Act (ESEA) of 1965, which established the Title I compensatory education program—the precursor of today's No Child Left Behind—to improve the performance of students in low-income schools. This marked the first major involvement of the federal government in funding and directing general elementary and secondary education. The law also mandated evaluation of the Title I program (the first time that federal legislation establishing a major social program required a formal program evaluation). In 1974 Congress established the Title I Evaluation and Reporting System (TIERS), which based required evaluations of Title I programs on students' scores on standardized, norm-referenced achievement tests.

In an unrelated action late in the 1960s, the federal government established the National Assessment of Educational Progress, a periodic assessment of nationally representative samples of students. NAEP has evolved in many ways since its inception; for example, in 1990 it was modified to provide the frequent comparisons among states—a form of norm-referenced reporting—that now receive prominent attention in the press. At the outset, however, NAEP was much more low-key. It provided information about the nation as a whole, regions of the country, and major subgroups of the population of young people (such as racial groups). But it was deliberately designed to be incapable of providing data at the state and district levels, where most decisions are made, so it was not useful for accountability. It was intended only to provide the public and policymakers with a description of student achievement and information about trends in performance over time.

Neither NAEP nor TIERS imposed consequences on students or teachers based on test results. Nonetheless, in retrospect it seems that these two federal programs marked the onset of a sea change in educational testing in the United States. They signified the beginning of a fundamental shift in the goals of testing, from diagnosis and local evaluation to large-scale monitoring of performance and, ultimately, to test-based accountability.[5]

The next step in this evolution—the minimum-competency

testing movement—was not long in coming. The first statewide minimum-competency testing program was created in 1971, and by the end of the decade there were programs in place in thirty-five states. Minimum-competency testing was designed to ensure that all students reached an acceptable minimal level of mastery of basic skills. Most minimum-competency tests were exit exams, tests on which students had to exceed a specified score, often called a *cut score*, in order to obtain a high school diploma. A smaller number of programs used cut scores on these tests as "promotional gates," that is, as requirements students had to meet for promotion between grades.[6] As their name implies, these tests were typically easy, and the cut scores established on them were low. Even though a few of these programs exist today—for example, as I write, New York City and Chicago use promotional-gate tests—states' use of minimum-competency testing waned during the 1980s.

Despite its brief lifespan, the minimum-competency testing movement had at least four important and lasting effects on large-scale achievement testing in the United States. First, and perhaps most obvious, it was another major step in the direction of using tests for accountability. For the first time since World War II, students in the majority of states were held directly accountable for their performance on a test, and while the standards were sufficiently low that only a modest percentage of students failed, the consequences for those who did were severe. Second, the movement initiated a dramatic increase in the number of states with mandated, statewide testing programs, a growth that continued after minimum-competency tests themselves fell out of favor. Although some states, such as New York, had long-standing testing programs, before the 1970s most states did not. By the end of the 1970s, 60 percent had statewide, mandatory testing programs, and twenty years later almost all did.

Third, the minimum-competency testing movement marked

the beginning of a shift toward reporting student performance in comparison with expectations rather than norms. These testing programs typically employed *criterion-referenced tests* (CRTs), performance on which is reported in terms of how well each student has mastered some established body of knowledge and skill (the criterion), not by comparison with other students. In practice, states and localities using CRTs usually established a cut score for performance—a single score that constituted a passing level on the test, like the scores on minimum-competency tests required for graduation. Norm-referenced reporting has since ebbed and flowed, but criterion-referenced testing with cut scores has persisted and, as I discuss below, is now required by federal law, albeit under a different name.

Less obvious but of even greater significance, the fourth lasting effect of minimum-competency testing was a fundamental change in the way tests are used to improve instruction. The idea behind traditional achievement tests, such as the ITBS, was that standardized tests should improve instruction by providing educators and parents with useful information they would otherwise lack. But the expectation motivating the minimum-competency testing movement was that instruction would be improved by holding someone—in this case, students, but it could also be educators—directly accountable for performance on tests. This deceptively commonsensical notion went by the name of "measurement-driven instruction."

The shift from using tests for information to holding students or educators directly accountable for scores is beyond a doubt the single most important change in testing in the past half century. Test-based accountability has taken varying forms from place to place and from time to time over the past thirty years, but the basic principle of shaping educational practice by means of accountability for test scores has grown only more central to educational policy in the United States (and in many other nations as well). It is not an exaggeration to say that it is now the cornerstone of American education policy. This trend culminated in the enactment of the No Child Left Behind Act in 2001, but there are a few additional important steps to document on the way there.

During the 1980s, the importance of testing was ratcheted up even further. This was an era of intense concern about the adequacy of American education. There was widespread discussion of discouraging evidence from achievement tests: a nationwide decline in test scores, particularly on the SAT, during the 1960s and 1970s; performance on NAEP that many considered inadequate; and international comparisons showing that U.S. achievement scores were lower than those in some other countries. These concerns led to the publication of the highly influential report *A Nation at Risk* and a nationwide surge in education reform known at the time simply as "the education reform movement."[7] The reforms were marked by an increased reliance on testing, a shift away from minimum-competency tests to harder tests, and a change in the consequences attached to scores. Although sanctions for individual students continued in some places (for example, in Indiana and Texas), the 1980s saw a shift toward sanctions for educators and schools, such as policies that permitted state agencies to take over the management of schools or districts that performed poorly on tests. A number of states, including California and Indiana, experimented with offering financial rewards to schools for strong test scores. At the time, these policies were considered revolutionary; ten or twelve years later, they had become commonplace.

The late 1980s also brought us the first public discussion of exaggerated scores on high-stakes tests. John Cannell, a physician in West Virginia, was perplexed by the depressed adolescent patients he saw who complained of having problems in school but nonetheless had fine test scores. He and his small staff started investigating and discovered that most districts and states were reporting average test scores that were above the national average.[8] This phenomenon quickly became known as the "Lake Wobegon effect," after Garrison Keillor's mythical town where the "all the women are strong, all the men are good looking, and all the children are above average."

In the technical literature, this exaggeration is called *score inflation*—increases in scores that are larger than the improvements in achievement they are supposed to signal. Score inflation has been the subject of intense debate. Many advocates of high-stakes testing dismiss the issue as unimportant, but they are simply wrong. The research on the topic, while limited, consistently finds score inflation, and it is often very large. Studies have also begun to shed light on the factors—other than simple cheating—that cause score inflation, such as focusing instruction on material emphasized by the test at the expense of other important aspects of the curriculum; focusing on unimportant details of a particular test; and teaching test-taking tricks. Score inflation is a preoccupation of mine, both because I have been investigating this problem for more than fifteen years and because I think it is one of the most serious hurdles we need to surmount if we are to find more effective ways of using tests for accountability. Chapter 10 provides a more detailed discussion of score inflation, and I return to it again at the end of the book in discussing sensible uses of scores.

Late in the 1980s, yet another major change occurred in large-scale testing programs: the widespread effort to supplement or replace the multiple-choice format with other forms of tests, many of which fell under the rubric of "performance assessment" or, more vaguely yet, "authentic assessment." The new tests were diverse and presented students with many types of tasks, including short-answer constructed-response items, items requiring more extensive written answers, hands-on performance (for example, with a scientific apparatus of some kind), tasks in which part of the work was conducted in a group and the rest by the student alone, and the portfolio assessments noted earlier.

Some of the individual tasks in these tests were modest in scope and could be completed quickly, but others were lengthy and complex. Some required parts of several school days to complete. For example, in 1996 New York introduced a variety of hands-on performance tasks for testing science in grades five through eight. One of these tasks, called "Creeping," was described as follows:

> Students will observe, measure, and graph a model of slow downslope movement representing soil creep.
>
> This task assesses students' abilities to collect, record, and organize data, set up graph axes, plot data points, draw line graphs, apply mathematics, infer based on observational data, predict based on a model, and apply models to other situations.
>
> This task is designed to take students approximately 30–40 minutes to complete.

Students were given a 250-milliliter beaker, a viscous material labeled "glop," a metric scale, a stopwatch, and materials with which to build a ramp. They were told to measure the glop's progress as it oozed down the ramp, tabulating the data they obtained. Afterward, they were to answer a variety of questions.

Some questions were quite narrow and closely tied to the task, for example:

> 3. a. Calculate the rate of movement of the glop during the first three minutes of observation to the nearest tenth of a cm / min. Show your work. Rate = distance / time.

Finding this answer required nothing more than rote application of the computational algorithm supplied in the question. But other questions required knowledge or speculation that went well beyond the activity itself, for example:

> 5. b. This activity presented a model for downslope movements like mudflows, soil creep, or glacier activity. In nature, what could happen to increase the rate of movement of sediment or ice in these earth features?*

Proponents of performance assessment sometimes got carried away. For example, some argued that tests ideally should be constructed from tasks that do not have a single correct answer, because important problems confronting adults in real life do not have single correct answers. At one conference of testing experts during those years, a prominent advocate of performance assessments presented a lecture in which she made precisely this argument. In such an extreme form, this is a silly position; while many real-world problems do not have single correct answers, innumerable ones do. The pilot who flew the lecturer to that conference, for example, had to decide whether the flaps should be up or down when landing the plane. Fortunately for the lecturer, the pilot chose the single correct answer. As the speaker was leaving the building after her presentation, she stopped and told me that she did not know which of the surrounding hotels was the Hilton, where she had a reservation. I pointed out that this was a question with a single correct answer, in response to which she left in a huff without letting me tell her which one it was.

The enthusiasm for performance assessment, which burgeoned remarkably rapidly, had several roots. One was implied by the

---

* This one excerpt, which is all that space permits, does not do justice to the complexity and diversity of performance assessment tasks. To get the full flavor, one must look at the administrative directions, the full descriptions (often illustrated) of the tasks, and the explanations of the rubrics used to score student performance. For a fascinating library of performance assessment tasks in science, check out the Performance Assessment Links in Science site maintained by SRI International, at http://pals.sri.com/. The task described can be found at http://pals.sri.com/tasks/5-8/Creeping/ (last accessed July 8, 2006).

term *authenticity*, a desire to evaluate students' performance on re-alistically complex tasks similar to those they would encounter outside of school. This was a reaction to the design of tradi-tional tests, in which skills and knowledge are deliberately broken into small pieces. The push for authentic assessment was gener-ally presented as new, even pathbreaking, but performance assess-ments were anything but new, and many of the arguments for and against this approach to testing had been clearly laid out nearly half a century earlier in the article by E. F. Lindquist described in the previous chapter.

A second reason for the interest in performance assessment during these years was the emphasis among education reformers on the related goals of establishing high standards for all students and focusing instruction on higher-order skills rather than basic skills and factual knowledge—in mathematics, for example, em-phasizing problem solving, reasoning, and communication rather than simple application of arithmetic procedures. It was widely thought at the time that performance assessments were better suited than multiple-choice tests to measuring these higher-order skills. There is something to this view, but it is overly simple. Re-search has shown that the format of the tasks presented to stu-dents does not always reliably predict which skills they will bring to bear, and students often fail to apply higher-order skills to the solution of tasks that would seem to call for them.

A third reason for the allure of performance assessment was the growing belief that "what you test is what you teach." Advo-cates argued that when you hold people accountable for scores on multiple-choice tests, you encourage teaching that resembles those tests—short reading passages, short problems, multiple-choice questions rather than questions requiring writing, and so on—and that this type of teaching is boring, cognitively unchallenging, and unproductive. There was no doubt that this was happening to some degree, not as a result of multiple-choice testing as such, but as a consequence of making teachers worry so much about scores on those tests. One newspaper reporter at the time spent several weeks observing unusually high-scoring schools in the Washington, D.C., suburbs that primarily served low-income minority students, and told me afterward that teachers in those schools began preparing students for the third-grade multiple-choice test while they were in kindergarten.

The response to this situation, advocates of performance assessment argued, should be "tests worth teaching to." These would be tests that assessed higher-order skills, such as complex problem solving, rather than the simple application of arithmetic computation, and they would embed those skills in complex, realistic tasks. Reformers argued that the new tests would encourage instruction not only by testing rich and demanding content but also by modeling types of tasks that would make for good instruction. That is, the assessment tasks themselves would exemplify types of work that teachers should include in their ongoing instruction. This represented a major change in the underlying notion of how tests should help improve instruction. In traditional achievement testing, tasks were designed to extract diagnostic information that would enable teachers to improve instruction, but there was no expectation that the tasks used in instruction should resemble those in the test.

The phrase "tests worth teaching to" had another connotation as well: tests would be designed such that preparing students for them—teaching to the test—would not lead to score inflation. But this was a logical sleight of hand. There is no reason to expect that a test that is "worth teaching to" in the sense of measuring higher-order skills and the like would be immune to score inflation. And as I explain in Chapter 10, research has confirmed that this expectation was false: even the scores on tests that avoid the multiple-choice format can become severely inflated.

Although the performance assessment movement has had lasting effects on large-scale testing programs, policymakers rapidly drew back from the more extreme forms of performance assessment. Such testing is expensive and takes a great deal of time. (Complex tasks take students a lot longer to complete.) It also poses serious technical difficulties. For example, performance assessments are often difficult to score reliably, and it is hard—in some cases, not practical—to make scores comparable in meaning from year to year or from school to school.

Another change in the form of testing—on the face of it, something that only a psychometrician could love, but actually very important and occasionally controversial—was the spread of *matrix-sampled assessments*. In conventional standardized testing, all students of a given type (say, all students in regular fifth-grade classrooms) are administered precisely the same test items. In matrix-sampled testing, the test is broken into a number of different parts that comprise different tasks, and these are then distributed randomly within classrooms or schools. Thus the test is not standardized for comparing individual students, but it is standardized for purposes of comparing schools or states. Matrix sampling is now common; it is used, for example, in NAEP, TIMSS, and some state assessments.

The significance of this seemingly arcane innovation is that it allows the testing of a broader range of knowledge and skills—a larger sample from the domain—within a given amount of testing time. Initially this approach was seen as advantageous simply because it offers richer information, but it offers an additional, critically important benefit when tests are used for accountability: it changes the incentives for students and teachers. The broader the test, the less incentive there is to narrow instruction inappropriately as a way of "gaming" the system and inflating scores.

So, many might say, if this esoteric change in test design gives us more comprehensive information about achievement and better incentives for teachers and students, why not just let the psychometricians have their way and use matrix sampling routinely? As is so often the case in testing, there is a price to be paid and a difficult trade-off between goals. A pure matrix-sampling design does not provide useful scores for individual students because students take different, and therefore not comparable, subtests. Hence the controversy. Many parents have argued that if their children are going to spend the time and effort participating in an assessment (not to speak of the often incomparably greater time spent preparing for the test), they want at least a test score in return. One compromise is exemplified by the Massachusetts Comprehensive Assessment System test: one portion of the test is common to all students and is used to provide individual scores, while the remainder is matrix-sampled and contributes only to scores for schools.

A more lasting wave of testing reform that overlapped with the performance-assessment era was the shift to *standards-based* or *standards-referenced* tests. The idea behind standards-based testing is that states or localities should begin by specifying *content standards,* which are statements of what students should know and be able to do, and *performance standards,* which are statements of how well students are expected to perform with respect to the content standards. Tests should then be aligned with content standards and should be designed to ascertain which students have reached the performance standards.

Advocates of standards-referenced testing consider it to be a major departure from traditional testing. (One sign of this is that some avoid the term *test* and instead refer to their measures as "assessments.") But in fact, standards-based tests are less of a departure from tradition than many believe. The construction of high-quality traditional achievement tests also begins with extensive efforts to clarify what students should know and be able to do, although this is generally called a "curriculum framework" rather than "content standards." In practice, states' standards-based tests vary markedly in content and format; some look quite similar to conventional tests, and for the most part, similar methods—for example, similar statistical procedures—are used to construct them.

Content standards do, however, differ in one important way from the curriculum frameworks of traditional tests: they are generally specific to individual states. Traditional achievement tests were designed by looking for common elements in the curriculum frameworks of many states so that the publishers could market their tests broadly and provide national norms. Proponents of standards-based testing generally call for close alignment of tests with the particular standards of each state, arguing that closer alignment will produce greater clarity about the states' educational goals and make the tests more sensitive to improvements in education. This creates pressure for states to use different tests. There is no free lunch, however, and this benefit comes with two serious costs. It worsens the crossing-the-Potomac problem with which I started this chapter. And it increases by a large amount the volume of tests that must be constructed, which strains the capacity of the small testing industry and creates a risk of lower-quality tests.

Building on the precedent of minimum-competency tests, standards-based testing also departs from tradition in the way in which performance is reported. Performance on these tests is reported primarily in terms of whether students have reached one or more of the performance standards. In a typical standards-based system with three performance standards, students are placed into one of only four categories: failed to reach the lowest standard, exceeded the lowest but fell short of the second, passed the second (usually, "proficient") but did not hit the third, and exceeded the highest. In contrast, traditional reporting relies on a variety of numerical scales that provide a large number of possible scores.

This innovation in scoring is now almost universally accepted, it has been incorporated into federal statute, and it is widely considered desirable because it focuses on expectations and is supposedly easy to understand. In fact, however, it exacts a very high, perhaps excessive, cost. The process of setting standards—deciding just how much students have to do to pass muster—is technically complex and has a scientific aura, but in fact the standards are quite arbitrary. The simplicity of this form of reporting is therefore more apparent than real, and most people do not really have a clear idea of what the standards actually mean. For this reason, one often finds norm-referenced reporting sneaking back in, for example to show how a school's percentage "proficient" compares with that of other schools. Standards-based reporting provides a very coarse and in some cases severely distorted view of achievement, and it can create the undesirable incentive to focus most on the kids who are nearest the standard that counts, to the detriment of others. (These issues are discussed further in Chapter 8.) It can be helpful to know whether students are up to snuff, but relying too much on performance standards—in particular, using them alone, without other more traditional forms of reporting—is a recipe for trouble.

The early 1990s saw a rapid increase in efforts to include more of the students with special needs—students with disabilities and with limited proficiency in English—in the assessments that states were administering to its general-education students.* Traditionally, many such students were excluded from the assessments because the assessments were not considered germane to their educational program, because the tests were too difficult for them,

---

* The term *limited English proficiency* (LEP) is much disfavored now, the usual substitute being *English language learner*, or ELL. However, as I explain in Chapter 12, the issue for purposes of good assessment is not whether a student is learning English. Even native speakers, when young, are learning English. What is important for assessment is whether non-native speakers have reached a level of proficiency in English that permits them to demonstrate their knowledge adequately on a test.

because their special needs made the standard form of the test inappropriate for them, or simply for fear that their inclusion would bring down average scores. The rationale for increasing their inclusion was straightforward: if tests were being used to hold educators accountable for improving the achievement of their students, teachers would have little incentive to focus on the achievement of students with special needs unless they, too, were tested. This change was first instituted at the state level, for example, in Kentucky and Maryland. It eventually became a matter of federal statute with the Individuals with Disabilities Education Act Amendments of 1997 and the No Child Left Behind Act of 2001.[9]

By the end of the century, state-mandated standardized achievement testing was nearly ubiquitous in the United States. Most states had created their own content and performance standards, although many used commercial, nationally marketed tests (sometimes with modifications) that they considered sufficiently aligned to their standards, rather than fully customized tests. Most programs reported achievement by comparison with performance standards, although many used other, more conventional reporting scales as well. The mix of formats varied, but it was common to find a combination of multiple-choice questions and modest constructed-response tasks, such as short-answer questions and essays. Most states used test scores to reward and punish schools in some fashion, and about half—the count changed almost continuously—used at least one high-stakes test for students, usually as a requirement for high-school graduation.

States had instituted a variety of approaches to hold educators accountable for scores. Some simply set a standard for performance and then monitored which schools met it. Another method, rare but increasingly a focus of interest, was a *value-added* approach in which students are tracked as they go through school, and schools or teachers are evaluated in terms of the gains students make from one grade to the next. This approach is intuitively appealing, but it confronts a number of daunting obstacles in terms of both testing and the statistical machinery used to analyze scores.

The most common approach employed by states during the 1990s, however, was simply to compare the performance of students in a given grade with previous cohorts of students in the same grade. For example, the percentage of this year's fourth-graders reaching the state's proficient standard would be compared with the percentage of fourth-graders attaining that level last year. This approach has numerous advantages, not the least of which is simplicity, but it has a number of shortcomings as well. One is that the scores of any given cohort of students are shaped not only by the quality of their education but also—and powerfully—by noneducational factors, such as social background. Schools serving disadvantaged students will score more poorly than comparably effective schools serving more advantaged children. The effects of changes in the characteristics of a community, such as rapid immigration or other demographic trends, are confounded with changes in educational effectiveness.

If educators are to be held accountable for scores, someone has to decide how much improvement is enough. These targets have generally been made up out of whole cloth, with no basis in hard evidence such as normative data, international comparisons, historical trends showing how rapid improvements are likely to be over time, or evaluations of large-scale interventions. In some cases, the resulting expectations have simply not been sensible. For example, many reformers have argued that students should be expected to reach a level of performance similar to the proficient level established for the National Assessment of Educational Progress. But fewer than one American student in four reaches the proficient standard in eighth-grade mathematics on the NAEP, and performance on the TIMSS international survey suggests that, in round numbers, something in the vicinity of 30 percent of the students in Japan and Korea would fall below it as well, if they were given the same assessment.[10] Do we really expect that over the short or even the moderate term, we can raise the performance of all students to a level that more than three-fourths of American students and about a third of the students in two of the highest-achieving countries in the world currently fail to reach? In one state, I found that the typical school was expected to make gains that in two decades would have put more than half of the students above a level reached by only 2 percent of students initially, and low-scoring schools were expected to do more yet. The enormous size of the gain expected of the average school can also be seen by comparing it to some of the particularly large group differences in performance we see in current data. The expected improvement was twice as large as the mean difference in mathematics between the United States and Japan on TIMSS. It was also about twice as large as the mean difference typically found between African American and non-Hispanic white students. No research suggests that we can be confident of making gains of this magnitude on a large scale.

In a system such as this, we also need to decide how quickly and consistently schools should progress toward the target. Many states set these expectations using a "straight-line" method. With the goal that all students would reach the proficient standard at the end of a given period of time, the interim targets for each school were set by drawing a straight line between the initial percentage proficient and 100-percent proficient at the end of the prescribed time. This required arbitrary rates of improvement and assumed (without evidence) that initially low-performing schools could maintain much faster rates of improvement than higher-scoring schools. It also assumed that teachers have the ability to create consistent and uninterrupted improvements. As someone who has taught at most levels from fourth grade through doctoral studies, generally with very favorable evaluations, I find this last expectation remarkably unrealistic. Real improvements in instruction are often erratic. If a teacher recognizes that a technique for teaching a topic has not worked well, there is no guarantee that the first alternative he tries will be a good one, and even if it is, he may need to try it a few times to get it right. It is hard to experiment with new methods that are promising but hold risk if you are expected to make constant gains in scores.

These approaches to improving performance also imposed identical expectations for all schools that had the same initial test scores. No effort was made to determine the particular factors leading to low performance in a given school or to tailor expectations for improvement to fit specific conditions. For example, consider two hypothetical schools with similar and unacceptably low test scores. School A has a stable student population comprising native speakers of English but has a terrible teaching staff. School B has a better teaching staff, but this is offset by the fact that a large proportion of its students are immigrants who are not yet proficient in English—plus, they come from many different language backgrounds, making it impossible to find bilingual teachers for all of them. In most states, the improvement targets for these schools would have been identical.

The extremity of the unrealistic expectations in this approach becomes clearer if one imagines trying something similar in another area of public concern, say, hospital quality. We would first set standards for "sufficiently healthy outcomes," using arbitrary and different methods in different states that yielded different answers and that were not based on any evidence about what current medical technology could produce. We would then tell all hospitals, regardless of their circumstances—for example, the age or health status of the patients they take in, the pool of available specialists in their geographic area, the resources available to them, and so on—that they had a set time, say a dozen years, to reach the point at which all patients would be discharged "sufficiently healthy." They would be rewarded or punished along the way on the basis of whether they were making linear progress toward this goal. It's hard to imagine such a proposal even getting serious consideration.

This brings us to No Child Left Behind, which is the most recent of the periodic, required reauthorizations of the Elementary and Secondary Education Act of 1965. The proposal for NCLB came from the White House, and it is presented by the administration and widely seen as President Bush's initiative. However, its political pedigree is a bit more complex. While NCLB was certainly President Bush's initiative, it was enacted with bipartisan support, in some measure because of the support of two influential liberal members of Congress, Senator Edward Kennedy of Massachusetts and Representative George Miller of California. As Miller said to me some time after the bill passed, efforts to improve the achievement of disadvantaged students had failed for decades, and it was time "to shine some light in the corners."

In some ways NCLB is pathbreaking, but in others, it represents a continuation of the trends in testing that preceded it. NCLB combined elements from common state policies for testing and accountability, added some others, and made the package a federal mandate for any state receiving funds under Title I of ESEA. (Under the common interpretation of the Constitution, the federal government has very limited power to mandate educational policy or practices, so the mechanism for compelling adherence to NCLB's provisions is that states cannot receive their substantial Title I funds unless they do. Several have considered giving up Title I funds in response, although none has yet walked the plank.) NCLB requires annual testing in mathematics and reading in grades three through eight and in one secondary grade. A requirement for science testing in a minimum of three grades will go into effect soon. It requires that all states use for this purpose a standards-referenced test and that results be reported in terms of performance standards, including one called proficient. It requires that virtually all students perform at the proficient level within twelve years and establishes a complex system for determining whether states and schools are making "adequate yearly progress" (AYP) toward that goal. (AYP may appear to be based on the straight-line growth models of some states, but it differs in that it requires the establishment of a single statewide target each year for all schools in the state.)

No Child Left Behind requires that nearly all students, including most students with special needs, be assessed with the same test and that nearly all be held to the same performance standards. It requires separate reporting at the state and school levels for racial and ethnic groups, for students with limited proficiency in English, for students with disabilities, and for economically disadvantaged students, unless the number of students in a group is so small that the results would be unreliable, and it treats any school as failing to make AYP if any one of these groups fails to do so. This is what Representative Miller was referring to when he talked of shining light in the corners. NCLB also requires that sanctions be applied to schools that fail to make AYP, and it specifies an increasingly severe set of sanctions as the failure to make AYP persists.

It is hard to overstate the impact NCLB has had on elementary and secondary education during its short life. In many ways, it is the culmination of the transformation that began at least as early as the minimum-competency testing movement, and perhaps earlier—from the use of achievement tests primarily for diagnosis and local evaluation to testing as a means of evaluating entire educational systems and holding teachers accountable for changes in test scores. Regardless of the arguments for and against test-based accountability, I believe that it is with us for the foreseeable future. Therefore, when I return at the end of the book to sensible uses of tests, one of the central questions will be how best to use tests to hold educators accountable.

Chapter 5

What Test Scores Tell
Us about American Kids

DEBATE ABOUT AMERICAN EDUCATION has been dominated by scores on standardized tests for more than a quarter century. Test scores have been used to tell us that the achievement of the nation's students has declined; that it is or is not improving again, depending on whom you listen to; that the gap between minority and majority students is or isn't narrowing; and that our students do or don't do well enough compared with students in other countries. Test scores have been a central focus of any number of prominent reports on education and economic reforms. Newspapers often place the results of state and local testing programs on page one, and they frequently give prominent coverage to large-scale national and international surveys of achievement.

But anyone who tries to follow this information by reading newspaper accounts, press releases, or public statements of education reformers or district and state administrators can be excused for being somewhat confused. Accounts are often inconsistent, even when the same data are referenced. Claims about scores are often exaggerated or simply wrong. Scores are routinely reported in forms that make it hard to know whether a change in scores or a difference between groups is relatively good news or unusually bad. Changes in context that should shape the interpretation of scores—such as trends in the mix of students tested—are typically ignored entirely. Completely unsubstantiated claims about the causes of changes in scores are ubiquitous.

It is important to get the story straight. In this chapter, I will draw on data from the past forty years to describe trends in the achievement of American students and to explore how our students compare with those in other countries. In the following chapter, I will discuss factors that influence test scores—in particular, the common notion that schooling has so large an effect on scores that one can assume that schools with higher scores offer superior education. But first it is necessary to explain a metric that is commonly used to evaluate the size of differences in scores and to compare findings from one test to another.

A Common Scale for Different Tests

In the measurements that we encounter in most aspects of daily life, we use scales that are so familiar, such as inches or centimeters, that we give them little thought. If we hear that one man is half an inch taller than another, we know that their heights are very similar because we understand the inch scale for length. If we learn that the day's maximum temperature is going to be 95 degrees Fahrenheit rather than 72, we know that the afternoon will be unpleasantly hot rather than delightfully warm. We are bemused only when we are confronted with an unfamiliar scale—for example, when travelers from the United States encounter the temperature scale used by virtually the entire civilized world and must figure out that a temperature of 35 degrees Celsius is uncomfortably hot, or when tourists arriving in the United States are confronted by summer temperatures of 95 degrees, which they think of as being near the boiling point of water.

The scales used to report students' performance on tests are not like this. Different tests are reported on different scales, and many of these are arbitrary. Consider the two competing college admissions tests, the SAT and the ACT. The SAT mathematics scale runs from 200 to 800, while the ACT mathematics scale runs from 1 to 36. What does this difference in scales indicate? Nothing at all. These scales are arbitrary, have no intrinsic significance, and are not comparable. To compare a 25 on the ACT with a 700 on the SAT requires converting one or both scores to put them on a common scale.

In addition to being arbitrary, most test-score scales are not familiar enough to make their meaning intuitively clear. For example, between 1999 and 2004, the average reading score of nine-year-olds on the National Assessment of Educational Progress long-term trend assessment went up 7 points, from 212 to 219. Is this a lot or a little? Even though this particular scale has been in the news many times for more than two decades, few people know whether a 7-point increase is substantial. Even the most familiar test-score scales are not entirely clear to most people. At least in the states in which the SAT is the dominant college-admissions test, few test-score scales are more familiar than the SAT scale. Parents of students applying to selective colleges in these states know that a math score of 750 on the SAT-I is a very high score. But if the average SAT score increases or decreases by 35 points, is that a large change? Comparing scores on different tests is even harder. If a group's average ACT score in mathematics increases 2 points out of a possible 36, how does this compare with an increase of 22 points on the SAT, which has a maximum score of 800? Unless we convert these numbers into some other form, we simply can't answer these questions—although that does not prevent many people from reporting changes on these scales as if their meaning were clear.

The most common solution to this problem, in educational testing as in many other sciences, is to convert everything to a single, well-understood scale based on the *standard deviation*, which is a measure of how much scores (or any other traits) vary—that is, how spread out they are. Once that is done, results from different tests can be readily compared, and they can also be translated into other, intuitively understandable forms, such as percentile ranks.

To illustrate this, let's start with some real data from the testing program of an anonymous state. Figure 5.1 shows the distribution of scores on a secondary-school reading test. This is a histogram, in which the height of each bar represents the actual number of students receiving a score in that particular range. Thus the tallest bar shows us that more than 400 students received a score of 500 or a bit above. The scale of this test is arbitrary, just like the SAT and NAEP scales, and I have changed it from the one actually used to obscure which state provided me the data.

Assume that we have encountered a difference on this scale— say, the difference between scores of 500 and 600, marked by the two vertical dashed lines in Figure 5.1—and we have to decide how large this is. Had I not given you the figure, you would have had no clue; a difference of 100 points might be either huge or small, depending on the (arbitrary) scale. The graph, however, gives us a hint that we would not have from the numbers alone, because it permits us to compare our difference of 100 points with the distribution of scores. It shows us that a score of 500 is about average, while a 600 is quite high relative to the distribution of scores—that is, not many students scored above 600. Similarly, not many students scored more than 100 points below the average, that is, below 400. Moving from 500 to 600 entails passing a large number of students, so in that sense, a difference of 100 points is large. (There is nothing magical about 100 points in this example; I chose it only because it is a convenient number given the arithmetic I used to compute this scale.) This figure illustrates a general point: knowing the *distribution* of scores gives you useful information about the size of any given difference in scores.

What we need is a way to be more precise in using information

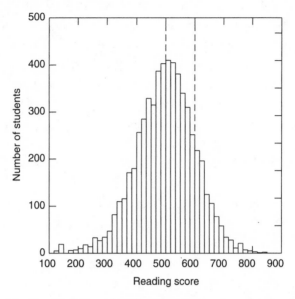

FIG. 5.1. The distribution of reading scores in an unnamed state.

about the distribution of scores. Let's superimpose on this distribution of actual test scores the notorious "bell curve," known properly as the normal or Gaussian distribution. You can see in Figure 5.2 that the bell curve fits this distribution very well. There are some bumps and wobbles in the histogram, but on the whole, the distribution does not depart very much from the normal distribution.

Over the years, the bell curve has picked up all manner of terrible connotations. Some insist that the bell curve is the malicious creation of psychometricians who want to create an appearance of differences among groups. Others associate it with the pernicious and unfounded view that differences in test scores between racial and ethnic groups are biologically determined. None of these associations is warranted. The bell curve is simply a way of describing a distribution that occurs very widely in nature (for example, the distribution of the circumferences of the heads of

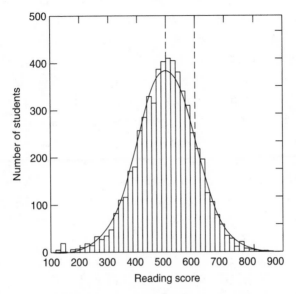

FIG. 5.2. The distribution of reading scores in an unnamed state, with the normal curve superimposed.

Egyptian mummies roughly fits the bell curve) and that has some mathematical properties that turn out to be very useful.

The fact is that we don't really know what the "true" distribution of reading or mathematics achievement really should look like, and we can design tests to change the shape of the distribution. For example, by changing the way the test is constructed or scaled, we can stretch out one of the "tails" of the distribution, giving very low- or high-scoring students scores that are farther from the mean. However, when several common conditions are met—when tests assess broad domains, are constructed of items that have a reasonable range of difficulty, and are scaled using most of the currently common methods—scale scores often show a roughly normal distribution, with many students clustered near the average and progressively fewer as one goes both lower and higher. Exceptions are not rare, however. If a test is easy for the students taking it, the distribution will not be normal—it will be asymmetrical, with a tail of low scores but many students piled up near the maximum score. A test that is too hard for the students taking it will have scores skewed in the other direction, with the greatest concentration of scores at the low end and a thin tail extending into higher scores. For example, in a study of a state testing program I conducted in the 1990s, I found that the distribution of scores for eleventh-grade students without disabilities was very nearly a bell curve, but the distribution of scores for students with disabilities was strongly skewed, with scores concentrated at the bottom of the range and a thin tail extending into the higher score range. The test was simply too hard for some of the students with disabilities.*

We can take advantage of the fact that the test scores in our example do fit the bell curve to solve our problem—that is, to put the scores on a scale that is not arbitrary and that allows us to compare results from one test to another. We'll do this with our actual reading data.

First, we will make use of the standard deviation, the measure of how spread out the scores are. The technical definition of the standard deviation is not important here.† What is important is that, provided that scores (or any other measurements) follow the bell curve, we know what proportion of the distribution falls within any range defined in terms of standard deviations. For example, if you set a cut at one standard deviation above the mean, 84 percent of all scores will fall below that line and 16 percent will be above it. This is symmetrical: if you set the cut one standard deviation below the mean, 16 percent of scores will fall below it. If you set a cut at two standard deviations above the mean, about

---

* Grade-equivalent scores in the early grades are another exception; because of their construction, they are right-skewed.
† The standard deviation is based on each observation's difference from the mean. Specifically, it is the square root of the average squared deviation from the mean.

95 percent of scores will fall below the cut. And this will hold true regardless of the original scale, so long as the distribution roughly fits the bell curve. Therefore, you can use standard deviations to place test scores on a scale that has a clear and well-understood meaning, provided that the distribution roughly fits the bell curve. If I say that an individual scored 633 on the mathematics portion of the SAT, only people very familiar with that test will know what that means. On the other hand, if I say that the student scored one standard deviation above the mean on the SAT, anyone familiar with standard deviations knows what it means: the student outscored roughly 84 percent of the students who took the test.

Our state reading data on the original scale shown in Figures 5.1 and 5.2 had a mean of about 500 and a standard deviation of about 100. This is why I chose scores of 500 and 600 for the dashed lines in the illustration: they are the mean and one standard deviation above the mean. If you were to count up the students represented by the bars above 600, you would find that roughly 16 percent scored in that range. The histogram is a bit bumpy, so this percentage is not exact, but the normal distribution gives us a pretty good approximation.

Psychometricians and other social scientists often take advantage of these properties of the bell curve by converting test scores and other variables to a *standardized* scale, which is a scale with a mean of zero and a standard deviation of one.* Standardizing the reading scores gives us Figure 5.3. The distribution shows exactly the same shape as in the earlier figures, but the scale on the bottom has been changed so that the mean is now 0 and the standard deviation is 1, and the dashed vertical lines are now at 0 and 1

---

* This scale is often called a *standard* scale, but I will use the term *standardized* here to distinguish it from a number of other, related scales, discussed in Chapter 8, that are also called *standard scales*.

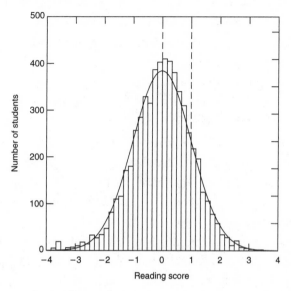

FIG. 5.3. The distribution of reading scores in an unnamed state, on a standardized scale.

rather than 500 and 600. Every student's score is now represented as the number of standard deviations (or the fraction of one standard deviation) it is from the new overall average score of zero.

Once we have transformed test-score data to this standardized scale, we have several ways to make sense of them. We can compare trends from one test to another. We can compare a change or difference in scores on a given test with other differences, such as the average differences between black and white students' scores in the United States or between the United States and high-scoring countries, such as Korea and Singapore (both of which are discussed below). We can also take advantage of our understanding of the bell curve to express differences in more concrete and easily understood terms. For example, let's say that the upper vertical dashed line in Figure 5.3 represents the average score of another group of students. That would show us that the average for that other group is one full standard deviation above the average of our group. (To give away a bit of the plot, this is roughly where the average scores in Japan and Korea fall on the distribution of math scores in the United States on some tests.) Initially, we would have known only that this group averaged 600 on our original scale, which would have told us very little. But now that we know that they average one standard deviation above our mean, we know that only about 16 percent of our students score above their average. That is clearly a very big difference in performance.

This example shows another way to use standardized scores, which is to re-express them as in terms of *percentile ranks*. The percentile rank is the percentage of scores falling below any given score. Suppose that we administered our forty-item vocabulary test from Chapter 2 to a large group of people and that 75 percent answered fewer than thirty of the items correctly. Then a student who answered 30 items correctly would be said to have a percentile rank of 75, meaning that she outscored 75 percent of the reference group. As the examples above show, the relationship between standardized scores and percentile ranks is fixed and well known, so once test scores have been standardized, it is a trivial matter to convert them to percentile ranks.*

If standardized scales are so handy, why are they never used to present test scores to the public? Because most lay people cannot abide fractional and, worse, negative scores. Imagine a parent receiving a report from her child's school that said, "Your daughter received a score of 0.50, which put her well above average." A standardized score of 0.50 *is* well above average—if scores follow the bell curve exactly, it represents a percentile rank of 69—but it certainly does not seem like it. It is easy to envision a worried parent responding that she does not quite understand how her child

---

* A table found in virtually all basic statistics texts and easily obtained on the Web, called a "standard normal table" or a "z-table," maps standardized scores to percentile ranks.

obtained a score of one-half and nonetheless ended up above average. Did half the class get no questions right? Or worse, imagine a report that said, "Your son's score on our math test was −.25." Less than zero? I'd hate to be that child at the dinner table the night that report went home. So in a great many cases, psychometricians start with a standardized scale—it is produced automatically by many current scaling methods—and then convert it to some other scale that they think will be more palatable, one with a larger standard deviation to avoid fractional scores and a high enough mean that no one gets a negative score.

⬭ Trends in the Achievement of American Students

With standardized scales in hand, we can compare the results of many different tests to obtain an overall view of trends in the performance of American students.

During the 1960s, the test scores of American students began to drop. Scores on the SAT began to decline in the 1963 school year; on the ACT, a few years later; and on other tests, at various times during the decade. Although public attention was focused on a few tests, in particular the SAT, the decline was startlingly pervasive. It appeared, with a few exceptions, on college-admissions tests, the National Assessment of Educational Progress, other nationally representative surveys conducted under contract with the federal government, state tests, a variety of special studies, and in national norming data from commercial achievement tests (data from the periodic nationwide testing undertaken to establish national norms for reporting scores). It occurred in Canada as well, and in both private and public schools in the United States.

It is hard to overstate the impact of this decline in scores. Although it became widely recognized only in the 1980s, after the decline had already ended, in this country its effects on the nation's view of the education system was profound. For example, it was a primary focus of the highly influential 1983 report *A Nation at Risk*,[1] which began by casting the matter in dire terms:

> Our Nation is at risk. Our once unchallenged preeminence in commerce, industry, science, and technological innovation is being overtaken by competitors throughout the world. This report is concerned with only one of the many causes and dimensions of the problem, but it is the one that undergirds American prosperity, security, and civility. We report to the American people that while we can take justifiable pride in what our schools and colleges have historically accomplished and contributed to the United States and the well-being of its people, the educational foundations of our society are presently being eroded by a rising tide of mediocrity that threatens our very future as a Nation and a people.

The report listed thirteen diverse "indicators of risk" to support this dismal appraisal, of which all but three were based on test scores. The poor showing of American students on tests administered internationally headed the list, but about half of the indicators were declines in test scores.

The concern about the adequacy of American education to which the score decline contributed so substantially has not abated over the intervening decades. The decline itself has lost much of its prominence, giving way to a greater focus on the now more frequent international comparisons and more recent data about trends in scores within the United States. However, the score decline has not entirely faded from view, and it still crops up here and there as a basis for judging current performance. For example, a recent article declared:

> In the wake of *A Nation at Risk,* educators pledged to focus anew on student achievement. Two decades later, little prog-

ress has been made. . . . Many areas of American life have changed for the better during the past two decades—except, it appears, the K–12 education system. Data from various sources—the SAT, the National Assessment of Educational Progress (NAEP), and international comparisons such as the Third International Mathematics and Science Study (TIMSS)—all reveal the same trend: despite 20 years of agitation and reform, much of it sparked by the *Risk* report, student achievement has at best stagnated, if not declined.[2]

One can find less negative and certainly less hyperbolic portrayals of the data, but in general, a pessimistic view of test scores has predominated in the public debate since *A Nation at Risk*.

The evidence, while hardly grounds for complacency, is less negative than this quotation suggests. The test data provide both good and bad news, and the picture they paint is complex, with a number of intriguing wrinkles. Moreover, there are a few complications that need to be borne in mind if we are to interpret the trends accurately.

Just how big was the decline in scores that put our nation at risk? There is no single answer, but painting with a broad brush and considering many different sources of data, it would be fair to call the drop "moderately large." The size of the decline varied markedly from one test to another, sometimes for understandable reasons but in many cases inexplicably. Most tests showed a total drop of between 0.25 and 0.40 standard deviation over the course of the decline. Using this scale allows us to clarify the size of the deterioration by estimating how the students tested at the end of the decline would have stacked up against their peers before the drop began. For an illustration, let's consider the student who reached the median—that is, the student who outscored half of the tested group and therefore has a percentile rank of 50—at the end of a decline of 0.35 standard deviation, which was a fairly typical drop. The score that placed this student at the median at the end of the decline would have been sufficient to reach only the thirty-sixth percentile rank before scores began to fall.

One of the largest declines was on the verbal portion of the SAT, where scores dropped almost half a standard deviation. This particular trend had a disproportionate influence on public debate because of the prominence of the SAT, but it was misleading, and the reason it was misleading—there were changes in the composition of the group of students taking the test—has much broader implications.

To illustrate the general problem that arises when the composition of the tested group changes, consider students who have special needs. For more than a decade now, federal policy and the policies of many states have pressed school districts to include more students with disabilities and more students with limited proficiency in English in the regular assessments administered to other students. The performance of students in these groups is highly variable, but on average they tend to score lower than the general student population. Now consider a hypothetical district in which the effectiveness of education remained constant and the characteristics of the total student population remained unchanged over a period of ten years. Suppose that this district had initially excluded a great many students with disabilities and with limited English proficiency from testing but had rapidly increased the proportion included over the course of the decade. Average scores would fall modestly. But what would that drop in scores signify? Not that schools had become less effective or even that students, for whatever reason, were learning less. The decline would signal nothing more than a change in the selection of students who were tested.

Such changes are called *compositional effects*—changes in performance arising from changes in the composition of the tested group. In general, if subgroups that are growing have substantially different average scores than those that constitute a decreasing share of the group, the result is a change in the overall average score stemming simply from these trends in composition. As the example illustrates, making sense of trends in the face of compositional effects requires some caution: some interpretations of the trends will be warranted, but others may not be.*

The characteristics of the American student population have changed in ways that have affected test scores. For example, immigration has increased the proportion of students with limited proficiency in English. Trends in graduation and drop-out rates have changed the composition of the student population in the secondary grades, as growing numbers of students who earlier would have dropped out have remained in school and therefore been tested. For example, between 1970 and 1985 there was a striking and consistent decline in the high-school drop-out rate for black students (as measured by one of numerous drop-out indicators, the so-called status drop-out rate, which is the proportion of individuals, age eighteen to twenty-four, who are neither high-school graduates nor currently enrolled in school).

The effect of compositional changes can be exacerbated when test taking is voluntary, and the decline in SAT scores was worsened by a major compositional change: a large increase in the proportion of SAT-takers drawn from historically lower-scoring groups. As college attendance became more common, the pro-

---

* Compositional effects are a special case of *Simpson's paradox*, the fact that treatment effects or other changes evident within groups may be inconsistent with or even reversed in direction from the effects that appear when the groups are combined. For example, a study may show that a medical treatment is effective for both males and females but appear misleadingly to show that it is ineffective when results for the genders are combined. Simpson's paradox has been discussed in statistics for many years—it is named for an article published by E. H. Simpson in the *Journal of the Royal Statistical Society* in 1951, and it had been recognized in the statistical literature for perhaps half a century before that—and it has been found in medical and social scientific studies too numerous to count. Nonetheless, the phenomenon has not become a commonplace, and lay readers of statistical results are often misled as a result.

portion of high-school graduates electing to take admissions tests rose, and many of those newly added to the rolls were lower-scoring students. This was studied in considerable detail by the College Entrance Examination Board in the 1970s, and the research showed clearly that a sizable share of the drop in SAT scores was the result of this compositional change. Had the characteristics of the test-taking group remained constant, the decline would have been much smaller.

Although compositional effects can be a particularly important issue when students choose whether to take a test, they can affect trends on other tests as well when the composition of the entire cohort changes over time. In recent decades, the composition of the U.S. student population has changed in numerous ways, and these changes have had a modest negative effect on scores, either exacerbating the decline or attenuating the increase that would have been seen if the population had been stable. One currently well publicized example is the rapid growth in the proportion of students who are not fully proficient in English. Based on an annual household survey, the Current Population Survey (CPS), the Census Bureau estimates that between 1979 and 2004, the percentage of children who spoke a language other than English at home increased from 9 to 19 percent of all children ages five to seventeen. During the same period, those who spoke English with difficulty roughly doubled, from 2.8 to 5.3 percent of the age group.[3] African American students have represented roughly 16 percent of public school students since 1978, but Hispanic students, who also have historically scored on average considerably lower than non-Hispanic whites, have increased in number from roughly 7 percent to 19 percent of enrollment.

Interpreting score trends in the presence of compositional change requires some care, but most commentators over the past forty years either have not been aware of this or couldn't be bothered with it. Consider again the SAT. The decline in SAT verbal scores that ended in 1980 provided a reasonable portrayal of the performance of the changing group of students taking the test, and this might have been relevant for some college admissions officers, who had reason to be concerned about the capabilities of whatever subset of graduates applied for admission. However, this trend in scores, if unadjusted for compositional changes, painted a biased picture of change in the performance of all graduates. And for the most part it was this latter use to which commentators put the SAT scores when they cited them as portraying the declining performance of American high-school graduates or, taking matters an unwarranted step further, used them to draw inferences about the quality of American high schools. For these purposes, the simple trend in SAT scores overstated the decline in performance among all high-school graduates—or, to be more precise, it overstated the decline in SAT scores one would have found if all graduates had taken the test, rather than the changing, self-selected students who actually did.

The ending of the decline—both its timing and its explanation—was a matter of some controversy among cognoscenti of the trends. Most commentators focused primarily on the SAT, which hit bottom in 1980 and began to show hints of an uptick two years later. This led them to hunt for possible causes, either educational or social, that occurred around that time. Some commentators even suggested that the conservative cultural and political changes in the nation at the time SAT scores hit bottom, reflected in the election of Ronald Reagan in 1980, arrested the decline in scores. They were hunting in the wrong place. The achievement of students graduating from high school represents the accumulated effects of twelve years of schooling, so some of the factors contributing to the end of the score decline would have antedated the bottoming out of the SAT by quite some time. As H. D. Hoover of the Iowa Testing Programs quipped, "If people are going to be dumb enough to attribute something like this to a president, then they will have to give the credit to Jerry Ford."

And examined more closely, the data show precisely that: the decline in scores ended earlier in lower grades, during the Ford administration. There was considerable variation from group to group and from one test to another, but looking across a wide variety of data, the nadir for scores generally occurred between 1974 and 1980. The students whose scores represented the low point appear to have been those born roughly in 1962 or 1963. The end of the decline first appeared in the mid-1970s, when these birth cohorts reached the middle-elementary grades, and it progressed through the higher grades in subsequent years as these students worked their way through school. This is an example of what social scientists call a *cohort effect:* a change that is tied to a particular birth cohort and follows them as they age. Cohort effects are common—for example, they occur in medicine when certain birth cohorts are exposed to particular conditions or medical interventions—but they did not figure prominently in the educational policy debates of the day. Rather, most commentators viewed the trends in terms of *period effects*—changes that are tied to a particular time, such as policies imposed on schools in a specific period, and that affect multiple cohorts at the same time.

In the early 1980s, after reading a paper in which I described these patterns, a senior writer for a major newspaper paid me a visit and asked: "Doesn't this indicate that the education critics who give credit for ending the decline to the conservative policies of the 1980s are full of garbage?" Well, yes, I told him, but the general implications are more important. First, it is essential to keep in mind that education is a long-term process, the effects of which accumulate over some time. Trying to explain changes in performance simply by reference to recent changes in policy or practice is a risky business. Second, as I will explain in the next chapter, these cohort patterns suggest that social as well as educational factors played an important role in bringing about the decline in scores and the subsequent upturn.

What has happened since the 1980s? One might expect that

with the huge increase in the amount of testing in recent years, we would know more about recent trends than about the decline of the 1960s and 1970s. Ironically, the reverse is true. While we have far more data now than we did twenty or thirty years ago, we have fewer sources of data that we can trust. The reason is simple: the increase in testing has been accompanied by a dramatic upsurge in the consequences attached to scores. This in turn has created incentives to take shortcuts—various forms of inappropriate test preparation, including outright cheating—that can substantially inflate test scores, rendering trends seriously misleading or even meaningless. This problem, which is discussed in detail in Chapter 10, has caused exaggerated gains in scores on some high-stakes tests that are sharply steeper than increases on lower-stakes tests such as the NAEP. Accordingly, to discern recent trends, we have to rely primarily on NAEP.

The National Assessment of Educational Progress is in many ways ideal for this purpose—it is very carefully designed to measure trends, it reflects a degree of consensus about what students should know, and its coverage of the measured domains is unusually broad—but it is nonetheless risky to rely so much on a single source, no matter how good. Even well-designed tests will often provide substantially different views of trends because of differences in content and other aspects of the tests' design. In fact, as I noted in Chapter 1, the two NAEPs—the "main NAEP" used to report detailed national and state-level results and the smaller survey used to assess long-term trends—have sometimes shown substantially different trends. NAEP can provide a broad picture of the trends, but we have to be careful not to place too much confidence in detailed findings, such as the precise size of changes over time or of differences between groups.

The NAEP paints a discouraging picture of trends in reading. In middle school and high school, there has been no substantial change in reading scores for more than thirty years. The trends in elementary school are slightly more positive, with gains during the 1970s and very small gains since 1999 or 2000. But current elementary-school performance is only very slightly higher than in 1980.

Mathematics is quite a different story: there have been large and rapid gains in elementary school math scores and substantial improvements in middle school. Scores for nine-year-olds on the long-term trend assessment began rising after 1982 and are now at the highest level ever recorded. The rise was so rapid that, despite a period of stagnation in the 1990s, the mean score in 2007 was 0.84 standard deviation higher than in 1982. This is shown by the solid line in Figure 5.4, which sets the first year of each trend to a mean of zero and then shows the increases as a fraction of a standard deviation. The main NAEP can be used to measure trends only for a shorter period, but it shows an even more rapid improvement. The average score for fourth-grade students on this assessment increased by roughly two-thirds of a standard deviation, but over a period of only thirteen years, from 1990 to 2003. (See the dashed line in Figure 5.4.)

One way to put this increase in perspective is to compare it with the decline that did so much to spark the ongoing concern about the condition of American education. The increases in NAEP elementary-school mathematics scores are far larger than most of the recorded decreases in scores and are about double the typical drop. Moreover, the annual rate of change in scores on the long-term NAEP assessment is roughly comparable to that observed during the decline, while the increase on the main NAEP is far faster. Two other useful standards of comparison are the gaps in average scores between African American and white students and between the United States and Japan in international assessments. The improvement of 0.84 standard deviation in elementary-school mathematics scores on the NAEP falls within the range found for the mean difference between African Ameri-

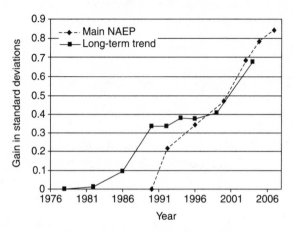

FIG. 5.4. Cumulative gain in elementary-school mathematics scores, NAEP.

cans and whites, and it is similar to the size of the gap between the United States and Japan in eighth-grade mathematics. Even the critics who insist that scores have not shown appreciable gains would call the gaps between African Americans and whites and between the United States and Japan large, and indeed they are. By the same token, the improvement in the mathematics performance of elementary school students has been substantial indeed.

The improvement in middle-school mathematics scores was less dramatic, but it too was respectable, and it puts current performance at the highest level since the assessment's inception. Mean scores for thirteen-year-olds on the long-term trend assessment showed a slower but less erratic gain than the gains shown by nine-year-olds: an increase of just over half a standard deviation during a period of twenty-six years, from 1976 to 2004 (Figure 5.5). The gain among eighth-grade students in the main assessment was about half a standard deviation over a shorter period, the seventeen years from 1990 to 2007. Again, these improvements are larger than the typical decline in scores that preceded them.

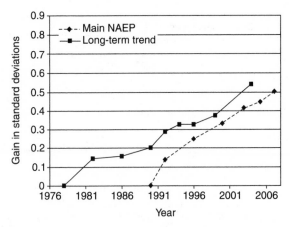

FIG. 5.5. Cumulative gain in middle-school mathematics scores, NAEP.

The bad news: trends at the high-school level have been much less encouraging. On both NAEP assessments, slower increases among seventeen-year-olds and twelfth-graders have been inter-spersed with brief downturns, and both assessments have shown total gains of only 0.2 standard deviation (Figure 5.6). Even this modest gain, however, is within the range of changes observed during the period of declining scores.*

The SAT paints a somewhat more optimistic view of trends at the end of high school than does NAEP. The SAT is less useful than the NAEP for gauging the achievement of American students overall because the test is not designed to mirror common high-school curricula and is taken by a self-selected and changing group of students, but it nonetheless warrants note and certainly plays a prominent role in public debate. SAT verbal scores have stagnated since they bottomed out, fluctuating a bit but ending only 6 points (0.05 standard deviation) higher in 2005 than in 1980.

---

* When this was written, the most recent data from the main NAEP on the mathematics performance of twelfth-graders were from 2000.

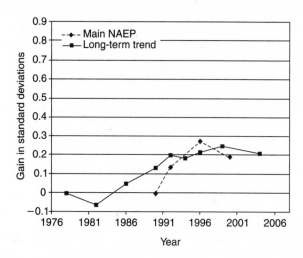

FIG. 5.6. Cumulative gain in high-school mathematics scores, NAEP.

In contrast, mean SAT mathematics scores have increased steadily but slowly since the end of decline. In 2005, the average score was 28 points (0.24 standard deviation) higher than in 1980 and was at the highest point since 1967.

Compositional changes have dampened these gains modestly. The attenuation of improvement on the SAT is evidenced by the fact that trends *within* racial and ethnic groups were often more favorable than the overall trend. Changes in the racial and ethnic composition of the test-taking group partially offset the improvement that would have appeared had the composition of the group remained fixed. Compositional effects have affected trends on the NAEP as well, although more modestly because a representative sample takes the assessment each time. For example, the NAEP reports that the improvement in the mathematics performance of seventeen-year-olds from 1973 through 2004 (a period that encompassed part of the decline as well as the subsequent rise) was too small to be statistically significant. That is, the rise was so small that it could well have come about from chance, rather than from real improvements in learning. (Statistical significance and related concepts are explained in Chapter 7.) Yet the improvements were statistically significant for whites, blacks, and Hispanics taken separately—even though trends in smaller groups are typically statistically less significant.[4] The explanation for this seeming paradox is that the increases within each group were partially offset by a change in the mix of students tested, with lower-scoring racial and ethnic groups growing as a share of the total school population.

Clearly, these data do not warrant the conclusion that "despite 20 years of agitation and reform, much of it sparked by the *Risk* report, student achievement has at best stagnated, if not declined." Even so, there are ample grounds for concern. Particularly important is the erosion of recent gains as students moved through school. These data show the same cohorts of students in different years—not the identical students, but nationally representative samples of students at each time. The NAEP cohort tested as nine-year-olds in 1982 reappears in the 1986 data as thirteen-year-olds and in the 1990 data as seventeen-year-olds. Therefore, if students were maintaining their early gains, one would see gains in elementary school echoed by gains in middle school four years later and in high school four years after that. This is what we saw with the end of the decline, but it is not what we see with the subsequent rise in scores. Given that we are ultimately concerned with the knowledge, skills, and dispositions that students accumulate over the course of their schooling and take with them into adulthood, this erosion is appropriately a focus of deep concern among educators as well as critics of the system.

How Variable Is Student Performance?

Most reports of aggregate test scores—scores of schools, states, districts, and even countries—focus on the horse race: who scores higher than whom? Often, newspapers simply report an average score or the percentage of students above some performance standard, along with rankings of schools, states, or even countries.

At least as important as these simple differences in the levels of performance is information about *variability*. What is the typical spread in performance shown by students on achievement tests? How consistent and how large are differences between socially important groups—for example, between racial and ethnic groups, between males and females, and between students from low- and high-income families?

Perhaps the single most discussed statistic about the variability of performance in the United States is the gap between African American and white students. Traditionally, this has been shown as the *mean difference*—the difference between the average scores of each group—but in recent years, it has often been reported as a difference in the percentage of students reaching some performance standard. I focus here on mean differences because changes in the percentage of students reaching a standard are very hard to interpret; they conflate the performance difference between groups with the level at which the standard has been set.

The mean difference between whites and African Americans has varied considerably from one source of data to another because of trends in the size of the gap over time, differences among the tests employed, and differences among the samples selected for testing. Nonetheless, the difference has been large in every credible study of representative groups of school-age students. Most estimates of the difference have been in the range of 0.8 to 1.1 standard deviation, although a few have been slightly smaller. To see just what this means, let's take one example, the mean difference between African Americans and whites on the 2000 main NAEP assessment of eighth-grade mathematics, which was 1.06 standard deviation. This standardized difference indicates that the median black student—the student who would outscore half of all black students—would score roughly at the twelfth percentile rank among white students. A mean difference of 0.8 standard deviation, which would be among the smaller of the score differences commonly found, would place the median African American student in only the twenty-first percentile among whites. Clearly, these are very large differences, large enough to have very serious implications for the students' later success.

While still distressingly large, the gap between blacks and whites has shrunk substantially, if erratically, over recent decades. Virtually all credible data showed the gap slowly narrowing from the 1960s or 1970s until 1990 or a bit later. During some periods, this narrowing of the gap reflected smaller decreases in scores among African Americans than among whites; at other times, greater gains. Progress paused around 1990, and over the next decade some data indicated that the gap was widening again. NAEP data indicate that in mathematics, the narrowing of the gap resumed again around the end of the 1990s in the elementary and middle-school grades, although the change among seventeen-year-old students was statistically uncertain. In reading, NAEP data indicate that the gap between black and white elementary school students began to narrow again at about the same time, but there is no sign of improvement at the high school level, and data about middle school are inconsistent.

On average, Hispanic students also lag behind non-Hispanic whites. At present, the mean difference between Hispanics and whites is generally smaller than that between blacks and whites, but it is nonetheless in some instances very large. For example, the 2007 NAEP eighth-grade mathematics assessment, which showed a mean difference of 0.90 standard deviation between blacks and whites, found a difference of 0.72 standard deviation between Hispanics and whites. Not all tests show differences this large between Hispanics and whites, but sizable differences are the rule.

The gap between whites and Hispanics, however, is more difficult to depict and interpret. Good data about the performance of Hispanic students are sparser and are available for a shorter time span than are data about black students. The Hispanic population is tremendously diverse, and some subgroups, such as Cuban Americans in Florida, show relatively high levels of educational attainment, while others show markedly lower levels of attainment. Perhaps most important, the Hispanic population is constantly refreshed by ongoing immigration, and new immigrants often differ substantially from those who have been in the United States longer. For example, the high dropout rate among Hispanic youth has been a focus of widespread concern for decades. From the 1970s through the 1980s, there was little consistent change in the high-school dropout rate for Hispanic students, but this stability masked two offsetting trends. Over the first several generations of residence in the United States, the high-school dropout rate for individuals in Hispanic families gradually declines toward the U.S. norm. This progress, however, has been partially obscured by the continuing influx of new immigrants, many of whom do not complete high school. Disentangling these trends is very difficult.

Despite the effects of rapid ongoing immigration, the test scores of Hispanic students have shown some gains relative to those of non-Hispanic white students. Before 1980, a number of different databases showed Hispanics gaining on non-Hispanic whites, although those gains were modest and sometimes inconsistent. Since that time, the National Assessment has provided an inconsistent picture. In reading, the NAEP long-term trend assessment, which has a small sample of Hispanics and is therefore vulnerable to fluctuations stemming from sampling error rather than true changes in achievement, shows few significant changes in the Hispanic-white gap in the younger age groups but hints at a worsening gap among seventeen-year-olds. The larger, main NAEP is more optimistic, showing a modest but statistically significant narrowing of the gap in grade four between 2000 and 2005. (It lacks data for twelfth-graders in 2005.) The results in mathematics are similar, except that they show some evidence that the gap is narrowing in middle schools as well.

Not all racial and ethnic differences favor whites. On tests of mathematics and science, one often finds whites lagging behind Asian Americans. For example, in the 2000 NAEP twelfth-grade mathematics assessment, the average score among white students was 0.31 standard deviation below the mean of the "Asian/Pacific Islander" group. Results for Asian American students, however, are also difficult to interpret, for the same reasons that the trends of Hispanics are. The rubric Asian/Pacific Islander subsumes a large number of groups that have relatively little in common other than the very large portion of the globe from which they originated and that show very different patterns of educational performance. Rapid immigration has made this the fastest-growing racial or ethnic group in the United States, with faster growth in percentage terms even than the Hispanic population, and that growth has brought with it dramatic changes in the mix of groups sharing the label—for example, combining under the same classification low-income immigrant Filipinos and well-established Chinese American and Japanese American families. Moreover, despite its rapid growth, this group remains relatively small nationwide, and data describing its performance are therefore limited.

It is essential to keep in mind what these data do and do not tell us. They indicate only that the average differences between racial and ethnic groups are substantial. But these average differences, even when very large, tell us nothing about individual students. The variability *within* any of these racial or ethnic groups is very large, almost as large as in the student population as a whole. There are some black and Hispanic students who score very high relative to the distribution of white students, and there are Asian American students who score well below the white average. Also, these data describe the differences between groups but do not explain them. The simple existence of a group difference, even if very large and persistent, tells us nothing about the causes of these differences. Academics and others have argued for decades about possible causes, including lower-quality schools, material deprivation, health problems, lower levels of parental education, and cultural differences. That argument is too large to address here.

Performance on tests and other measures of educational achievement also varies with socioeconomic status, often abbreviated SES, a somewhat amorphous term coined by sociologists to describe the social placement of individuals and households. Socioeconomic status is often misconstrued as a synonym for income, but it properly refers to more than that, and it is often measured by a composite of income, educational attainment, and occupational status. In descriptions of test scores, SES is often gauged by whatever measures are at hand or can be gathered easily, and these are often weak. School districts and states can collect only limited information about the characteristics of students—imagine being told by your elementary school principal that you have to provide her with information about your annual income—and even most of the large-scale surveys that include achievement tests, such as NAEP and TIMSS, have only weak information about socioeconomic status. For example, NAEP does not survey parents, which precludes collecting usable information on family income. Therefore, we usually have to make do with weak proxies for the data we would really want—for example, using students' eligibility for free and reduced-priced lunches as a proxy for poverty or income more generally, and students' estimates of the number of books in their homes (how well could you estimate this?) as an indicator of the educational background and orientation of the family.

Even though the effect of this weak measurement of SES is to make its relationship with scores appear weaker than it ought, we typically find striking differences in performance associated with socioeconomic status. For example, in the 2000 NAEP twelfth-grade assessment of mathematics, the mean performance of students eligible for free or reduced-priced lunch was 0.71 standard deviation below the mean score for other students. Even weaker measures of socioeconomic status, such as students' estimates of the number of books in their homes, typically predict scores.

International Comparisons of Student Performance

For years, international comparisons of students' scores on achievement tests have provided some of the most potent grist for criticism of the American education system. While international comparisons provide reason for concern about the performance of American students, the picture is both less bleak and more complex than some critics would have you believe.

Systematic international comparisons of student achievement began at least as early as 1959, with infrequent ad hoc surveys that administered common tests to students in whichever countries mustered support for the effort. Since the mid-1990s, these endeavors have become institutionalized in three ongoing series of studies. One of these is TIMSS, which originally stood for Third International Mathematics and Science Study but has since been renamed, in recognition of the current repetition of the study at four-year intervals, the Trends in International Mathematics and Science Study. TIMSS has assessed students at as many as five grade levels, although its most extensive coverage has been of the eighth grade. The TIMSS tests are designed to reflect common elements of the curriculum, and they bear a considerable resemblance to the NAEP tests. Although heavily supported by the U.S. Department of Education, TIMSS operates under the auspices of the International Association for the Evaluation of International Achievement (or IEA), an international consortium of government agencies and research organizations. A second effort, operated by the same group, is an assessment in reading called the Progress in International Reading Literacy Study (PIRLS). The third assessment program, operated by the Organisation for Economic Co-Operation and Development (OECD), is called the Programme for International Student Assessment (PISA). PISA, which focuses primarily on mathematics and reading, has a somewhat different purpose: assessing the real-world competencies students have developed by the time they are nearing the end of secondary school. The framework from which the PISA tests are constructed does not as closely reflect school curricula, and the tests are organized by broad themes, such as "change and growth," rather than curricular areas, such as geometry.

The results of these international assessments are frequently reported as a straightforward ranking of countries, and one will often encounter summary statements such as this one from the U.S. Department of Education: "On the [first] eighth-grade TIMSS assessment, U.S. students scored somewhat above the international average in science and somewhat below average in mathematics."[5] International comparisons, however, are a tricky business, and simple conclusions such as these are unwarranted.

The first complication is that the tests used for international comparisons are, like all others, small samples of content, and the decisions about the sampling of content and the format of its presentation matter. For example, what percentage of mathematics test items should be allocated to algebra? (The decision was approximately 25 percent on the TIMSS test and NAEP tests but only 11 percent on the PISA test.) What aspects of algebra should be emphasized, and how should they be presented? What formats should be used, and in what mix? TIMSS and NAEP are roughly two-thirds multiple-choice while PISA is one-third.

These decisions about the construction of tests can have an appreciable effect on results even within one country or state, but they are particularly important when making comparisons among countries, because of the often large differences among their curricula. PISA and TIMSS are substantially different tests that rank countries quite differently. For example, when results for the twenty-two nations participating in both middle-school mathematics assessments were compared, Scotland, New Zealand, and Norway ranked considerably better on the PISA assessment than on TIMSS; the Netherlands, Hong Kong, Korea, and the United States had quite similar ranks on both tests; and Russia and Hungary ranked much higher on the TIMSS assessment than on PISA.[6] This is in substantial part a reflection of differences in the content and skills sampled by the two tests. Even within the constraints of any one test, sampling matters. For example, the ranking of countries' averages can be changed, although not greatly, simply by altering the relative emphasis given to the five content areas making up the TIMSS mathematics test.[7]

A second complication is that international comparisons do not provide a consistent and logical norm group for comparison. In norm-referenced reporting, the comparison group should be one that gives the comparison a useful meaning—for example, reporting a student's performance as her percentile rank in a nationally representative sample of students, or a school's mean score relative to the distribution of schools' scores throughout the state. With international studies, however, the comparison group is a matter of happenstance—it comprises whichever countries happened to pony up the money, effort, and class time to participate, and it changes from survey to survey, grade to grade, and year to year. Statements such as "the United States scored at the international average" do not mean much when the international average can move up or down depending on which countries elect to participate in a given assessment. This is not just a theoretical possibility. For example, in the report of the 1999 iteration of TIMSS, the United States was shown as scoring above the "international average" of countries that participated in that year. A few pages later, the report showed the United States scoring well below the average of a different norm group, the countries that had participated in both 1995 and 1999.[8] This is one reason why PISA provides a somewhat gloomier view of American performance than do some of the TIMSS results.

These complications do not render the findings of international comparisons useless by any means, but they do call for a more cautious approach to interpreting the findings. Simple comparisons to an "international average" are not useful because that average is fortuitous, and some differences between countries are ambiguous because a different but entirely reasonable test could cause the rankings to shift.

So how is one to make good use of international comparisons? First, rather than comparing performance with the average of whichever countries happen to participate, we should compare U.S. performance with specific countries that are for some reason pertinent. For example, it is useful to compare the United States with countries that are in many respects similar—say, England and Australia—and with particularly high-scoring countries we might want to emulate. If we do this, fortuitous changes over time in which countries participate will have no effect on our conclusions.

Second, treat the results of any one assessment as no more than what they are: the somewhat error-prone findings of one particular sampling of student achievement. This has two implications. Large differences and general patterns are more trustworthy than small differences, so pay little attention to the latter. For example, the wide gap between the United States and Japan in the most recent TIMSS assessment is large enough to be both substantively important and robust. The very small difference between the United States and Australia (the country ranked just above the United States) is neither.[9] And be alert for inconsistencies between assessments—for example, between PISA and TIMSS results—that may be larger than expected. Two sources of data—or more—paint a fuller and more trustworthy picture than one.*

Developed East Asian countries consistently dominate the top end of the distribution in international comparisons of mathematics performance. In the 2003 TIMSS, for example, the highest mean scores were obtained by students in Singapore, Korea, Hong Kong, Japan, and Taipei. The U.S. average fell well below those of these East Asian countries but was similar to the means of numerous other nations that might be considered competitors. For example, in the 2003 TIMSS assessment of eighth-grade mathematics, countries that had average scores statistically not significantly different from that of the United States included Russia, Australia, England, Scotland (tested as a separate country in TIMSS), New Zealand, and Israel. The highest-scoring European countries scored well above the United States but closer to our mean score than to the mean scores of those Asian countries. At the bottom of the distribution were primarily less developed countries, such as South Africa, the Philippines, and Saudi Arabia, although there were some exceptions, such as Chile.[10] Put in standardized form, the gap between the U.S. mean and the means of the highest-scoring countries, such as Japan and Korea, has been roughly 1 standard deviation, although it has varied somewhat from one iteration of the TIMSS survey to the next.

PISA, administering a different test to an older group of examinees, paints a very different picture. On the 2003 PISA test, Hong Kong, Korea, and Japan again scored at the top end of the distribution, but Canada and several European countries, including the Netherlands and Belgium, scored in the same general range. Also

---

* Recent international assessments provide information on statistical significance to discourage readers from paying heed to differences that are too small to be trustworthy, but this information reflects uncertainty *given the design of the test* and does not take into account differences that may appear when a differently designed test is used.

in contrast to the TIMSS results, Australia and New Zealand did substantially better than the United States in the PISA assessment. The U.S. mean score was much farther down in the distribution, similar to those of Latvia and Spain.[11]

Thus, taken together, the two international testing programs leave us somewhat uncertain about the relative performance of our students in mathematics. We can be confident that our students perform markedly worse, on average, than those in developed East Asian countries such as Korea. Our standing relative to European countries, however, is unclear. There has been a good deal of conjecture about the reasons for our weaker performance on the PISA test compared with the TIMSS, but it is nothing more than speculation at this point. The two tests were designed to share virtually no content. This precludes our conducting a convincing analysis of the effects of differences in the construction of the tests. We can say only that the disparate results reflect some unknown combination of dissimilarities between the tests and differences in the samples tested. Something more than a repetition of the TIMSS and PISA tests, as they are currently designed, would be needed to explain the differences between their findings.

International comparisons of achievement in reading have garnered less attention but place the United States in a better light. One little-noted international study a decade and a half ago showed that the reading performance of American students was relatively strong in middle school and second-best among twenty-eight tested countries in the elementary grades.[12] Some cynics suggested at the time that this study garnered little attention because the good news it offered was not helpful to those who insisted that American schools were failing. The Progress in International Reading Literacy Study, modeled in many ways after TIMSS, also shows the United States to be doing quite well in reading in fourth grade, the only grade tested by PIRLS. The United States was in a cluster of high-scoring countries the mean scores of which were very similar and statistically not significantly different from each other, including Canada, Germany, and Italy. Only three countries, Sweden, the Netherlands, and England, had average scores significantly higher than the United States. The two developed East Asian countries that participated, Singapore and Hong Kong, had significantly *lower* average scores, but this may reflect the difficulties of learning to read a nonalphabetic language.

Given that our focus should be on the knowledge and skills students possess when they leave school, it would be useful to know whether the standing of U.S. students compared with those in other nations improves or deteriorates as they move through school. Many commentators have asserted that it does deteriorate, but in fact the information addressing this question is very sparse. Several of the international studies tested only a single age or grade level, and comparing different tests administered at different ages (such as PISA and the middle-school TIMSS) is risky because discrepancies in the findings could stem from disparities between the tests rather than from age-related differences in performance. TIMSS tested students at three ages—elementary school, middle school, and near the end of high school—but the samples of high-school students are so different from one country to another that I find it hard to draw conclusions with any confidence. This leaves us with a handful of comparisons of elementary- and middle-school students.

The best comparisons are provided by the TIMSS mathematics data pertaining to elementary and to middle-school students. These data show that the gap between students in the United States and those in the highest-scoring countries tends to widen with age. For example, the TIMSS shows the difference in performance between the United States and both Japan and Singapore to be larger in grade eight than in grade four. This is hardly surprising. After all, the gap appears in fourth grade because students in Singapore and Japan are learning at a faster rate than those in the United States in the earliest grades, and there is no reason to expect their rate of growth to slow to the U.S. pace once they enter the fifth grade. This does not mean that the U.S. education system is worse, relatively speaking, in the higher grades. If the factors that contribute to faster learning in Singapore and Japan—both educational factors, such as the quality of the curriculum, and noneducational factors, such as the culture—are consistent across the grades, one would expect consistently faster growth in Singapore and Japan, which would cause the gap between those countries and the United States to widen from one grade to the next. But in general, we simply do not know enough about the relative growth in the performance of U.S. students as they move through school.

Finally, international comparisons counter a commonly held misconception about the variability of student performance in the United States, although this fact rarely garners any attention. The distressingly large achievement differences among racial/ethnic groups and socioeconomic groups in the United States lead many people to assume that American students must vary more in educational performance than others. Some observers have even said that the horse race—simple comparisons of mean scores among countries—is misleading for this reason. The international studies address this question, albeit with one caveat: the estimation of variability in the international surveys is much weaker than the estimation of averages. This stems from both the design of the samples and arcane aspects of the mathematical models used to place the test scores on a scale. Therefore, it is meaningless to offer conclusions such as "the standard deviation of performance in Japan is 10 percent larger than that in the United States." We are limited to more general conclusions, along the lines of "the standard deviations in the United States and Japan are quite similar."

Which they are. In fact, the variability of student performance is fairly similar across most countries, regardless of size, culture, economic development, and average student performance. For example, thirty-one of the countries that participated in the first TIMSS assessment of eighth-grade mathematics met the data-quality standards for the survey. Of those, all but four had a standard deviation of scores in the range of 73 to 102 points. Contrary to the speculation that the United States would show particularly large variability because of our social heterogeneity, the U.S. variation was fairly close to the middle of the pack, with a standard deviation of 91. Similarly, in the 2003 PISA assessment of mathematics, the variability of performance of U.S. students was very close to the average of twenty-nine OECD countries.

Yet more surprising was the ordering of countries: by and large, the social and educational homogeneity of countries does not predict homogeneity of student performance. Some small and homogeneous countries—for example, Tunisia and Norway—do have relatively small standard deviations of scores, but many do not. For example, in all three TIMSS surveys, the standard deviation of scores in Japan and Korea—both countries that are socially more homogeneous than the U.S. and that have more homogeneous education systems through the eighth grade—was roughly similar to the U.S. standard deviation. The PISA assessment also confirmed this general finding, showing the variability of performance in the United States to be a tad larger than that in Korea but smaller than that in Japan. The TIMSS and PISA results also showed that the relationship we find in the United States between test scores and socioeconomic background is pervasive. Although there are some exceptions—for example, Macao and Iceland in the 2003 PISA assessment—a substantial relationship between scores and SES appeared in most countries in both assessments, despite the weak measurement of socioeconomic status in both.

This is not to say that the huge variability we see in student performance on tests is immutable. However, these data do show that the underpinnings of this variability are complex and that wide variations are to be expected even in high-performing and more equitable education systems. This, as we will see, is an issue in setting expectations for educational reform in the United States.

Chapter 6

What Influences Test Scores, or How Not to Pick a School

IN 1990, THE FIRST STATE-LEVEL RESULTS from NAEP were released, with states ranked by their average scores. The top of the
distribution saw an overrepresentation of states from the north-
central region and New England, including Minnesota, Maine,
Vermont, Massachusetts, and North Dakota. States in the Southeast, including Mississippi, Alabama, Arkansas, and Louisiana, were
disproportionately clustered at the bottom. While there were a
few unexpected results, this regional pattern was no surprise, having appeared in other, less publicly accessible data for a long time.

These results generated a great deal of discussion. It seemed
that nearly everyone who responded publicly—state commission-
ers of education, education reformers and critics, writers for the
media—had an explanation in hand for the standing of the states
that concerned them, usually crediting or blaming some aspect of
the states' educational systems. One state commissioner, for example, immediately announced that it would be necessary to replace his state's mathematics curriculum. Almost lost in the crowd
was the commissioner from a north-central state that had scored

near the top, as states in that region typically do. Asked why his students had done so well, he responded that there were no beaches or mountains in his state to distract them. Was he serious or simply poking fun at the claptrap around him? I never had a chance to ask.

It is hardly surprising that all of these commentators clutched at supposed explanations of the differences in performance among states. After all, only a few of us are interested in descriptions of achievement for their own sake. Most people want to know what result is OK, what is not OK, whom or what to credit or blame, and how to fix whatever is broken. Improving the educational system requires that we identify effective and ineffective programs, schools, and systems, so that effective programs can be emulated and ineffective ones terminated. If we are going to continue to reward and punish educators for scores on tests, fairness requires that we identify the right schools for both.

Nonetheless, their assertions were, for the most part, hogwash. Test scores describe what students know and can (or can't) do. And in most cases, that is *all* test scores do. Except in unusual circumstances, such as a planned experiment with random assignment of students, scores by themselves do not explain *why* students know what they do. For that, we need additional data, and those additional data are rarely available to the commentators who are so quick to tell us why students can or cannot perform as we wish. Some of those commenting on the NAEP results may have been correct, but when they were, it was usually by chance.

The reason their claims were generally groundless is simple: a great many things other than the quality of schools influence educational achievement, and the impact of these noneducational factors can be huge. When a school performs well or poorly on an achievement test, the reason can be the quality of education, any number of noneducational causes, or—more likely—both. Figuring out which is the case is not always easy. These commentators and policymakers were just like the frustrated home buyer I described in Chapter 1: eager to infer school quality from test scores alone, without doing the hard work of digging up the additional data one would need to identify differences in educational effectiveness.

This is not merely an academic concern. People routinely misinterpret differences in test scores, commonly attributing more to quality of education than they ought. Trends in scores over time, whether down or up, are often influenced by social factors and, in the case of seeming improvements, by inappropriate teaching to the test. Not all low-scoring schools offer as weak an educational program as their scores might suggest. By the same token, if your neighborhood schools have high scores, that may mean less about the quality of their programs than you'd like. The huge variability in scores shown by American students is not anomalous, and its causes are somewhat different than often thought. Understanding these complexities can do more than help parents choose schools sensibly; it can also help us evaluate the success or failure of education policies and set reasonable targets for reforms.

Everyone who studies educational achievement knows that differences in scores arise in substantial part from noneducational factors. A huge body of research collected in the United States over half a century documents this, and the United States is not unusual in this respect. At present, there is a heated argument about the *relative* impact of educational and noneducational factors. Much of the research suggests that variations in social factors account for the bulk of the variability of scores, while some researchers maintain that this reflects flaws in the design of the studies, such as weak measurement of educational quality, and that some educational factors—in particular, variations in the quality of teachers—have a large influence on scores.* This argument is not entirely resolvable at present, in part because differences in educational quality are strongly confounded with the social factors that influence test scores. The quality of educational resources is on average lower in poor and high-minority neighborhoods than in wealthier ones, and it is extremely difficult to disentangle the effects of the educational and social factors. But it remains unarguable that social factors have a very substantial impact on test scores, even if the precise proportion of the variability they account for cannot be ascertained.

The impact of noneducational factors on test scores is an example of what a classmate from my graduate training called a "grandmother finding," something you could have learned by asking any reasonably astute grandmother without the bother of conducting scientific studies. For example, imagine two hypothetical schools. School A has a stable population of students, all native speakers of English from moderately advantaged backgrounds. In contrast, many of the students in School B are immigrants, most with a limited command of English, and the rate of transience is very high, so the staff has limited opportunity to work with some of the students before they leave and are replaced by newcomers. Now suppose that these two schools have the same average test score, or in the metric of No Child Left Behind, the same percentages of students above the proficient standard. In terms of most of our current educational accountability systems, these two

---

* This controversy is linked to another that has received some prominent attention from policymakers and the press: whether schools should be evaluated based on cohort-to-cohort changes in scores (for example, comparing this year's fourth-graders to last year's, as mandated by No Child Left Behind) or by so-called value-added analysis that tracks students and evaluates how much they have improved over the course of the school year. Several value-added studies purport to show very large effects of variations in teacher quality. A recent review of these studies in which I participated reached a more cautious conclusion, arguing that they indeed show an important effect of teacher quality but that the results are not yet sufficient to ascertain its size well. See D. F. McCaffrey et al., *Evaluating Value-Added Models for Teacher Accountability*, MG-158-EDU (Santa Monica, CA: Rand, 2003).

schools are treated identically. But it defies logic to assume that the quality of education is similar in the two schools. The staff at School A has a much easier job than the staff at School B, and if they were working as effectively, they would have produced far higher average scores. Given the additional information I provided about the students in the two schools, it seems likely that the quality of education is lower in School A than in School B, but scores alone could not have revealed this.

As obvious as it is, the impact of noneducational factors on test scores is widely ignored—by politicians who want to claim credit or place blame; by the press, which wants to tell a compelling story; by both consumers and agents in the real estate trade; and, all too often, by educators. Some people seem not to know better; others understand that noneducational differences matter but don't think them important enough to worry about. One often hears phrases such as "the perfect is the enemy of the good," implying that worrying too much about the accuracy of the data (or, to be more precise, the accuracy of the inference based on the data) stands in the way of gleaning useful information.

In 1984, the U.S. Department of Education released the first of its so-called Wall Charts, which compared states in terms of average SAT scores. The intention was to show which states had better educational systems. I and innumerable others protested that this was a fundamentally misleading comparison for many reasons, the most important of which was that the proportion of students taking the test varied dramatically from state to state. States with small and highly selective groups taking the test—in those days, for example, in some midwestern states very few students took the SAT, and they were mostly high achievers interested in getting into competitive universities on the East or West Coast—rose in the rankings simply because of the characteristics of the kids taking the test. Attributing these differences in mean scores to putative differences in educational quality was arrant nonsense. No one could offer a good, substantive rebuttal; this problem was well known, and simple arithmetic was enough to show its severity. Instead, the response we were given was that the perfect was the enemy of the good.

"The perfect is the enemy of the good" is reasonable guidance if flawed data provide an approximately correct answer. But it is very bad advice if the flawed data suggest fundamentally misleading answers, as was true of the Department of Education's Wall Charts and, to a lesser degree, the simple comparisons of state means on NAEP. Often, lay people and experts disagree about where the line lies between results that are useful but not precise and those that are so far off as to be fundamentally misleading. This may help account for the propensity to ignore noneducational influences on test scores. A few years ago, I was asked to attend a meeting at a newspaper to discuss the paper's routine reporting of results from the state's standardized test—reporting that included tables showing the percentages of students in districts and high schools scoring at or above certain performance standards. Many on the staff wanted to focus on whether they were using the correct metric, but a few of us, all social scientists, insisted the issue was more serious: the inference many readers would draw from these tables—that the schools with higher scores were better—was unwarranted and in some instances badly misleading. We made little headway. I don't think anyone in the room was willing to countenance misleading results; I think we researchers simply had not persuaded the others that the results as presented would in fact be substantially misleading. The others were still on the "the perfect is the enemy of the good" side of the line.

Some critics of education disregard noneducational explanations of test scores, not because they have credible evidence to the contrary, but because they believe that such explanations let schools off the hook. Many conservative critics don't want failings of the educational system as a whole to be obscured, while some liberal critics fear that recognizing these influences will excuse the low performance of schools serving low-income and minority students. To be fair, some of these critics are not really denying the impact of noneducational factors but, rather, are turning a blind eye to them for fear of diverting attention from the variations in educational quality that do matter.

Ironically, these critics usually miss the flip side of the coin: ignoring noneducational causes of variations in scores—that is, assuming that scores are a direct indication of school quality—lets some *high-scoring* schools off the hook. Some schools have high test scores because of the students they serve rather than the quality of the education they offer, but those who are convinced that scores most reflect educational quality consider them good schools regardless. My own children attended some of the highest-scoring schools in our state. They did indeed have some truly superb teachers, but they also had some mediocre ones and a few I thought should not have been allowed to teach at all, including one English teacher whose grammatical and vocabulary errors during parents' visiting day were so egregious that they sparked repeated and audible protests from the parents sitting in the back of the room. Test scores were nevertheless always high, a reflection in part of the very high education level in the community, which was full of attorneys, physicians, academics, economists, foreign diplomats, biomedical researchers, and the like. Another grandmother finding. Not only did these parents provide—on average—environments highly conducive to academic achievement, but many also provided supplementary instruction, either by re-teaching material themselves or by paying for the services of neighborhood tutoring firms.

A concrete example: when my son was in the seventh grade, he took a math class that was not well taught. (I went and watched, to confirm my hunch.) One evening he told me that he was confused by his math homework, which was part of an introduction to probability and statistics. I first tried to clarify the homework, but I soon realized that he was missing a few key notions. I asked him for his class materials, looked them over, and retaught him some of the core concepts, and after that he was able to handle the homework. I went back to the kitchen to clean up from dinner, but he soon called me upstairs again. He had just auditioned successfully for the school's jazz band, and he was having trouble counting out rhythms in the piece he was supposed to practice. I counted them out for him, but he still found them confusing (as I had too, many years earlier, when I first tried playing jazz). So I fetched my own horn and played the music at about half tempo, while he counted it out. That worked. As I resumed scrubbing pots, my wife turned to me and said, "There you have it: social class differences in educational achievement."

Critics who ignore the impact of social factors on test scores miss the point: the reason to acknowledge their influence is not to let anyone off the hook but to get the right answer. Certainly, low scores are a sign that something is amiss; after all, finding out where performance is strong or weak is one of the primary reasons for administering tests. But the low scores by themselves don't tell *why* achievement is low and are usually insufficient to tell us where instruction is good or bad, just as a fever by itself is insufficient to reveal what illness a child has. Disappointing scores can mask good instruction, and high scores can hide problems that need to be addressed. This is particularly the case now, when high-stakes testing can lead to severe inflation of test scores, as explained in Chapter 10. Low scores, like a fever, are an indication that we need to explore further to find out what is really wrong and what interventions might be useful in addressing the problem. Used properly, test scores can provide invaluable descriptive information that can be used to improve education, but incorrectly evaluating schools or educational systems, placing credit or blame where it does not belong, will not help.

Identifying the Causes of Scores

Neither I nor my wife is a doctor, so when one of our children developed a fever, we generally had little idea why. The child's temperature indicated that he or she was ill but was not sufficient to indicate the cause. Sometimes we had hunches, but rarely good enough ones that we were willing to act on them. Lots of illnesses, after all, can cause a sudden fever. Instead, we called our pediatrician. He would ask us for the descriptive information we had gathered, such as how high the fever was, and typically asked us for more—perhaps details of the child's gastroenterological symptoms, whether the child had a headache, and so on. He then ventured his hypothesis about the cause of the symptoms or told us to bring the child in so that he could gather more data. Often his answer was not definitive but was instead more along the lines of, "This is enough to rule out X and Y, which were the troubling possibilities; it is most likely just Z, so let's treat for that and see what happens over the next twenty-four hours."

We often go through a similar process when our cars malfunction. When I was younger, when cars were simpler and I seemed to have more time, I tuned and sometimes repaired my car myself. These days, given the complexity and computer control systems of modern cars, I turn my car over to my mechanic. His process of diagnosis, while incomparably more expert, is fundamentally the same as the one I used, and it is the same as the one used by my pediatrician: coming up with possible explanations for the observed problem by gathering descriptive information, referring to expert knowledge, and ruling out alternative explanations.

For wonderful examples of precisely this sort of reasoning, listen to Click and Clack, the car guys on National Public Radio's *Car Talk*.

Thus, most of us are somewhat familiar with the process of moving from descriptive data to an explanation, and we realize that it is often arduous work. But because this common process turns out to be so controversial when the data to be explained are test scores, it is worth spending a little time here to highlight some of the formal principles that govern this scientific process.

Hidden in the commonplace examples above is a principle that is axiomatic for scientists but often unclear to others. Most people think that a hypothesis is confirmed when the data gathered are consistent with it. That is only part of the process, however. *A hypothesis is only scientifically credible when the evidence gathered has ruled out plausible alternative explanations.* This is fundamental to science, and you can hear it played out every week in the arguments between Click and Clack (both of whom have MIT degrees), in statements like, "No, it can't be a wheel bearing because the noise stops when she depresses the clutch."

A failure to recognize this principle is perhaps the most important reason why many people assume that test scores are in themselves enough to indicate the effectiveness or quality of a school. To the many people who used test scores to argue that my kids' schools were high-quality schools, a competent social scientist would have answered: "Perhaps, but have you taken into account the *other* factors that could plausibly account for these high scores, such as the educational level of the parents in the community?"

The question is not either/or: both quality education and noneducational factors, such as parents' education, could have contributed jointly to the high scores in my kids' schools. (I believe that a careful study, which has not been done, would have revealed precisely that.) The point is that one cannot give all the credit or blame to one factor, such as school quality, without investigating the impact of others. Many of the complex statistical models used in economics, sociology, epidemiology, and other sciences are efforts to take into account (or "control for") other factors that offer plausible alternative explanations of the observed data, and many apportion variation in the outcome—say, test scores—among various possible causes. True randomized experiments are considered the gold standard in many kinds of research because they eliminate most alternative explanations (because the groups being compared are equivalent except for the treatment administered).

Even though most of us have encountered this process of buttressing a hypothesized explanation by ruling out plausible alternatives, it does not seem to be how most people think about test scores in education. Instead, they most often note one or two factors consistent with some pattern in the scores and then announce that they can explain them. And most often, the factors that get credit or blame are aspects of schooling.

This leads directly to a second principle for uncovering causes: *a simple correlation need not indicate that one of the factors causes the other.* For example, consider the following finding from the National Assessment of Educational Progress: "In 2000, eighth-grade teachers who reported that they assigned 45 minutes of homework had students with higher average scores than did students with teachers who assigned lesser amounts of homework."[1] This is a positive correlation—a term that has a technical meaning but in lay parlance means that more of one factor (homework) is associated with more of another (test scores). (A negative correlation means that more of one factor occurs with less of the other—if more homework were associated with lower scores, for example—and a zero correlation means that there is no relationship between the two factors.) The positive association between homework and scores is a common finding, and a common interpreta-

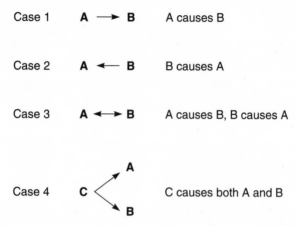

FIG. 6.1. Four causal explanations of a simple correlation.

tion is that homework causes an increase in scores. Maybe, but maybe not.

There are other, plausible explanations for the observed relationship. Figure 6.1 shows four general cases, where *A* is one variable (let it be homework in this example) and *B* is the other (in this case, test scores). More homework may cause higher scores (case 1). Alternatively, the reverse (case 2) may be true: higher achievement may lead to more homework. This possibility may seem at first a bit of a stretch, but it isn't really: perhaps the teachers who are assigned high-achieving kids reason that their students can do more and profit more from it, so they give them more homework. Case 3 simply says that the causal process can work in both directions at once.

Case 4 lays the credit or blame at the feet of some other factor entirely: something else (factor *C*) may cause both more homework and higher scores. For example, perhaps the homework is not causing scores to rise but, rather, some attributes of certain parents, such as more concern with academic achievement, lead their kids to score higher and their teachers, concerned about parental approval, to assign more homework. (This process was certainly going on in my children's middle school. When I complained about greatly excessive homework one year, the principal responded by saying that some parents would complain if there were less.) Dick Darlington, a professor at Cornell, used to give this example in his statistics classes: the amount of salt applied to the roads is correlated with the rate of traffic accidents. Does salt (say, factor A in Figure 6.1) cause accidents (factor B in Figure 6.1)? Of course not. The missing element is factor C, snow. When there is snow on the roads, the road crews apply salt, but this is not enough to fully compensate for the slipperiness caused by the weather, and the accident rate increases.

The point is not to argue for one of these explanations; rather, the point is that there are many possibilities, *and without additional information, we cannot tell which is correct.* People will often simply pick the explanation that seems most reasonable on its face. Unfortunately, people don't agree about what is most reasonable, and in any event, their guesses are often wrong.

This principle is all too easy to ignore when a causal explanation seems commonsensical—shouldn't more homework improve achievement?—but looking at a wider variety of correlations helps make it clearer. Many years ago, I starting writing a spoof, based on real research findings, entitled "The Effects of Irrelevant Coursework." The research literature shows many correlations between coursework and test scores. For example, more coursework in mathematics is associated with higher mathematics test scores. This sort of finding is occasionally trumpeted in the news media and gets a good bit of attention in the policy community. The interpretation is consistent: kids should take more courses in subject X to improve their performance in that subject. This conclusion is obviously reasonable up to a point: the reason to take a course in algebra is to learn algebra, and students who study it more will learn more. This is not, however, quite the whole story. The complication, usually ignored in press reports, is that more coursework in some subjects predicts higher scores in *other* subjects as well. For example, years ago, H. D. Hoover, then director of the Iowa Testing Programs, showed that high-school students who take more math courses have higher scores on the ACT mathematics test, but they also have higher scores on a composite of the other three ACT tests (English, science, and social studies). The same pattern is found with science courses.[2] Other research found that study of foreign languages predicts test scores in reading and English vocabulary. One might conclude that students are learning the meaning of root words through studying Romance languages, but wait: it also predicts scores in mathematics.[3] Why is this? Does learning French conjugations really facilitate learning algebra? Does taking more courses in science improve reading skills and knowledge of social studies? Perhaps a bit, but certainly not much. The key is a third variable: the characteristics of the kids who take lots of mathematics courses and study foreign language early. These kids tend to have high motivation for achievement, and they tend to be high achievers. As one colleague once put it simply, in politically incorrect terms, "Smart kids do well on tests."

Failure to take this particular factor into account—that is, the characteristics of the people with higher values on one of the variables—is a classic problem in social science, formally labeled *selectivity bias*. Consider this example: years ago, when a large proportion of students did not take algebra, a study was released showing that students who took algebra were more likely to complete college than those who did not. In the education-policy community, this was generally interpreted as *A* causes *B:* taking algebra *makes* students more likely to complete college. Algebra became known as a "gatekeeper" course, and great efforts were made to increase the proportion of students taking it. This endeavor was all for the good, in my opinion: learning some algebra is a good thing, it can help people understand all manner of problems in real life, and it opens doors for students both in later studies and in the world of work. The interpretation of this particular study, however, was suspect because of selectivity bias: students who took algebra in those days were unlike students who did not, and some of the differences between the groups could have contributed to the observed correlation. For example, students who wanted to go to competitive colleges—mostly high achievers—generally took algebra.

As these examples begin to show, when we want to explain test scores, there can be many missing third factors such as the one labeled C in Figure 6.1, presenting us with a variety of plausible explanations of scores that need to be rebutted. The list of factors that have been shown to predict achievement, including scores on tests, is long and diverse. It includes, for example, the health of children taking the tests, parental education, income, family configuration, and cultural influences. The list is too long, and the controversy about the evidence too extensive, to address here. But you might ask: can't we in principle "control for" or adjust away the effects of these many factors in order to isolate what people really want to measure, which is the effect of educational quality on scores?

The answer is: not very well. To see why, let's consider socioeconomic status, or SES, which is universally acknowledged to predict test scores. SES is a somewhat amorphous term coined by sociologists to describe the social placement of individuals and households. It is not uncommon to treat some measure of income as if it were a measure of socioeconomic status, but SES refers to more than that, and it is properly measured by a composite of income, the parents' educational attainment, and their occupational status. All three of these variables strongly predict test scores, even when taken separately. For example, in the 2000 NAEP twelfth-grade assessment of mathematics, the mean performance of students eligible for free or reduced-priced lunch was 0.71 standard deviation below the mean score for other students. That is a large difference—nearly as large as the difference in eighth-grade math between the U.S. and Japan, and about three-fourths of the typical mean difference between African American and white students.

Because high-SES kids generally don't go to the same schools as low-SES kids, isolating the effects of school quality would require disentangling them from the effects of SES. Efforts to do this are too numerous to count, but they run into two obstacles: SES is usually poorly measured, and even when well measured, it does not tell us all we need to know about the social factors that influence test scores.

In the databases that include test scores, SES is often gauged by whatever measures are at hand or can be gathered easily, and these are often weak. As I explained in Chapter 5, school districts and states are allowed to collect only limited information about the characteristics of students, and even most of the large-scale testing programs gather only weak information about socioeconomic status. (NAEP relies on students to provide this information, but—another grandmother finding—kids don't provide accurate information about many aspects of family background.)[4] Therefore, we usually have to make do with weak proxies for the SES data we would really want—using indicators such as students' eligibility for free and reduced-priced lunches, for example, and their estimates of the number of books in their home. Despite the weaknesses of these proxies, they do predict scores, and strongly—just not well enough. There remains some argument among social scientists about how adequate a job one can do if one combines enough of these flawed measures, but that is no help to most users of scores—politicians, the press, parents—who usually have access only to the very limited data collected by states and local districts.

A more fundamental problem, also often ignored by social scientists, is that socioeconomic status is really not quite the right thing to measure anyway. Even if measured perfectly, SES is itself largely a proxy for the variables, usually unmeasured, that directly influence student achievement. For example, within limits, income itself does not directly affect students' learning, but other factors that are influenced by income, or that determine income, do. Higher incomes enable families to provide children with better nutrition and health care, more educational resources in the home, and greater access to resources outside of the home, such as music lessons and after-school tutoring. The factors that enable parents to achieve a higher income, such as higher levels of schooling, achievement motivation, and an acceptance of delayed gratification, can also help their children achieve more in school. And the educational attainment of parents, which has been shown in many studies to be a powerful predictor of the academic performance of children, is itself a marker of other things. A mother's college degree does not convey an automatic advantage to her children on achievement tests. Highly educated parents, however, will often behave differently than less well educated parents in many ways that foster achievement: using language more and in different ways, placing greater value on academic success, and so on. Of course, there are many poorly educated parents (my immigrant grandparents, for example) who do precisely those things needed to encourage academic achievement and many educated parents who do not, but the probability of finding those types of behavior increases with higher parental education.

Any number of studies have shown the complexity of the noneducational factors that can affect achievement and test scores. For example, one rather uplifting study in the early 1990s, during the influx of Southeast Asian "boat people" to the United States, attempted to uncover factors could help explain why the children of poor Indochinese immigrant parents outscored their neighborhood peers by a very large margin. Some of the most striking results were grandmother findings: for instance, parents in the immigrant communities generally stressed the importance of educational achievement as a path to a better life, expected their children to study regularly, despite their meager standard of living, tried to provide both a place and a regular time for studying, and so on.[5] This study reminded me of an anecdote my mother wrote about years ago. During the Great Depression, my immigrant grandmother, who had never had the opportunity to gain an advanced education, prepared food for some striking workers in town and told my mother to take it to them. My mother balked, not because of any disagreement but because of what she saw as the potential for acute embarrassment: like many adolescents, she did not want to stand out from the crowd. She protested that carrying food to the strikers was not going to address the fundamental problem. My grandmother answered, "That's why you are getting an education, so you can change conditions. Meantime, carry the soup."

A second study, at least as depressing as the study of boat people is inspiring, describes in truly painful detail the enormous differences in the linguistic environments provided to children in two nearly adjacent communities, one impoverished and poorly educated, and another highly educated and much more affluent. Researchers found dramatic differences in the frequency and types of verbal interactions in the two communities, and these were paralleled by huge differences in the typical rates of the children's acquisition of vocabulary.[6] Simply controlling for the income level of school populations does not fully capture these sorts of influences on students' test scores.

A third principle for identifying the causes of test scores is just a special case of the second: *simple concurrence in time does not estab-*

lish causality.* In recent years, despite astonishing denials from certain quarters, evidence has clearly shown that carbon dioxide has been building up in the atmosphere, temperatures have been rising, and the polar ice caps have been melting. Math scores have also been rising at the same time, but it is a safe bet that melting ice caps should not get the credit. You might say that no one with any sense would attribute the rising scores to melting ice caps, but that would be missing the point. Often a concurrence *appears* more plausible, and this leads people to make causal arguments that actually have no more basis than this absurd illustration. If you follow coverage of educational testing in the press, you will find frequent explanations of scores based on a simple concurrence—for example, assertions that a policy is (or is not) successful because scores have (or have not) increased. These explanations may be wrong or they may be right, but they are always unwarranted: without additional information, we cannot know whether they are correct.

And finally, a fourth principle arises when one attempts to discern the effects of educational quality on test scores: *don't trust scores on high-stakes tests without other evidence to confirm them.* Scores on high-stakes tests—tests that have serious consequences for students or teachers—often become severely inflated. That is, gains in scores on these tests are often far larger than true gains in student learning. Worse, this inflation is highly variable and unpredictable, so one cannot tell which school's scores are inflated and which are legitimate. There are several reasons for this, in-

---

* The second principle refers to a "cross-sectional" correlation, a relationship that appears at a single point in time. At a given time, kids who do more homework also tend to get higher scores. This third principle refers to a correlation as well, but one that occurs over time. An example would be an increase over time in the amount of homework done, accompanied by an increase in scores.

cluding inappropriate test preparation and simple cheating. The problem, its causes, and its severity are discussed in Chapter 10.

The problem this creates for evaluating schools is obvious: how can you identify the effective schools and programs, those that warrant recognition and emulation, if you can't tell which schools' higher scores are bogus? It is also not news. Some experts in measurement, most notably George Madaus at Boston College, warned about this at least four decades ago; in a report published by the Congressional Budget Office twenty years ago, I warned that it was a growing problem that would erode our ability to monitor trends in student performance; it has been confirmed by several careful empirical studies since 1991; and it has been discussed in the public media and the education trade press since at least 1988, although far less frequently than is warranted. Nonetheless, score inflation is routinely ignored when people use scores in an effort to identify effective schools or school systems, not only by politicians and the news media but also by educators and by some social scientists who ought to know better.

This fourth principle is a bit different from the others because it calls on you to question the descriptive information itself, rather than being cautious about making the leap from trustworthy test data to an inference about its causes. It also might seem different in that it appears to be specific to test scores, but it really is not; inflated measures appear in all sorts of other areas as well, such as diesel truck emissions and health care cost containment. Again, more on this in Chapter 10.

⬭ Causes of Some Important Patterns in Test Scores

Often—as in most of the examples above—people search for explanations of specific test scores that are, for whatever reason, of particular interest to them. Parents want to identify effective schools for their children; politicians want to claim credit for successful initiatives or to use low scores to justify reforms; newspapers want to highlight supposed differences in school quality; critics want to identify failures; educators want to claim success; and so on.

But public debate about education and other social policies is shaped by concern about broad patterns in student performance—national secular trends upward or downward in scores, the large differences between racial/ethnic and economic groups, other aspects of the variation of student performance, differences in average scores between countries, and so on. These patterns provide a context for the discussion, shaping people's understanding of the issues and their expectations for reasonable improvements. And purported explanations of the patterns often play a central role in these debates. Here I look at the evidence pertaining to two of the most important patterns: overall trends in scores over the past four decades, and the huge variability in the performance of American students.

Trends in test scores over time may well be the most discussed results from large-scale testing programs. These have been a staple of public and political debate for more than a quarter century, and much of the discussion focuses on their putative causes. Most of the explanations that have been offered, whether in fact correct or not, are not supported: the principles described above are widely ignored, and scores alone are presented as evidence of changes in the quality of education.

This was perhaps most striking early in the 1980s, when widespread and intense public debate focused on the pervasive decline in test scores that had occurred during the 1960s and 1970s, the end of the drop, and the relative gains shown by minority students. Social scientists and other commentators offered a remarkable diversity of explanations for these patterns. They pointed to both educational factors and social and other noneducational factors, but noneducational explanations gained much less traction in the public debate. Among the explanations proffered were a watering down of required coursework in secondary school; insufficient time devoted to core subjects; the putatively low academic quality and poor preparation of teachers; the growing proportion of students living in single-parent families; changes in family size (research suggests that in many social settings, children in larger families score lower); an increase in time spent watching television; radioactive fallout from atomic tests (one study argued that the decline was worse where fallout was heavier); changes in the ethnic composition of the student population; desegregation, Head Start, and the Title I compensatory education program (all put forward as causes of the relative gains of minorities); and minimum-competency testing and the conservative policies of the 1980s (both suggested as having caused the end of the decline). And this list is not exhaustive.

Most of these explanations, regardless of whether they were correct—or, to be more precise, I should say "partly correct," since no one factor seems sufficient to explain these trends—were put forward without much evidence to support them. Often the only justification for an explanation was just simple concurrence: we think that X changed about the time that scores declined, so X must have caused the decline. And, of course, this concurrence by itself does not tell us much; a great many changes in all manner of things happened to be roughly concurrent with the decline in scores, and almost all of them were entirely irrelevant. Very few commentators acted like a competent pediatrician—or a competent auto mechanic, for that matter—by searching for evidence that would rule out alternative explanations. Few even mentioned alternatives.

Worse, many of these commentators did not even get the timing right and therefore pointed to concurrences that did not really exist. Because the debate focused unduly on tests at the high-school level, in particular the SAT, critics tended to focus on explanations that were concurrent with changes in scores in those grades. This ignored the earlier end of the decline in lower grades, as described in Chapter 5. It also failed to take into account the fact that educational performance at the end of high school represents the accumulated effects of twelve years of schooling, so some of the relevant causes—for example, factors that helped end the decline—would have antedated the actual change in scores in the high-school grades, sometimes by many years.

More careful studies of the possible causes of these score trends suggest two generalizations: numerous factors appear to have played a part, each contributing modestly, and the causes appear to be social as well as educational. The evidence strongly suggests this to be true of both the onset and the ending of the score decline of the 1960s and 1970s. The evidence is of two types: broad patterns in the trends, and research exploring specific possible causes in detail.

The broad patterns shown by trends in scores are not by themselves enough to establish the causes, but they offer some useful clues and rule out some possible explanations. One pattern is the truly remarkable pervasiveness of the decline in scores. The drop occurred throughout the nation's highly decentralized school system, affected students of many types and ages, appeared in private as well as public schools, and even occurred in Canada. That pretty well puts the kibosh on those who would like to lay all of the blame at the feet of education policies and raises the possibility that larger social forces were also at work.

A second pattern is the uniformity of the decline among subject areas. I believe this issue was first raised by the sociologist Christopher Jencks. The logic is straightforward and, to my way of thinking, persuasive: if only educational policies and practices were at fault, one would expect to see larger declines in subjects taught primarily in school (mathematics) than in those that are more influenced by "indirect instruction" outside of school, such as reading and especially vocabulary. This was not observed:

there was no consistent difference in the decline across subject areas. This stands in marked contrast to the improvements of the past two decades, which have been striking in elementary-school mathematics, modest in secondary-school mathematics, and insubstantial in reading.

The final pattern is the cohort effect described in Chapter 5: the decline ended first in the younger (mid-elementary) grades, and the nadir gradually moved up through the grades as these cohorts moved through school. Jencks was the first to point this out as well: cohort effects of this sort are more consistent with some social explanations than most educational ones.[7]

The available evidence about specific hypothesized causes of the score trends is not sufficient to evaluate all of them, but it is adequate to rule out some of them and to estimate the size of the effects others might have had. The evidence suggests that a variety of both social and educational factors may have contributed to the trends but that no one factor can account for more than a modest share of the total. For example, by my estimate, changes in the demographic composition of the student population may have accounted for 10 or 20 percent of the decline and somewhat damped the subsequent increase in scores. Changes in family composition may have contributed to both the decline and the upturn. Some changes in educational practice, such as a softening of course requirements and course content, could have played a role, particularly in the higher grades. Changes in homework may have had a small effect.

The relative gains of African American students also appear to reflect several factors. Research suggests that social factors, such as an increase in the educational attainment of parents, contributed to the gains but are insufficient to account for them entirely. Evaluations of Title I, Head Start, and desegregation suggest that they, too, may have contributed, albeit modestly. Research generally finds their long-term effects to be fairly small, if even positive, and the impact of the former two on the relative gains of African Americans is lessened by the fact that many of the students served by these programs are white.[8]

Taken together, then, the evidence suggests that the trends in student performance reflect a complicated confluence of a variety of factors, both educational and social. With hindsight, perhaps this is a grandmother finding as well. The American educational system is complex, even fragmented, and the development of children's cognitive capabilities is a staggeringly complicated process that we are only beginning to understand. Why should we expect a single factor to have a very large impact on development across a wide variety of contexts nationwide, and all of the manifold other influences on student learning to stand still in the meantime? Or, to put this same question in more forward-looking terms, why should we expect a single package of education reforms to create upward trends in scores even larger than the decline (which has been the goal of numerous recent policies)?

The simplistic debate about the great decline could serve as a cautionary tale, but so far it has not. The debate about the causes of student performance has not grown a great deal more sophisticated—perhaps *realistic* is a better word—since then. You can see this in the pronouncements about the purported success or failure of No Child Left Behind. NCLB was not even signed into law until January of 2002, and it took some considerable time for states to respond—for example, to purchase and administer the additional tests required by the law. If the program is successful, it should take a while for its effects to be felt. Nonetheless, when the results of the 2004 NAEP (administered roughly two years after NCLB was signed) were released to the public, supporters of NCLB pointed to an increase in math scores as an argument that the policy was succeeding, while critics pointed to the lack of an increase in reading scores to show that it wasn't. That mathematics scores had been increasing at a rapid clip for years before

NCLB was not noted at all, and the possibility that something else—many other things, actually—could be going on at the same time generally escaped mention. Worse, some commentators did not rely on the NAEP at all, instead accepting at face value the increases in scores on state tests that educators were determined—in some cases, desperate—to achieve.

A second question that is less often explicitly debated but nonetheless implicitly plays a major role in shaping education policy is this: what causes the huge variability in test scores shown by American students? Asking this question is essential to setting targets for improvement. What does it mean to say that "all students can achieve to high standards"? In various forms, this statement has been repeated, mantra-like, by reformers and education policymakers for years. You will find it in the federal Education Department's explanation of No Child Left Behind and in statements by various state departments of education.

When this statement became a staple of education policy about fifteen years ago, I started asking the people using it what it meant. I pointed out that "all children can achieve to high standards" could mean at least three things. First, it could mean that the variation in student performance would remain enormous but that the whole distribution would rocket upward, such that kids at the low end of the distribution would end up doing better than most kids do today. Second, it could mean that the bottom part of the distribution—all the kids whose scores are strung out below the average—would get scrunched up toward the average, or even higher, but the high-scoring kids would remain dispersed. Third, it could mean that everyone would become more alike, so the high-scoring kids would get scrunched down toward the average as well.

The initial reaction to my question was usually puzzlement. Given a moment to think, they replied that they expected a combination of the first two outcomes: everyone improves, but the low-scoring kids improve even more, bringing their scores up relative to the rest. No one wanted to say that high-achieving kids would become more mediocre, of course, so we would let their scores remain spread out.

However, the distribution of performance is very wide—that is, a great gap separates low-scoring from high-scoring kids. Therefore, if the performance target is high or even just middling relative to the current distribution, a great deal of upward movement of the whole distribution and compression of the distribution— kids toward the bottom moving up relative to higher-scoring kids—would be needed to push most kids above it. I addressed the issue of unrealistic expectations for overall improvement earlier. Here I would like to consider the issue of compressing the distribution of performance.

Many of the performance targets set in recent years seem to rest on an expectation that the distribution of scores can be reduced dramatically. I call this the myth of the vanishing variance. If one looks at the data, it is hard to see how the distribution could be compressed so much. It could shrink, yes, but dramatically? No.

I believe that the tacit reasoning underlying these expectations is a view that educational inequities are the root of much of the performance variation in the United States. Only if this is so would it make sense to argue that education reforms can make the performance distribution shrink dramatically.

There can be no denying that educational opportunities in the United States are enormously, and in my view unconscionably, inequitable. There is ample research documenting this, but these too are grandmother findings: they document, in awful and systematic detail, what one can't help but observe just by walking into a handful of schools. And while there is academic debate about how much the various disparities in resources and opportunities affect performance, the proof is in the pudding, or, as economists would put it, in revealed preferences. Most well-educated people who know schools won't put their own kids in most of the schools serving predominately disadvantaged children.

From this unavoidable fact, it is a seemingly small leap to assume that if we reduced these inequities, the variability of student performance would shrink, and the performance of some kids at the bottom would move up toward the average (or beyond). And this is indeed a reasonable expectation. What is unreasonable is to expect that the variability of performance thereafter would be dramatically smaller. The reason for this is straightforward: there are many things in addition to educational inequities—glaring social inequities, for example—that also contribute to the variability in student performance.

One piece of evidence supporting more modest expectations has already been noted (in Chapter 5): the findings of international studies, such as TIMSS. These studies do not show a strong and consistent relationship between the educational and social heterogeneity of nations and the variability of their students' scores. For example, both Japan and Korea have more equitable educational systems than does the United States at the eighth-grade level, but their students have roughly as wide a range of scores as do American students (only at a much higher level).* There is some variation among countries in this regard, which suggests that it should be possible to shrink the variability of stu-

---

* In TIMSS but not PISA (which tests older students and groups them by age rather than grade), an interesting pattern appears that is consistent with the view that educational opportunities are more equitable in Japan and Korea. While the total variability of students in these two countries is similar to the variability in the United States, the breakdown of that variation is not. There is much less variation *among* classrooms in Japan and Korea than in the United States. That is, the mean scores of classrooms are more similar to each other in both Japan and Korea. However, the variability of their students *within* the average classrooms is correspondingly greater. This is what one would expect if educational opportunities and social background are more similar across classrooms in these two countries than in the United States. The state of Iowa also shows less variation among schools than is common in the United States as a whole.

dent performance somewhat. But the fact that most countries show variability that is not dramatically different from that in the United States suggests setting modest expectations in this regard.

Another piece of evidence comes from examining the effect of racial and ethnic group differences. Some of the best known and most troubling symptoms of social and educational inequities in the United States are the very large mean differences in test scores among these groups, in particular among African Americans, Latinos, and non-Hispanic whites (see Chapter 5). Some years ago, I presented a talk at a conference in which I made the argument, based on TIMSS and other data, that we cannot expect a dramatic shrinking of the variability of student test scores. A decrease, yes, but not a dramatic one. I was taken aback by the hostility of the reaction from some in the audience. Afterward, one of the questioners explained the tenor of the reaction: he and others had thought that I was arguing that racial and ethnic group differences in achievement are fixed, perhaps innate, and cannot be reduced. I was shocked and appalled. My argument was not this at all.

Since then, when I know this issue will come up, I come armed with two slides, which I also use every year in one of my introductory classes. I start by posing the following question: if we simply obliterated the current average differences in test scores between the major racial and ethnic groups in the United States, such that the distribution of scores in every other group looked just like the distribution among non-Hispanic whites, how much would the total variability in scores—the variability in the total student population—shrink? Usually, no one ventures a guess; it must be apparent that I would not ask the question unless I expected that people's assumptions would be wrong. The answer: very little. I calculated this four times: for eighth-grade reading and math, and using data from both the National Assessment of Educational Progress and the National Education Longitudinal Study of 1988, one of the federal Education Department's infrequent nationally representative longitudinal surveys. The reduction in the variability (technically, the standard deviation) ranges from about 0.5 percent to 9 percent across the four cases.

How can this be? It is predictable from statistical theory, but it is counterintuitive, given how large the mean differences between these groups are. The reason is that the variability *within* each group is very large and simply swamps the impact of the average differences among groups. Eliminating (not just reducing) racial and ethnic group differences would slightly reduce the overall variability of student performance, and eliminating other inequities, such as the average disparity in performance between poor and affluent whites, would slightly reduce it further. But in the end, we would still confront a tremendous variability in performance, and we would still need an educational system able to serve students across that wide range of performance.

In many ways, then, a careful examination of the big picture leads to some of the same lessons as a conscientious effort to explain test scores in a particular school or school system. The development of educational achievement is a complex process that is influenced by a great variety of factors, some of which are far beyond the control of educators. Simply attributing differences in scores to school quality or, similarly, simply assuming that scores themselves are sufficient to reveal educational effectiveness, is unrealistic. And more generally, simple explanations of performance differences are usually naive. All of this is established science. I would go one step further: this suggests that to be realistic, we often need to set more modest targets for improvements in performance than many policymakers of late have been wont to do. I will return to this at the end of the book.

Chapter 7

Error and Reliability: How Much We Don't Know What We're Talking About

SHORTLY AFTER LEAVING graduate school, I worked on an evaluation of a federal program designed to contain costs in the Medicare and Medicaid programs. I was then an analyst with the Congressional Budget Office (CBO), and a House subcommittee chair who was skeptical of the program had requested that we evaluate it. The Department of Health and Human Services (HHS), which administered the program and by all signs wanted to preserve it, prepared a very similar evaluation to ours. The CBO and HHS were both asked to present the results of their studies at a subcommittee hearing.

Washington being what it is, there was no question of my actually presenting the testimony; I was far too junior and nowhere nearly equal in rank to the person presenting for HHS. However, being the most knowledgeable analyst on the team, I wrote the testimony and, as is customary, accompanied the person testifying to the hearing on the off chance that he would get a question he could not handle without my help.

The CBO and HHS evaluations were similar in results as well as approach. HHS concluded that the program was saving a small amount of money, something like 10 cents on the dollar. In contrast, our CBO report concluded that the program was losing roughly 10 cents on the dollar.

The fly in the ointment was that neither evaluation could support a conclusion as precise as "for every $1.00 spent, $1.10 (or $.90) was saved." The studies relied on a variety of arguable assumptions and decisions about methods, and they used less-than-ideal data based only on samples. Therefore, in writing our testimony, I did not claim that the program lost money. Instead, I wrote that "within any reasonable estimate of the margin of error," the two evaluations reached much the same conclusion: the program was roughly a wash, neither saving nor losing an appreciable amount of money. Those who wanted to preserve or terminate the program, I argued, should look to rationales other than cost.

The dry phrase "within any reasonable estimate of the margin of error" attracted much more attention than I had expected or wanted. The chair of the subcommittee leaned forward from his seat on the dais, stared at the person presenting my testimony (my boss), and said something along the lines of, "What the hell is this 'margin of error' stuff? Doesn't that mean you don't know what the hell you are talking about?"

My boss remained unfazed—fortunately, because I was far too inexperienced and unnerved by this outburst to figure out a response on the spot. One came to me only after the hearing had ended and I was safely out of the room: "Yes, the 'margin of error' is a way of quantifying the degree to which we don't know what the hell we are talking about."

This degree of uncertainty, second nature not only to social scientists but also to scientists in many other fields, is what is called *error* in educational measurement and all other statistical disciplines. In educational testing, it takes two analogous but distinct forms, called *measurement error* and *sampling error.*

The amount of error in turn determines the *reliability* of a test score: the higher the error, the lower the reliability. The importance of error and reliability is now widely enough recognized that they are even occasionally referenced in the law. For example, the No Child Left Behind Act of 2001, which is the single most important statutory influence on K–12 achievement testing today, states that the assessments it mandates "shall . . . be used for purposes for which such assessments are valid and reliable," and it states that the performance of groups of students with a school—such as minority students—need not be considered separately in calculating whether a school has made adequate yearly progress "in a case in which the number of students in a category is insufficient to yield statistically reliable information."[1]

What does "reliable information" really mean? In common parlance, the word *reliable* can signify many things, such as trustworthy, dependable, or consistent. In educational measurement, however, the term has a specific and critically important meaning. The key to understanding reliability is to understand what experts in measurement and other statistical sciences mean by "error."

Measurement Error

Several years ago, parents in Massachusetts whose children took the Massachusetts Comprehensive Assessment System test received a score report that looked like the one in Figure 7.1. The student's score was denoted by a small, vertical black bar (here, it appears to be a score of about 247, according to the scale at the bottom of the figure), and a longer horizontal bar (extending from 240 to about 255 in the example) was labeled the "probable range of scores." A guide to these reports, made available to parents, explained that "student performance is shown as a range of

1. How did   do on this test?

SUBJECT AREA	PERFORMANCE LEVEL	SCALED SCORE	DISPLAY OF SCORE AND PROBABLE RANGE OF SCORES			
			Warning	Needs Improvement	Proficient	Advanced
Mathematics	Proficient	280				

FIG. 7.1. A sample MCAS report to parents. Massachusetts
Department of Education, *MCAS Tests of Spring 2002, Parent/
Guardian Report.*

scores. The bar in this section shows where your child's score falls
within a performance level range. The vertical line in the middle
of the bar represents your child's scaled score . . . on each test.
The horizontal bar shows the range of scores your child might receive if the test were taken many times."[2]

This horizontal bar, labeled the "probable range of scores" in
the figure, represents measurement error. To put it in the terms
used by that subcommittee chair years ago, the width of the bar
quantifies how much we don't know about this particular student's performance on the MCAS from this single instance of testing. All test scores have a range of uncertainty such as this—some
larger, some smaller—and many other testing programs report
this information, although not always in a form similar to this or
with this much explanation. The efforts by Massachusetts and
some other states and districts to convey this uncertainty to parents, the press, and others are laudable. I know from experience,
however, that many people find this sort of information perplexing, understanding neither the sources of the uncertainty nor the
meaning of the range described.

In the language of measurement, what precisely is meant by
"error"? In common speech, error often refers to a measurement
that is systematically wrong. For example, in discussing a bathroom scale that typically reads roughly five pounds too high, peo-

ple might say, "I actually have lost more weight than this scale indicates, because it has an error of five pounds." People might use
exactly the same phrase if they stood on the scale only one time.
In that case, however, they would not know whether the discrepancy of five pounds is consistent over time or a one-time fluke. It
might be, for example, that the first time they stood on the scale it
just happened to register five pounds too high, and if they had
climbed on again, the second reading would have been pretty
much on target or far too low.

This seemingly subtle distinction between consistent and inconsistent inaccuracy is critically important in testing and, for that
matter, in any application of statistics. Error in these fields—both
sampling error and measurement error—generally signifies uncertainty or imprecision. That is, it refers to *inconsistency*, not systematic inaccuracy. This uncertainty is inherent in any single measurement, such as the "probable range of scores" above. It also shows
up in any single public opinion poll, such as the one discussed in
Chapter 2: additional polls would have provided different estimates than the one Zogby presented. Taking repeated measurements, such as by administering repeated polls to different samples, or testing a student multiple times, would reveal this
inconsistency. In contrast, a systematic error, such as a scale that
consistently reads five pounds too high, is called *bias*. In educational testing, the practical implications of this difference are hard
to overstate.

To make this distinction concrete, let's go back to cheap bathroom scales. If your scale is of low quality, it is probably notice-
ably inconsistent from one measurement to the next. You weigh
yourself, and it reads 165 pounds; you step off and on again, and it
reads 164 pounds; you try again, and it reads 165.5 pounds. The
scale's inconsistency is, for all practical purposes, random and unpredictable. You do not know at any time whether the next reading will be higher or lower, and you don't know whether the next

discrepancy between two readings will be larger or smaller than the previous one.

This inconsistency is measurement error. One effective if neurotic way to quantify the problem—to find out how much you don't know what the hell you are talking about when you estimate your weight by standing on the scale only once—would be to get on and off the scale many times, say, 100 times. The distribution or spread of the 100 measurements would give you an idea of the degree of uncertainty in any single measurement. In fact, the "range of probable scores" in Figure 7.1 is a similar estimate: it reflects the distribution of scores the student would get by taking the MCAS math test many times.

The difference between measurement error and bias sometimes appears slippery to the uninitiated, but a simple thought experiment distinguishes the two. If you were to take repeated measurements and the average of those repeated measures gradually approached the right answer, you would have measurement error. If the average of repeated measures stayed incorrect, even with a great many measurements, you would have bias. For example, given the inconsistency in your cheap scale, if you weighed yourself *only once,* the single reading would likely be either too high or too low, and this discrepancy from your actual weight could be the effect of either bias or measurement error; with only the one time on the scale, you could not know which. The cause would become clear if you climbed onto the scale repeatedly and kept taking the average of your repeated measurements. If the scale has measurement error but is not biased, the average would approach your true weight as the number of readings became larger. The random fluctuations in the readings would gradually cancel each other out. However, if the scale is biased, this average would be wrong no matter how many times you stepped on the scale. Either way, as the number of estimates increased, the average would stabilize around a single number, but in the case of bias, that number would remain wrong.

In educational testing, measurement error is much more important than it is in the case of your bathroom scale, and its causes and effects have been the subject of many decades of research. Three questions about measurement error are particularly important for interpreting and using test scores. What causes this inconsistency? How is it measured—that is, how do we quantify how much we don't know what the hell we are talking about when we have only one measurement? And, for practical purposes, how much does it matter?

In Chapter 2, I noted three sources of inconsistency in test scores. The source of error that has received by far the most attention in technical psychometrics is variation in performance from one sample of items to the next, illustrated by *feckless* and *parsimonious* in the vocabulary test example. The technical reports accompanying most large-scale assessments usually include estimates of reliability, called *internal consistency* reliability statistics, that take into account only the measurement error that arises from the selection of items to construct that particular form of the test.

The second cause of measurement error is noted in the explanation of the probable range of scores offered by the Massachusetts Department of Education: fluctuations in students' performance over time. If students were given the exact same test multiple times—assuming they did not remember its contents and did not become fatigued or simply fed up with testing—they would score differently from one occasion to the next for many different reasons, including variations in their own conditions (illness, amount of sleep, test anxiety, and the like) and external factors (conditions in the testing room, and so on). When students take the SAT multiple times and find that their scores fluctuate, that inconsistency reflects both of these sources of error: differences in the items selected for successive forms of the SAT, and the students' own good days and bad days.

A bathroom scale can also illustrate both of these sources of measurement error. The problem of getting a reliable estimate of your own weight is not just a matter of random inconsistencies in the scale's behavior at 6:30 a.m. on any particular morning. There is another problem as well: your true weight will fluctuate considerably from day to day, even if there is no underlying trend in your weight, as a result of what you have eaten and drunk, how much you have exercised, and so on. This is the reason for the common but misguided advice that if you are trying to lose weight, you should weigh yourself only infrequently rather than daily. This is poor advice because if you compare only two measurements, say one week apart, the randomness of your scale's behavior and the fluctuations in your own weight together will add error to both estimates and create a substantial risk that the comparison will be entirely misleading unless your weight change has been large enough to overwhelm these inconsistencies. A better, if compulsive, approach would be to take frequent measurements but to ignore differences from one time to the next, instead of taking averages or looking for underlying trends.

The third common source of measurement error is inconsistency in scoring. This obviously does not come into play in the case of machine-scored multiple-choice tests unless something malfunctions, as it did in a recent, well-publicized case in which moisture caused students' SAT answer sheets to expand so that the bubbles on the answer sheets did not line up properly with the sensors on the scanners. However, inconsistencies in scoring can be important in any testing program that requires people to score students' work, particularly when the products they have to score are complex. This issue appears routinely in discussions of assessments such as writing tests, other essay tests, and portfolio assessments. It is often referred to as interrater agreement, interrater consistency, or interrater reliability. The last, as we shall see in a moment, is a potentially misleading term.

Variations in scoring provide a good illustration of the distinction between bias and measurement error. Scoring variations take several forms. One is consistent differences in the severity of raters. As a graduate student, I was a teaching assistant in a large class that had three sections, each taught by a different graduate student. Partway through the semester, a number of students in my section complained that my grading of assignments was consistently and substantially harsher than that of the other two teaching assistants. I checked, and they were right. (I then adjusted the entire distribution of my grades to better match those of the other two sections.) Individual raters may also change their behavior over time, often unpredictably. Faced with many essays to grade, for example, one scorer may become crankier and hence more severe over time, while another may become more lenient, just wanting finish the work. And yet another may produce a progressively narrower range of scores as time goes on. Raters who are comparably tough on average may nonetheless differ in leniency from one student to the next. For example, two raters may be swayed to a different degree by grammatical errors or even sloppy handwriting, as a result of which they will rank specific students differently even if their average severity is the same. Raters may also be swayed by characteristics of the student other than the work at hand, such as their demeanor in class. Clear scoring rubrics and careful training can lessen but not eliminate these inconsistencies. (For this reason, all work in my classes is graded anonymously, with students identified solely by ID numbers, and students take their exams on computers to avoid issues raised by handwriting. We add names only at the end of the semester so that we can take other factors into account in assigning final grades, such as class participation and extenuating circumstances.)

Clearly, some inconsistencies in scoring are systematic rather than random. When do they produce bias, and when just measurement error? Let's consider one example of each. First, suppose a student takes an admissions test that involves hand scoring. She takes the test only one time and has it scored, unbeknownst to her, by Rater A at the testing company. Rater A is relatively lenient among the scorers employed by the testing company, and so the student's score is a bit higher than it would have been if many of the other raters had scored it. The assignment of the student's exam to Rater A is for all practical purposes random, and if the student takes the exam again, she will very likely not get Rater A the second time. Therefore, if she took the test repeatedly and then averaged her scores, the inconsistencies in scoring would cancel out, and the average would tend toward her "true" score— or at least, her score purged of the effects of rater inconsistency. Accordingly, we can consider this inconsistency just measurement error, and it would contribute to a band of uncertainty extending both ways from the true score, just as in the MCAS example in Figure 7.1.

But now take another case: a testing program in which students' own teachers score their exams. This is how New York State's Regents Examinations are scored, it was the system used in the 1990s for scoring Kentucky's portfolio assessment of writing, and it was used briefly when Vermont instituted portfolio assessments of writing and mathematics. If the test score is important enough, teachers have an incentive to score leniently. What happens if they succumb to this temptation? The distortion in a student's score would not average out if the student were repeatedly tested, because she would draw the same rater—her own classroom teacher—each time. This is precisely what happened in the case of Kentucky's portfolio assessment. When samples of portfolios were rescored by other raters in a state audit of scoring, it was discovered that the scores assigned by many classroom teachers to their own students were substantially too high.[3] Because this distortion would not wash out with repeated testing, it was bias, not measurement error. For reasons no one has ascertained, this sort of bias did not arise in the Vermont portfolio assessment program. (To my knowledge, there are no recent, systematic studies indicating whether scoring bias is a problem for the New York State Regents Examination.)

Users of test scores will encounter three different approaches to quantifying or displaying measurement error and reliability. The first approach is exemplified by the horizontal bar in Figure 7.1. The bar expresses measurement error as a range of uncertainty (240 to 255) on the same scale as the student's estimated score (247). Technically, this is quantified with a statistic called the *standard error of measurement* (SEM).

To make this approach concrete, let's take another hypothetical example. I simulated data to represent what would happen if a student, whose "true" score is 550, repeatedly took a hypothetical test that had approximately the same amount of measurement error as is in the verbal and mathematics sections of the SAT, which is a highly reliable test (that is, compared with other tests, the SAT has relatively little measurement error and a relatively small standard error). Figure 7.2 shows what the distribution of scores might look like if one student took the test 500 times. (This assumes the impossible: no effects of practice or fatigue, and seemingly limitless testing time and patience.) Each circle represents a single score.

Any single score that the student would have obtained taking the test only once could be quite far from the desired score of 550, and even though this is a relatively reliable test, some of the scores in the figure are far off. The average score over these simulated tests, however, was almost exactly 550, which is the "true" value for this hypothetical test-taker, the score purged of measurement

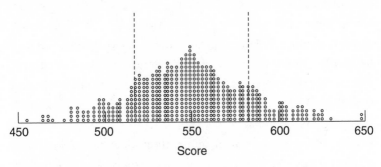

FIG. 7.2. Measurement error in a hypothetical test.

error. As in the case of the bathroom scale, with many measurements, the error apparent in individual scores washed out. (If you were to do this exercise repeatedly, you would find that it does not always wash out exactly, but the average would almost always be very close to 550 because of the large number of observations.)

As the plot shows, scores slightly above or below 550 are numerous, while scores far from that level are relatively rare. This translates into the probability that our poor test-taker, if allowed only one attempt, would obtain a score far from her true score of 550. She has a reasonably high probability of getting any score within a range of, say, 25 or 35 points of 550, while a score more than 50 points off is unlikely.

This figure illustrates the answer to the question asked by the irate subcommittee chairman decades ago: it shows how we quantify how much we don't know what the hell we are talking about (in this case, from a single test score). The dashed lines represent a distance of one standard error of measurement above or below the average. The range in this particular case is 66 points, 33 in each direction from the mean, which is similar to the standard error of measurement on the SAT. Roughly two-thirds of the simulated observations lie within that range. This is true in general: an examinee with any given true score, taking a test once, has a probability of about two-thirds of getting a score within the range from one SEM below that score to one SEM above, and a probability of one in three of obtaining a score more than one SEM away from the true score. Extending the range to two standard errors above and below the mean—in this case, from 484 to 616—would encompass about 95 percent of the scores our indefatigable examinee would obtain. The range of uncertainty reported can be plus or minus either one or two standard errors (I don't know which was the case in the example in Figure 7.1). This is a "margin of error," analogous to the one that set off the subcommittee chair years ago (but not identical, as we will see).

One aspect of this error that some people find unsettling is that even with a wide band—say, plus or minus two standard errors—there is no certainty that the true score is actually within the band.* We can say only that it is probably within that band. This is not a problem specific to educational measurement; it is true of all statistical inference. For example, a single study can rarely tell us with absolute certainty that a new medication is effective in treating a specific disease. Rather, research will typically indicate that a difference in outcomes between a group treated with the new medication and one not treated is so large that it is very unlikely to have occurred by chance and therefore is probably a result of the treatment. Over time, we may accumulate so much evidence from numerous studies that the uncertainty becomes negligible, but in practice, it is always lurking in the background.

---

* This way of presenting error is technically incorrect, but the correct description is cumbersome, and people routinely use this simpler description. To be strictly correct, what we are estimating is not the probability that the true score that we want is within some range of the estimated score the student obtains. Rather, we are answering the following question: if the score initially observed is actually the true score, what is the range of scores we would obtain with repeated testing?

In the case of a single educational test, the uncertainty is rarely negligible.

This illustrates one of the common ways of quantifying how much we don't know from a single score, but for most readers, this will not answer the third question posed above: is this range of uncertainty big enough to worry about? The answer to this question requires that we know how spread out scores are on the particular scale used. For example, unless we know something about the variability of scores on the scale on which the MCAS results are reported, there is no way to know whether the "probable range of scores" of 15 points shown in Figure 7.1 is large or small. On some tests (such as the ACT, which has a maximum score of 36 for each test), 15 points would be an enormous range of uncertainty. On others (for example, the SAT, which has a range from 200 to 800 on each scale), 15 points would be a very small margin of error.* The hypothetical example in Figure 7.2 might have more meaning for readers familiar with the SAT because it was constructed to be quite similar to the SAT in terms of scale and reliability. To those readers, it will be apparent that the margin of error on the SAT is not negligible—to have even a 5 percent chance of scoring more than 66 points above or below the true score is not trivial. And I repeat that the SAT is a very well-

---

* Technically, the issue is not the total range of scores—because the range of scores can be extended arbitrarily—but rather the variability of scores, typically measured with the standard deviation. The standard deviation, which is described in Chapter 5, is a measure of variability such that if scores follow the bell curve, approximately two-thirds of all scores fall within a range from one standard deviation below the mean to one standard deviation above. (The standard deviation and standard error of measurement are analogous: the former quantifies the variability in a set of scores—for example, the scores of a group of many students—while the latter quantifies the variability in a set of multiple measures of one person.) The standard deviation of SAT mathematics scores is 115 points, while that of the ACT mathematics test is 5 points. Thus, a range of 15 points is small relative to the variability students display on the SAT but huge—twenty-three times as large—relative to their variability on the ACT.

constructed, highly reliable test. The uncertainty is greater in the case of many other educational tests.

The practical impact of this range of uncertainty depends on how the scores are used. Let's assume that our hypothetical test in Figure 7.2 is a college-admissions test. If one were to set a fixed cut score—for this example, say the cut is 545—and simply reject anyone with a score less than 545, even a very small margin of error will have serious consequences for students, such as our hypothetical one, whose true scores are near that cut score. Those students would have a reasonably high probability of being incorrectly rejected or accepted simply because measurement error caused their scores to be somewhat lower or higher than they should have been. However, if scores on the test were used as only one piece of information contributing to the decision to admit or reject students, a modest amount of measurement error would have little impact. This is one of several reasons that the College Board counsels admissions officers to take reliability and measurement error into account in using SAT scores and to treat them as "approximate indicators" of students' strengths. The Board advises them specifically to use the scores in conjunction with other information about students' capabilities (such as grades and written statements), not to make decisions based on small differences in scores, and not to impose a minimum cut score unless it is used in conjunction with other information.[4]

Reliability is often presented using a second statistic, the *reliability coefficient,* which is useful for experts but harder for laypersons to grasp. The reliability coefficient, unlike the standard error, is not expressed on the scale of the test. Regardless of the test or the scale on which scores are placed, the reliability coefficient always varies from 0 (a score that is nothing but measurement error—that is, random noise) to 1 (a perfectly consistent score, with no measurement error at all.) This makes the reliability coefficient comparable from one test to the next, even when the scores are expressed on different scales. This coefficient also has other mathematical properties that make it useful for those doing technical evaluations of test scores, and it is the reliability statistic most often reported in practice. However, for all its technical advantages, the reliability coefficient has a major drawback: unlike the standard error of measurement, it does not directly communicate to untrained users how much error is inherent in the score.

Users of test scores are often given rules of thumb for deciding how high reliability coefficients should be, but these are arbitrary, and it may be more helpful to have standards of comparison instead. In large-scale assessment programs, the most reliable tests have reliability coefficients in the range of .90 or a bit higher. For example, the internal consistency reliabilities of the math and verbal portions of the SAT—the estimates of reliability that take into account only measurement error stemming from the sampling of test items—are both in the range of .90 to .93, depending on the form.[5] The reading and mathematics tests in the Iowa Tests of Basic Skills, one of the oldest and most widely used commercial achievement tests, have even less measurement error from selection of items and slightly higher internal-consistency reliability coefficients.[6] Some custom-developed state tests have similarly high levels of reliability. In 2003, the internal-consistency reliability of the tenth-grade MCAS mathematics test, on which a passing score is required for obtaining a high-school diploma, was estimated to be .92.[7] Shorter tests and "subtests" (for example, the score on the computation portion of elementary-level mathematics tests) are generally less reliable, as are many innovative or otherwise unusual assessments. For example, in 2001, an early administration of the state of Washington's alternate assessment for students with severe disabilities found internal-consistency reliabilities in the range .72 to .86, in addition to substantial error from scoring.[8]

While such comparisons help show the level of reliability one might hope for, they do not explain just how good or bad the numbers are. The answer is that even when the reliability coefficient is high, substantial measurement error remains. There are several ways of clarifying this. One is to ask, for a given reliability coefficient, how large is the band of error around an individual score? For example, even though the SAT is a highly reliable test, with a reliability coefficient over .90, the standard error of measurement is more than 30 points, similar to that shown in Figure 7.2. A reliability coefficient of .80 indicates an error band roughly 40 percent larger, and a reliability coefficient of .70 indicates an SEM almost 75 percent larger than that in Figure 7.2. A second way is to ask, with a given reliability coefficient, how well can you predict a second score by knowing the first? If one has a first set of scores for a group of students, a reliability coefficient of .90 indicates that these first scores allow you to predict about 80 percent of the variability in the second scores. With a reliability coefficient of .70, one can predict only about half of the variability in a second set of scores.

A third way of showing reliability, particularly relevant to the standards-based testing that dominates state-mandated testing today, is the consistency of the classification or decision based on scores. This arises only when scores on a test are broken into discrete categories, as with a single pass-fail cut score or the small number of categories created by reporting performance in terms of a few performance standards, such as the "proficient" standard mandated by NCLB. This latter type of reporting is now ubiquitous and was common even before NCLB. When performance is reported in this way, one can ask: if you classify a student as being in one category (say, not proficient or proficient) based on one test score, how probable is it that you would reclassify the student as being in the other category if you tested her a second time? The more measurement error there is in the test—that is, the less reli-

Table 7.1   Percentage of students whose pass/fail status would be changed
with a second testing at various combinations of passing rate and
reliability

Percent passing	Reliability		
	.70	.80	.90
90	11	9	6
70	22	17	12
50	26	21	14
30	22	18	13
10	11	09	6

Source: Adapted from Stephen P. Klein and Maria Orlando, CUNY's Testing Program:
Characteristics, Results, and Implications for Policy and Research (Santa Monica, CA: Rand,
April 27, 1999), Table 2.

able the score—the higher the probability that the classification
would be inconsistent from one time to the next.

The disquieting answer is that classification is inconsistent more
often than one would like. Table 7.1, which is adapted from a
study done by two social scientists at Rand for the City University of New York, shows the percentage of students who would
be classified inconsistently as passing or failing by two instances
of testing. The rows indicate different levels of standards, with
harsher standards toward the bottom. The top row represents a
very lenient standard that would let 90 percent of students pass;
the second row, a standard that would allow 70 percent of the students to pass; and so on. The three columns represent different
levels of reliability, measured by the reliability coefficient. Let's
stick with the .90 column, which is close to a best-case scenario.
The table shows that unless the standard is set either very low or
very high, a substantial number of students would be reclassified
if retested. If the standard is set near the middle, so that anywhere
from 30 to 70 percent of students pass, 12 to 14 percent of students would be classified differently if tested a second time.

Just how important is this inconsistency? Once again, it depends on how the scores are used, but for some uses, it would matter a great deal. If the single score were used alone to make an important decision, such as denying a high school diploma or rejecting a student's application to college, even the inconsistency inherent in a highly reliable test would be troubling. For example, in the case of a passing rate of 50 percent on a test with a reliability of .90, half of the inconsistently classified students—7 percent of all students taking the test—would fail the first time but would pass if tested again. This is one reason many states that impose a test-score requirement for graduation from high school permit students to retake the test, often several times.

The reliability statistics provided with test scores tend to understate the problem of measurement error because these statistics often take only one or two of the sources of error into account. Error is therefore underestimated—because error from some sources is ignored—and reliability is correspondingly overestimated. For example, it is common to provide users of test scores with internal consistency estimates of reliability that take into account error from the sampling of items but do not reflect inconsistency over time or, where relevant, inconsistencies in scoring.* Most of the examples above are of this sort.

In the case of assessments for which scoring is difficult, one will sometimes encounter reports in which statistics representing the consistency of scoring—often misleadingly labeled "interrater reliability"—are given without any other information about error and are treated as if they represent the reliability of scores, even though they ignore both fluctuations over time and the effects of sampling items. Some years ago, in response to this latter misrepresentation, H. D. Hoover, then senior author of the Iowa Tests

---

* Internal consistency estimates of reliability can often be identified by name, even if they are not described as such. The most commonly reported estimate is *Cronbach's alpha*. *Kuder-Richardson* reliability coefficients are essentially the same thing, but applied only to multiple-choice or other items scored simply as right or wrong.

of Basic Skills, a multiple-choice achievement test battery, commented that if interrater consistency is enough to indicate the reliability of test scores, scores on the ITBS are perfectly reliable because they have no error from scoring: the optical scanning machines would cough up identical scores as often as you put the answer sheets into them.

What makes a test score more or less reliable? When scoring is required, improving the consistency of scoring will lessen overall measurement error and increase reliability. This can be done by carefully designing and evaluating the rubrics that raters use to score students' work, by training raters rigorously, and by monitoring the scoring process to catch and correct problems (for example, by conducting a second "read-behind" rating of a random sample of papers). Standardizing test administration procedures will help lessen fluctuations in performance from one occasion to another.

Another factor that influences reliability of scores is the consistency of the content of the test, called its internal consistency (hence the name of the reliability statistics discussed above), or *homogeneity*. Recall that in the vocabulary test, the choice of words—*feckless* versus *parsimonious*—caused variations in the ranking of students taking the test. Now consider a test of fourth-grade mathematics. This is a broad domain, and the selection of items will cause some fluctuations in performance, and hence some measurement error. But suppose you designed the test to include nothing but two-digit subtraction problems without carrying, presented in the vertical format, for example:

$$\begin{array}{r} 57 \\ -25 \\ \hline 32 \end{array}$$

Because all of the possible items of this type are very similar, it would make little difference which you picked, and the resulting fluctuation in scores—measurement error—would be small. The cost, however, would be substantial: you would have designed an extremely narrow test that might be useful as a weekly quiz in a math class but would be highly misleading as a test of fourth-grade mathematics. This is yet another of the unavoidable trade-offs in measurement. In designing a test of a large domain such as fourth-grade mathematics, one would want reasonably broad coverage of the domain to support the conclusions in which you are interested, but that breadth of content will reduce reliability. As the reliability coefficients above suggest, with careful work, the authors of tests of broad domains can in fact attain high levels of internal consistency reliability, but this is nonetheless constrained by the breadth of the test.

One of the most important influences on reliability is the length of the test. In discussing the example of the cheap bathroom scale, I pointed out that if you weighed yourself enough times and averaged the readings, the measurement error in individual readings would wash out, and the average would be a pretty good measure of your actual weight. In educational testing, the individual items in a test are analogous to individual readings on your scale. The more of them you include in the test, the more the measurement error in each one of them will average out and the more reliable the test score will be. This entails a trade-off as well: longer tests are more expensive and, even more important, require more testing time and therefore more disruption and loss of instructional time.

Considering both test length and homogeneity helps shed light on one of the most contentious recent arguments about educational testing: the best mix of formats to use. Since the late 1980s, there has been widespread interest among educators, reformers, and measurement experts in going well beyond the multiple-choice formats that had dominated achievement testing from the end of World War II until that time. As noted in Chapter 4, the additional formats tried were diverse and included items requiring short written responses; items requiring longer essays; hands-on performance tasks (e.g., science tasks requiring an experiment or other manipulation of apparatus); portfolio assessments based on work generated in the course of instruction; and hybrid tasks that required both group and individual effort. In general, if testing time is not increased, using more complex formats will often (although not invariably) decrease reliability. There are two related reasons. First, the more complex the tasks are, the less homogeneous they are likely to be. Two hands-on science tasks, for example, are likely to differ in many respects that are not necessarily central to the aspects of performance about which conclusions will be drawn. Second, because complex tasks take more time, there will be fewer per hour of testing time and hence less opportunity for measurement error to wash out. This too is a trade-off because even when they reduce reliability, complex formats may offer other important advantages, such as an ability to tap skills not readily measured with formats such as multiple choice.

Sampling Error

More familiar to most people than measurement error is a second, closely analogous form of error: sampling error. While measurement error is the inconsistency that arises from one measurement of a person to the next, sampling error is inconsistency that arises from the selection of particular people (or schools or districts) from which one takes a measurement. When scientists or newspapers write about error, they are usually referring to sampling error, and it was a concern with sampling error that led to my comment about a margin of error that provoked the subcommittee chairman years ago to say to my boss, "Doesn't that mean you don't know what the hell you are talking about?"

One of the most common examples of sampling error is the results of polls and other surveys. Anyone who reads a newspaper in the months leading up to an election confronts frequent poll results, usually written in a form such as this: "In the newest poll by [name a polling organization], 52 percent of likely voters said they would vote for Candidate X if the election were held today. Thirty-eight percent said they would vote for Candidate Y, and 10 percent were undecided. The poll surveyed 658 likely voters and had a margin of error of plus or minus 3 percentage points." Even the subcommittee chairman made irate by my testimony decades ago would have understood this one; after all, politicians live and die by poll results.

The margin of error reported for most polls reflects inconsistencies arising from the sampling of people who are interviewed. Each time you draw a sample to interview, there will be random fluctuations in the types of people who respond. One day, one might by chance nab a few extra conservatives, the next day, a few extra progressives, and so on. The result will be some fluctuation in the results. The uncertainty is present even if one samples only once—and indeed statisticians can estimate the sampling error from a single sample, if they know the sample design—but drawing repeated samples would make it apparent.

Of course, polls and other surveys also suffer from biases that do not wash out over repeated samples. Survey results can be biased if the questions are poorly worded, even if accidentally. Bias can arise if the sample of respondents is not well designed to be representative—for example, if the design results in sampling too many elderly voters or highly educated ones. Yet another, more insidious bias can arise from nonresponse. Not everyone contacted by a pollster agrees to respond. (How do you respond to phone calls from survey administrators at dinnertime?) The people who refuse to participate are often systematically different from those who agree to answer, and those differences can create a powerful bias in the results unless the response rate—the proportion of individuals approached who agree to participate—is very high. In practice, these response rates rarely make it into the lay media. When they do, you will sometimes see that they are low, which should be a warning to take the results with a very large grain of salt or even ignore them altogether. But this takes us afield: the issue I want to clarify here is sampling error and its relevance to educational testing.

Traditionally, sampling error was not a major concern in educational testing. The primary purpose of most testing programs until fairly recently was to estimate the proficiency of individuals, and therefore the primary focus in evaluating error was measurement error—the reliability of estimates of individuals' scores. When my parents were given my ITBS scores decades ago, sampling error was not an issue—the score was simply about me—but measurement error was. This has changed in recent years because of the rapidly evolving uses of test scores. As explained in Chapter 4, a major use of scores is now to describe and evaluate groups: schools, districts, and entire states.

And this gives us sampling error: instability in these aggregate scores resulting from sampling students. The second of the two quotations from the NCLB statute at the beginning of this chapter is an explicit recognition of the problem of sampling error in estimating annual changes in performance.

Sampling error in aggregate test scores, as in all sample-based statistics, is a function of the size of the sample. The more people questioned in a poll about likely voting, the smaller the margin of error—or at least the error that stems solely from the random sampling of survey respondents.* This is analogous to the impact of test length on measurement error. A longer test has more items and hence more opportunity for chance differences between items—measurement error—to wash out. A larger sam-

---

* Specifically, for a mean, the margin of error shrinks as a function of the square root of the number of observations.

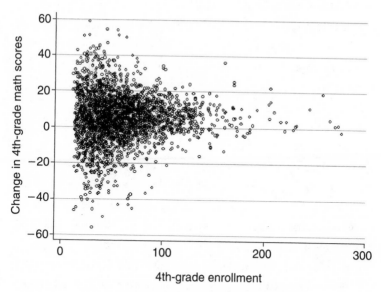

FIG. 7.3.   One-year change in mean test scores of fourth-grade
students in mathematics, California STAR assessment.
Adapted with permission of the authors, from Thomas J.
Kane and Douglas O. Staiger, "The Promise and Pitfalls of
Using Imprecise School Accountability Measures," *Journal of
Economic Perspectives* 16, no. 4 (2002): 91–114.

ple includes more individuals and therefore offers more opportunity for chance differences between people—sampling error—to
wash out.

This sampling error can be very large. One illustration of this
can be found in studies conducted by my colleague Tom Kane, in
collaboration with Douglas Staiger of Dartmouth College. During the period leading up to the enactment of NCLB, Kane and
Staiger published a series of papers investigating the reliability of
aggregate measures based on test scores. They found that simple aggregate scores are highly unreliable in many schools because
the number of tested students is small. An example is shown in
Figure 7.3, which is adapted from one of their studies.[9] This graph

shows the annual change in the average score on a fourth-grade mathematics test in California between 1999 and 2000. The vertical axis on the graph is the change in average score. Each circle represents the change in average score for a single school. The horizontal axis of the graph is the fourth-grade enrollment of the school.

One can see from this figure that the scores of the largest schools—say, those with more than 200 students in the grade—are quite stable, showing very little change in either direction from 1999 to 2000. Very few elementary schools, however, have this many students in one grade. Most, as shown by the mass of circles toward the left side of the graph, have relatively small enrollments, most often only one, two, or three classes in that grade. For these schools, particularly those with only one or two classes, the annual changes are highly variable, with many schools showing a large change in one direction or the other. Additional studies confirm that these changes are erratic from year to year. Thus, for the most part, these changes represent the greater sampling error when relatively few students are tested, not meaningful changes in the performance of small schools. In other words, it is not really the case that many small schools are rapidly improving or deteriorating while the performance of larger schools is remaining stable.

The problem of sampling error in aggregate scores is compounded by the requirement under NCLB to report "disaggregated" scores, that is, the scores of specified groups of students, such as minority students and students with disabilities. As some of the proponents of the legislation made clear, the purpose of this requirement was to force schools to attend to the performance of historically lower-scoring groups and to make it impossible for schools to get off the hook by improving only the performance of the higher-scoring students, who are easier to teach. Although I have been an outspoken critic of many aspects of NCLB, I (and some other critics of the statute) agree that this pressure is important, and there is at least anecdotal evidence that this requirement is indeed leading many schools to pay more attention to the performance of groups of students at higher risk of scoring poorly.

The fly in the ointment is that the statistics reported for these groups, which are usually much smaller than the school populations shown in Figure 7.3, are often highly unreliable. Therefore short-term trends in these scores can be misleading, and apparent progress, or lack thereof, will often be illusory. It is this concern that sparked the statutory language at the beginning of the chapter. NCLB recognizes this problem and exempts from reporting groups small enough that their performance would be unreliable, but it largely leaves it to the states to decide how many students must be included in a group—that is, how reliable scores have to be—before separate reporting for that group will be required.

Kane and Staiger showed another, less obvious consequence of this requirement: the more groups a school has that must be reported separately, the more likely it is that the school will fail solely because of sampling error. NCLB requires that every single reported group must make adequate yearly progress if the school is to be credited with making AYP. The more groups that are reported separately, the more likely that at least one will fail to make AYP simply because of chance, primarily sampling error. For example, say that in a given year, a school happened to have a couple of highly successful minority students and a couple of highly unsuccessful students with disabilities. And assume, as is often the case, that these patterns reflect sampling error: by chance, this year, the minority subgroup is relatively high-scoring and the disabled group relatively low-scoring, compared with other cohorts of those groups in the same school in other years. The annual change in performance for minority students will look somewhat better than it would without these few students, and the change for students with disabilities will appear somewhat worse.

When reporting the overall results for the entire school, the sampling error in the scores of these two groups would average out. However, disagreggated reporting does not allow their scores to average out. Because NCLB requires that all reporting groups make AYP, the school could fail to meet its target because of these specific students with disabilities, even if its overall performance is fine and the failure of that one group is a result of sampling error.

A few readers might be wondering: if all students in a school (or at least nearly all) are being tested, where does sampling error come into play? After all, in the case of polls, sampling error arises because one has in hand the responses of only a small percentage of the people who will actually vote. This is not the case with most testing programs, which ideally test almost all students in a grade.

This question was a matter of some debate among members of the profession only a few years ago, but it is now generally agreed that sampling error is indeed a problem even if every student is tested. The reason is the nature of the inference based on scores. If the inference pertaining to each school in Figure 7.3 were *about the particular students in that school at that time,* sampling error would not be an issue, because almost all of them were tested. That is, sampling would not be a concern if people were using scores to reach conclusions such as "the fourth-graders who happened to be in this school in 2000 scored higher than the particular group of students who happened to be enrolled in 1999." In practice, however, users of scores rarely care about this. Rather, they are interested in conclusions about the performance of *schools.* For those inferences, each successive cohort of students enrolling in the school is just another small sample of the students who might possibly enroll, just as the people interviewed for one poll are a small sample of those who might have been.

A story given to me by another researcher provides a nice illustration of the importance of sampling in interpreting test scores. In a meeting some years ago, teachers in a small school in Maryland were puzzling over a noticeable drop in scores that lasted a single year in each grade and moved up one grade each year, much as a recently consumed rat might be seen moving through a python. One teacher offered this explanation: "That's Leo." She was referring to a disruptive student who managed to bring down the performance of every class he was in. Whether or not she was correct in the specifics, I don't know, but her explanation was reasonable in pointing to sampling error as the likely culprit. When I mention this in one of my classes that includes many former teachers, most laugh knowingly, and the "Leo effect" has become our shorthand for short-term fluctuations in aggregate scores caused by sampling error.

Statistical Significance

Reports of test scores are often accompanied by statements about the "statistical significance" (or lack thereof) of the findings—say, an improvement in test scores from last year, or the difference in scores between two districts or states. These references also appear in the reporting of many other scientific findings, such as the results of research on the effects of a medication. It is not clear how many newspaper writers understand what these phrases mean or what they expect readers to do in response to them. One journalist who took one of my courses while on leave from his job gave me one of his own articles about differences in test scores as an example. He had written the article before taking the course and showed it to me in order to discuss how he might word things differently in the future. He had included in the article a single sentence warning that some of the differences were not statistically significant. However, once he understood measurement error and sampling error, he decided that the reference to significance was pro forma and that he had written it with no clear expectation that readers would know what to do with the information.

The term *statistical significance* is just another way of quantifying how much we don't know what the hell we are talking about. Let's again climb on the cheap bathroom scale. Suppose you are trying to loose weight. At the start of your diet or your exercise regimen, you weigh yourself and get a reading of 144. A week later, you weigh yourself one more time and get a reading of 143. You have lost a pound, according to your scale.

But should you believe it? Maybe the apparent loss of weight is the result of nothing more than measurement error. That is, because of measurement error, the apparent improvement on the scale *may be the result of chance.* If the scale is really terrible and has a lot of measurement error, the probability of getting a one-pound "improvement" just by chance is high. The more reliable the scale is, the less likely it is that a given result would arise simply from chance.

An entirely different example comes from a lesson I once prepared for one of my kids' middle-school math classes—a lesson I was not allowed to present, despite the teacher's invitation, because of the severe embarrassment this would have caused. (Parents of middle-school students will understand that the embarrassment had nothing to do with a concern about how well I would teach.) For this example, you have to imagine being a twelve-year-old who is somewhat reluctant to challenge a teacher openly. Suppose I stand in front of the class and explain that I am going to flip a penny repeatedly and write the results on the board. I alone can see the results of the coin toss, so you have to take my word for the results. The task is to decide after each toss whether the results are so improbable that you are willing to walk the plank and declare openly that you think I am fudging the results, either by using a loaded coin or simply lying. Let's let p be the probability of the string of results I get. The first toss is heads. That has a probability of .5 (one out of two), so there is no reason to speak out yet. The second is also heads, and the probability of two heads in a row is one out of four, or .25. You can see this in

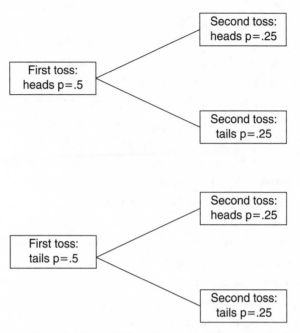

FIG. 7.4. The probabilities of all combinations of two tosses of a fair coin.

Figure 7.4: half the time, one will get heads on the first try, and of that half, half again will lead to heads on the second flip. The general rule for independent probabilities (if the coin is fair, the probability of heads on the second flip is independent of the results of the first flip) is that the probability of a string of equally probable events is p^n, where n is the number of events. So with two flips, there is still no cause to do anything; the probability of obtaining this result with a fair coin is quite high. The third flip also turns out to be heads, and the probability of this string of heads is $.5^3$ or .125. The results are becoming more unlikely but still probably not worth the potential cost of calling the teacher a fraud. The fourth toss: also heads, $p = .5^4 = .0625$. This is a tougher call. The fifth toss: also heads, $p = .5^5 = .0313$. Now we are getting to a result that is highly improbable: if the tosses were truly random and I repeated this exercise over and over, I would get this string of five heads only about three times out of a hundred.

At some point, someone in the class would say that these results are simply too improbable to be credible and that she believes the coin toss is rigged. In other words, this string of results is *unlikely to have arisen simply by chance*—in this case, the random chance of a series of coin tosses. The student does not *know* that the results did not arise by chance, but they are so unlikely that she will argue that the outcome *probably* stems from something other than chance (in this case, my cheating).

Statistical significance is simply a statement about the probability that whatever result is at issue might have occurred by chance alone because of sampling error, measurement error, or both. The lower this probability, the more confidence one would have in the explanation that entails some cause other than chance, and the higher the statistical significance. By convention, most scientists set as a minimum threshold a probability (the p in my coin toss) less than 0.05, but this is simply a convention. (Initially this may be confusing: the *lower* the probability that the results could have arisen from chance, the *higher* their statistical significance, and the more confidence we have that something other than chance caused the results.) Those who were arguing for a cheating effect in my class would have crossed the conventional threshold for statistical significance at the fifth toss of the coin.

So what should you do with this information when confronted with test scores? There are two common misconceptions to avoid. The first is that statistically significant results are real and nonsignificant results (statisticians usually don't call them "insignificant") are not real. Unfortunately, we are playing the odds—a fact that can be quite unsettling in some cases of statistical inference, for example, in deciding whether to prescribe a given medical treatment. A finding that is statistically significant is less likely than a nonsignificant one to have arisen by chance. However, there is still a possibility—just a small one—that a statistically significant finding *did* arise by chance. There is also a possibility that a statistically nonsignificant finding *did not* arise by chance. The less information we have—the less reliable the test or the smaller the sample of people—the more likely it is that we will be deceived by a lack of statistical significance.

To make this concrete, Figure 7.5 presents the average fourth-grade mathematics scores of several states on the 2000 National Assessment of Educational Progress. Each state is represented by a sample of roughly 2,500 test-takers. This figure is the top left corner of a much larger figure that displays the results for each state participating in the assessment. This and similar NAEP figures are often called "pantyhose charts" because the white area in the middle looks like the run in a stocking. Each row and column represents a state. For example, the top row and left-most column represent Minnesota (MN), which was the highest-scoring state that year. The second column and row represent Montana (MT), the second-highest-scoring state, and so on. Reading down the first (Minnesota) column, you will see that MN, MT, and KS are in white, while all of the boxes below those three are shaded. Any comparison in this white range is not statistically significant. Thus, for example, even though Minnesota outscored Kansas, the difference could have occurred by chance—or, to be more precise, it was too likely to be a result of chance to count as significant. By contrast, the average performance of Minnesota was significantly higher than that of Maine.

This does not indicate that the averages of Montana and Minnesota really are the same. If one tested many more kids in both states, one might find that Minnesota's students really do perform a little better—or vice versa. Rather, it means only that, given the error in these data, you can't have a great deal of confidence that the observed difference in scores is real. The probability is too

Minnesota (MN)	Montana (MT)	Kansas (KS)	Maine (ME)	Vermont (VT)	Massachusetts (MA)	North Dakota (ND)	Indiana (IN)	Ohio (OH)	Connecticut (CT)	Oregon (OR)	Nebraska (NE)	North Carolina (NC)	Michigan (MI)	DoDEA/DoDDS (DI)
MN	MN	MN	MN	MN	MN	MN	MN	MN	MN	MN	MN	MN	MN	MN
MT	MT	MT	MT	MT	MT	MT	MT	MT	MT	MT	MT	MT	MT	MT
KS	KS	KS	KS	KS	KS	KS	KS	KS	KS	KS	KS	KS	KS	KS
ME	ME	ME	ME	ME	ME	ME	ME	ME	ME	ME	ME	ME	ME	ME
VT	VT	VT	VT	VT	VT	VT	VT	VT	VT	VT	VT	VT	VT	VT
MA	MA	MA	MA	MA	MA	MA	MA	MA	MA	MA	MA	MA	MA	MA
ND	ND	ND	ND	ND	ND	ND	ND	ND	ND	ND	ND	ND	ND	ND
IN	IN	IN	IN	IN	IN	IN	IN	IN	IN	IN	IN	IN	IN	IN
OH	OH	OH	OH	OH	OH	OH	OH	OH	OH	OH	OH	OH	OH	OH
CT	CT	CT	CT	CT	CT	CT	CT	CT	CT	CT	CT	CT	CT	CT
OR	OR	OR	OR	OR	OR	OR	OR	OR	OR	OR	OR	OR	OR	OR
NE	NE	NE	NE	NE	NE	NE	NE	NE	NE	NE	NE	NE	NE	NE
NC	NC	NC	NC	NC	NC	NC	NC	NC	NC	NC	NC	NC	NC	NC
MI	MI	MI	MI	MI	MI	MI	MI	MI	MI	MI	MI	MI	MI	MI
DI	DI	DI	DI	DI	DI	DI	DI	DI	DI	DI	DI	DI	DI	DI

FIG. 7.5. A comparison of states' average eighth-grade mathematics scores, NAEP. Adapted from James S. Braswell et al., *The Nation's Report Card: Mathematics 2000* (Washington, DC: U.S. Department of Education, Office of Educational Research and Improvement, August 2001), Figure 2.9.

high that it could have arisen from sampling error. Similarly, these results do not necessarily mean that Maine's performance would really be lower if everyone were tested and the test had no measurement error. Rather, it indicates that Maine's average is far enough below that of Montana that the difference is not likely to be the result of chance.

The second common misconception is that statistically significant findings are "important" or "substantial" and that nonsignificant results are unimportant. This is never a safe conclusion. For example, a difference between two states that is too small to be of any practical import may nonetheless be statistically significant, and conversely, a substantively important finding may turn out to be nonsignificant in a particular instance. One of the several reasons for this is that statistical significance depends on the size of the sample as well as the size of the result in question. A larger sample leads to less sampling error, which in turn produces a higher level of confidence or statistical significance. So a substantively small difference may be statistically significant if the sample is large enough, and a substantively large difference may be statistically nonsignificant if the sample is small enough. Statistical significance tells you only that a given result was unlikely to have arisen by chance.

The appropriate way to use information about statistical significance, then, is to treat it as one indication of how much confidence you should place in the results. If you suspect that a nonsignificant finding (the difference between two schools or districts, for example) is not a matter of chance despite the lack of statistical significance in one set of data, one option would be to look for other data addressing the same question—other data on performance in the same year, or results from subsequent years.

◯ Responding to Error in Using Scores

The ubiquity of measurement and sampling error is not a reason to forgo testing, but it does indicate the need to use scores carefully and not to treat them as solitary, complete, and perfectly reliable indicators of students' knowledge and skills. However valuable it may be, a test score represents only a single sample from the domain—think back to the vocabulary test—and a single occasion of measurement. The resulting error is one reason why it is axiomatic in the field of measurement that, to the extent possible, important decisions should not be based on a single test score— an axiom widely ignored in practice, although clearly stated in the *Standards for Educational and Psychological Testing* published by leading professional associations.[10] Using scores along with other information and ignoring small differences, as the College Board advises, are reasonable responses to measurement error. When cut scores are used, a common response to measurement error is to allow students who fail the test a second chance to take it, to lessen the probability that students will fail only because of measurement error. When looking at aggregate scores, such as a report of the percentage of students in a state's schools who reach a proficient standard, some of the effects of measurement error may be reduced, but one has the additional problem of sampling error and the uncertainty it produces. I'll return to these issues at the end of the book when I discuss sensible uses of test scores.

Chapter 8

Reporting Performance: Standards and Scales

EARLY IN THE FILM *This Is Spinal Tap*, one of the protagonists, the rock musician Nigel Tufnel, shows the filmmaker Marty DiBergi a room full of his equipment. They discuss Nigel's favorite amplifier:

Tufnel: It's very special because if you can see, the numbers all go to 11—right across the board . . .

DiBergi: And most of these amps go up to 10.

Tufnel: Exactly.

DiBergi: Does that mean it's louder? Is it any louder?

Tufnel: Well, it's one louder, isn't it? It's not 10. You see, most blokes will be playing at 10, and you're on 10 here, all the way up, all the way up, you're on 10 on your guitar, where can you go from there? Where?

DiBergi: I don't know.

Tufnel: Exactly! Nowhere! What we do is, if we need that extra push over the cliff, you know what we do?

DiBergi: Put it up to 11.

Tufnel: Exactly. Exactly. One louder.

DiBergi: Why don't you just make 10 louder, and make 10 be the top number, and make that a little louder?

Tufnel: [Long pause.] These go to 11.[1]

This dialogue illustrates the central problem of *scaling,* the process of assigning numbers or labels to whatever one is measuring—in Nigel's case, volume, and in ours, student achievement. Nigel fails to grasp the distinction between actual volume and the scale—the numbers printed on his amplifier—used to represent it. Perhaps he would also think it is always much hotter on the U.S. side of the border than it is a few feet away in Mexico because we use the Fahrenheit temperature scale and the Mexicans use Celsius. (For those unfamiliar with the Celsius—or centigrade—temperature scale used virtually everywhere but in the United States, 95 degrees Fahrenheit corresponds to 35 degrees Celsius.)

The humor of the scene in *Spinal Tap* lies in the obviousness of Nigel's misunderstanding of the volume scale—he is portrayed repeatedly as less than the sharpest knife in the drawer—but in the case of achievement testing, the problem of scaling is highly complex, and misunderstandings are neither infrequent nor quite so obvious. Diverse scales have been devised over the years to serve a variety of different purposes, and a basic familiarity with them is essential for understanding the patterns of achievement that tests are designed to portray.

The many scales people have devised for describing performance on tests are of two types. One approach is to choose several levels of performance on the basis of judgment, split the distribution of performance at those points, and then report achievement in terms of the resulting categories. This is what is done in all current standards-based testing systems: judgment is used to establish levels like "basic" and "proficient," and students' performance is reported simply in terms of the resulting bins into which their scores fall. Most advocates of this type of reporting do not consider a set of performance levels to be a scale, but it is—although, as we will see, it is not a very good one. The alternative and traditional approach is to create some sort of numerical scale to represent the range of performance on the test. There are many of these, such as arbitrary numerical scales (for example, the SAT scale, which runs from 200 to 800), percentile ranks, and grade equivalents.

In this chapter, I work backward in time, starting with the more recent approach of reporting in terms of standards and only afterward turning to more traditional scales. I do this because standards are (or at least they seem to be) much simpler, and they are currently more in vogue, so some readers might want to give short shrift to the more complex, traditional numerical scales. However, standards-based reporting looks a great deal less appealing close up than it does from afar, and seeing its limitations may give readers more appetite for coming to grips with traditional scales.

Performance Standards

Standards-based reporting of student achievement is now ubiquitous in the United States. Virtually all parents will at some point be told that their children are "advanced," "proficient," "partially proficient," or the like in subjects such as mathematics and language arts, and newspapers are full of stories reporting the percentage of students reaching one or another of these performance standards, most often the one labeled "proficient."

Politically, this sort of reporting gained traction because of the widespread dissatisfaction with the nation's schools that sparked the various education reform movements of the past several decades. To many critics of public education, traditional ways of reporting student performance were unacceptable. Traditional scales, as we will see, are purely descriptive and do not inherently reflect any judgment about expected levels of performance. In addition, many of the traditional scales are norm referenced and compare the achievement of any student or group with the current distribution of performance. Many critics argued that the current distribution of performance was unacceptably low and that the use of norm-referenced reporting entailed a tacit acceptance of this undesirable status quo. In their view, to label a student above average creates a false sense of success if the average itself is unacceptably low. And beyond that, the critics of norm-referenced reporting did not want value-neutral, purely descriptive reporting. They wanted to evaluate performance by comparing it with explicit goals.

The solution, they argued, was to create tests that report students' results in terms of performance standards. In the jargon that spread rapidly and remains current, *content standards* are statements of *what* students should know and be able to do, and *performance standards* indicate *how much* they should know and be able to do. Proponents of standards-based reporting argue that their approach will focus everyone's attention on the goal of improving student achievement. Many maintain that it will also create a system in which all students can succeed, because they believe that almost all students can be raised eventually to a level above the standard. Few of the advocates of this new approach to reporting test scores had any understanding of the Pandora's box they were opening.

The past two reauthorizations of the Elementary and Secondary Education Act have made standards-based reporting a matter of federal statute. The Improving Americas Schools Act, the 1994 reauthorization of ESEA, called for states to implement systems for content and performance standards; No Child Left Behind requires that the state tests used to fulfill its requirements be reported in terms of these standards, mandates that one be labeled "proficient," and stipulates that schools must be sanctioned based on a complex system for determining whether the percentage above "proficient" is adequate in terms of the targets established by the law.

This type of reporting rapidly became popular with the press and educators as well, because it is simple, seemingly clear, and allows us to determine whether students are living up to expectations. We know what "proficient" means, even if we don't know what a scale score of 156 means. Or rather, most people believe they know what "proficient" means, although I hope that after a few more pages, you will doubt that most people really do understand it.

In addition to being exceedingly popular among education policymakers and newspaper writers, standards-based reporting has received a reasonably hospitable welcome in the measurement field. In part, this simply reflects the fact that measurement is primarily a service profession: if governments insist that performance on their tests be reported this way, the people hired to construct the tests will have to oblige. But it goes beyond this; many members of the profession are enthusiastically contributing to the shift toward standards-based reporting.

I find this puzzling, because standards-based reporting is seriously problematic. Because of the ways in which performance standards are set, their meaning is far less clear than most people believe. Reporting test performance in this way obscures some important information, exaggerates the importance of other information, and can provide a seriously distorted view of differences and trends. And it also can create highly undesirable incentives for teachers.

Let's start with how performance standards are set. Reporting student achievement in terms of a few performance standards requires one to decide just how much achievement is enough to make the grade. A typical achievement test provides many possible scores. At what score should a student abruptly change from "not proficient" to "proficient?" From merely "proficient" to "advanced?" How are these decisions—the choice of where the performance standards are placed—actually made?

The procedures most often used to set the standards are complex and arcane, and this leads some users of the standards to assume that the process is "scientific" and therefore trustworthy. The impression I often get when listening to people describe performance standards—that is, people who don't know the details of how standards are set—is that they almost always believe there is some underlying truth about performance, some real but hidden level of achievement that constitutes being "proficient," that is somehow revealed by the complex methods used to set standards. Or, at the very least, that the standards set clearly break the continuum of performance into unambiguous categories. One can see this, for example, in innumerable newspaper articles. To pick a handy one, an article published in the *Boston Globe* as I was writing this chapter stated: "Massachusetts students lead the nation on national standardized tests in math. Still, *fewer than half of the state's students demonstrate a solid command of math* on those tests" (emphasis added).[2] The reporter did not offer more details, but I believe she was referring to the most recent NAEP, which showed that only 43 percent of Massachusetts eight-graders reached or exceeded the proficient "achievement level" (performance standard).[3] That seems unambiguous, doesn't it?

A closer look at the process, however, shows us otherwise. The old joke holds that there are two things no one should see being made, laws and sausages. I would add performance standards.

Although many standards-setting methods are carefully reasoned and conscientiously documented and monitored, the results—just what level of performance is required to be called, say, "proficient"—remains a matter of judgment. The judgment is somewhat obscured by the complexity of the process, but it is not supplanted by some scientifically validated criterion. Moreover, although the results of standard setting appear clear-cut—a small number of usually simply described and seemingly clear descriptions of performance—they are anything but. A brief sketch of two of the methods most commonly used to set standards in K–12 testing will illustrate this.[4]

One of the most common methods, variants of which are used in the National Assessment of Educational Progress and in some state assessments, is called the *Angoff* or *modified Angoff* method (after the psychometrician William Angoff). In the NAEP version of the modified Angoff process, as implemented in the 2000 assessment of mathematics, panels of judges began by considering very short descriptions, called "policy definitions," of the standards. These definitions were as follows:

- *Basic.* This level denotes partial mastery of prerequisite knowledge and skills that are fundamental for proficient work at each grade.
- *Proficient.* This level represents solid academic performance for each grade assessed. Students reaching this level have demonstrated competency over challenging subject matter, including subject-matter knowledge, application of such knowledge to real-world situations, and analytical skills appropriate to the subject matter.
- *Advanced.* This level signifies superior performance.[5]

These definitions are very vague, as any similarly brief definitions of performance standards would necessarily be. How good does performance have to be to be "superior"? What subject matter qualifies as "challenging"? What is "proficient work"? In the NAEP process, the panelists themselves added some flesh to these bones. They first took the actual test themselves, and then they revised and elaborated the definitions of the standards based on brainstorming about what they believed performance should be.

Then, after two hours of training in the Angoff method, they rated each of the items. For each of the standards—let's consider only the proficient standard for illustration—the panelists were asked to envision a group of students who just barely exceeded that standard. That is, they imagined students whose performance barely qualified as proficient. Then they had to estimate the probability that these imaginary, marginally proficient students would answer each item correctly.

Notice that up to this point, the panelists had no actual data about student performance to help them. They had a definition of the standard, elaborated somewhat by their brainstorming; they had in their minds an imagined group of students who just barely meet that vague standard; and they had a set of test items. They had no examples of students who actually meet the standard. They had, up to this point, no information on the actual difficulty of the test items for students, although they did know how hard they themselves found the items. (Difficulty for adults may be quite a misleading guide to difficulty for students still in school, and the difference may go in either direction, as parents of secondary-school students routinely discover when they try to dredge up details from their long-past math classes to help their kids with homework.) Absent data, teachers from the grade in question had their own experience as a guide. However, standard-setting panels often include people who are not teachers, and these individuals generally have little or no first-hand experience to go on.

To make the difficulty of the panelists' task concrete, you can try it yourself with the mathematics item shown in Figure 8.1. This item was used in the 2003 fourth-grade National Assessment of Educational Progress. NAEP does not make publicly available the percentages of students marginally above each of their standards who answer items correctly, so let's change the task slightly to match the data they do provide. NAEP has three standards, basic, proficient, and advanced, and thus four levels of performance:

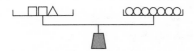

13. The objects on the scale above
     make it balance exactly.
     According to this scale, if △
     balances ○○○, then □ balances
     which of the following?

     A) ○
     B) ○○
     C) ○○○
     D) ○○○○

FIG. 8.1. A mathematics item from the 2003 fourth-grade National
Assessment of Educational Progress.

below basic, above basic but below proficient, above proficient but
below advanced, and above advanced. Referencing the definitions
above to explain what the standards mean, try to estimate the percentages of each of these four groups that answered this item correctly. The actual percentages appear in the footnote below.*

After the first round of ratings, the procedure used by NAEP
and many other testing programs does introduce some actual data
about performance, called *impact data*. Panelists are given the actual percentage of students who answered each item correctly—
the percentage of all students, not the percentages of students in
the imagined groups just above each of the standards, which have
not yet been set. This adds a norm-referenced element to the stan-

---

* Below basic, 14 percent; basic, 29 percent; proficient, 67 percent; and advanced, 92 percent. Note that the panelists' task was a bit easier because they had elaborated definitions
of the standards to reference, but not all standard-setting procedures provide those.

dards because the impact data are in fact normative data about performance. NAEP also provides panelists with data about the variation in ratings among the panelists.

With this additional information, the panelists rated the items a second time. They then were given another round of feedback and rated the items a third time. At the end of this process, a mathematical procedure was used to link the final ratings of judges to the original NAEP reporting scale in order to determine how high on that scale one had to go to reach each of the three standards. For example, in the eighth grade, the basic standard was set at a scale score of 262, the proficient standard was set at 299, and the advanced standard was set at 333.

Another approach to standards setting that has rapidly grown in popularity—and is now the most common in state testing programs—is called the *bookmark* method. To start this process, the test publisher ranks all of the items on the test in terms of their actual difficulty. As in the Angoff method, panelists are given short definitions of the standards, and they are asked to envision students who have reached a given level of performance. These students may be those who just barely reach a given standard, or they may be all of those who have exceeded that standard but have not reached the next level. Again, let's use proficient as the example. They are then asked to go through the items in order of difficulty and to stop at the item that they believe would be answered correctly by a specified percentage of the marginally proficient students they have imagined. This percentage, called the *response probability,* is often set at 67 percent, but there is no compelling reason why it has to be, and panels have used a variety of response probabilities ranging at least from 50 percent to 80 percent. I'll return to some data about the effects of this choice shortly, but for now, let's assume a typical response probability of 67 percent. Because the items are ranked by their difficulty, panelists are necessarily making the judgment that all preceding items would be answered correctly by more than 67 percent of the imaginary students in the group, and all subsequent items, by fewer than 67 percent. At their root, the cognitive demands placed on the panelists using this method are similar to those posed by the Angoff: estimating percentages correct for imagined groups of students, in the absence of actual performance data. Here again, however, panelists may be given feedback, including impact data for the total tested population, and they may go through several iterations of the process. At the end, the difficulty statistic used to rank the items provides a link to the scaled score that will then be treated as equivalent to the proficient standard.

My short descriptions do not do justice to these methods. A great deal of thought and effort has gone into refining them. But these sketches are sufficient to illustrate that judgment remains at the core of standard setting and that the basis for these judgments—in the case of these two common methods, estimates of the item-level performance of imagined groups of students—is not entirely confidence-inspiring. Whatever the pros and cons of these methods, they are not a means of uncovering some "true" or objective standard that is waiting to be discovered.

This makes the resulting standards a lot less compelling than many people think they are, but it need not render them worthless by any means, and in fact there is a long-standing debate among measurement experts about their utility. One piece of this debate is an argument about whether the standards are arbitrary and capricious. Two leading measurement experts, Jim Popham and Ron Hambleton, have separately argued that "arbitrary" has both a positive meaning connoting an appropriate use of judgment and a negative meaning indicating capriciousness. They each made the case that, when done carefully, the setting of standards is arbitrary in the first, positive sense but not capricious.[6]

This argument is correct so far as it goes but misses the main point. Most standard-setting procedures are conducted with great care, and few would claim that they are capricious. This does not imply, however, that we should be unconcerned about their arbitrariness. The issue is whether the standards, despite their arbitrariness, provide information that is clear, useful, and not misleading.

One basis for judging whether the standards measure up in this regard is whether the results are robust enough that users of the scores can have confidence in them. For example, we saw earlier that only 43 percent of Massachusetts eighth-grade students reached the NAEP proficient level in the most recent National Assessment of Educational Progress. This finding is intended to tell people something clear about the performance of Massachusetts students, and certainly the *Globe* reporter took it that way: she concluded, gloomily, that fewer than half of the students "demonstrate a solid command" of mathematics. But what if the results reported are highly sensitive to details of how the standards are set—details that are entirely irrelevant to the conclusions readers are basing on the results? What if another method would have given readers of the *Globe* the news that "75 percent [to pick a number out of the hat] of the state's students demonstrated a solid command of mathematics"?

Unfortunately, this example, while hypothetical, is realistic: the results of standard setting are not generally robust. And this throws into doubt the interpretation of performance reported in terms of these standards. Should readers of the *Globe* be more or less pessimistic about our eighth-graders, depending on the method chosen? And how many readers of a morning newspaper would have any idea, when confronted with as definitive a statement as that quoted above, that the findings depend not only on students' achievement but also on the choice—for all practical purposes, an arbitrary one—of methods used to set standards?

This point is likely to sit poorly with some readers, so a bit of empirical evidence may make it go down more easily. In 1989,

Richard Jaeger, then unquestionably one of the world's leading experts on standard setting, published a comprehensive review in which he showed that the results of standard setting are generally inconsistent across methods. He reviewed thirty-two published comparisons and calculated the ratio of the percentages of students labeled as failing by different standard-setting methods. In the typical case (the median), the harsher method of standard setting categorized fully half again as many students as failing as did the more lenient method, and some studies found far larger ratios.[7]

More recent research has not provided any more grounds for optimism. For example, studies have shown that methods in which judges evaluate one item at a time, such as the Angoff method, yield results inconsistent with those in which a body of actual work by a student, such as part or all of a completed test, are evaluated. Worse, choosing particular method for setting standards, for whatever reason, does not mean you're home free, because a growing body of research indicates that the details of how you implement that method—here again, details that are generally irrelevant to the conclusions people base on the results—can cause the performance standards to vary considerably. Differently composed panels of judges, for example, often produce appreciably different standards. And judges tend to move their standards up or down depending on the mix of item formats (multiple-choice and constructed-response). Judges also have been found to underestimate the difficulty of hard items and overestimate the difficulty of easy items, which can lead them to set higher standards when the items they evaluate are more difficult.[8] Changing the response probability used with the bookmark method—an arbitrary choice—can have dramatic effects on the placement of the standards.[9]

A comparison of current state performance standards makes the arbitrariness all the more apparent. As any number of commentators have pointed out, the percentages of students reaching a given threshold—say, the proficient standard—varies dramatically among states. One might hope that this variation represents real differences in achievement, but that is clearly not the case. For example, a recent article pointed out that the percentage of students reaching proficient in fourth-grade reading according to state standards is 81 percent in Massachusetts, 83 percent in Alabama, and 53 percent in Maine. For anyone familiar with test scores, these results would raise a red flag because states in New England and the north-central region generally outscore states in the deep South by a large margin. And indeed, the most recent NAEP results order these three states as one would expect: the percentage of students reaching the NAEP's proficient level is twice as high in Massachusetts as in Alabama (44 versus 22 percent). In eighth-grade mathematics, the inconsistencies are even more striking. A recent paper asked whether it is credible that the percentages reaching proficient are 63 percent in Alabama, 53 percent in Mississippi, and 16 percent in Missouri. NAEP confirms that it is not. Missouri, although in the same region, is a substantially higher-scoring state on the NAEP, and the percentages proficient by that barometer are 15 percent in Alabama, 13 percent in Mississippi, and 26 percent in Missouri.[10] So what is a concerned citizen in Alabama to believe? Are nearly all of the state's students "proficient" or hardly any? A detailed statistical analysis of state standards confirms that these are not flukes: the percents deemed proficient are largely unrelated to states' actual levels of student achievement.[11] A recent study compared the standards established for three nationally normed achievement tests to those set for the NAEP and found similarly dramatic inconsistencies. For example, the 2000 NAEP classified 17 percent of twelfth-graders as "proficient" or "advanced"; the percentages for the three other national tests ranged from 5 percent to 30 percent.[12]

Performance standards are also often inconsistent across grades or among subjects within a grade. In most standard-setting approaches, a given panel of judges considers only one subject and grade. There is usually nothing in the process to link panels' efforts from one grade or subject to another. Even though the same process is typically used for all subjects and grades within a single testing program, the resulting performance standards are often substantially and sometimes dramatically different across grades or subjects. Some states are now experimenting with methods to reduce these inconsistencies, but these are as yet unproven, and their impact remains unclear.

To be fair, the arbitrariness of performance standards need not render them useless. It can be helpful to have a formal statement of expectations. And even an initially arbitrary standard may accrue meaning over time, with experience. A score of 700 on the SAT verbal scale was initially just an arbitrarily chosen number, but with experience, it has gained meaning (albeit a norm-referenced one): high-school students, teachers, parents, and admissions officers all know that this is a very high score, good enough to keep a student competitive at even highly selective colleges. Similarly, over time, an arbitrary standard labeled "proficient" may accumulate meaning as people learn what level of work it requires and which students reach it.[13]

This accrued meaning, however, can take one only so far. The labels chosen for performance standards, such as "proficient," have their own meanings independent of their use with the standards, and these clearly influence how people interpret the results they are given. The *Boston Globe* quote above is an example: having a "solid command" of math is a pretty good synonym for "proficient," isn't it? Such inferences are generally unwarranted, however, and are sometimes clearly misleading. For example, the level and description of standards used with one of the federal government's surveys of adult literacy led many people to infer unreasonably high rates of illiteracy among American adults.[14] Inconsistencies in standards across subjects or grades often lead to conclusions such as "our schools are much more effective in English than in mathematics" or "our elementary schools are less effective than our middle schools" when the data may simply reflect differences in standard setting. And regardless of how they are interpreted, the standards now imposed by states have serious practical impact. Whether some schools are "failing" under the terms of NCLB, and in some states, which students obtain a high-school diploma, can vary depending on irrelevant aspects of the methods used to set performance standards.

Even leaving aside all of these many inconsistencies, standards-based reporting has a serious drawback: it obscures a great deal of information about variations in student performance. This is a consequence not of the judgmental nature of standards but rather of the coarseness of the resulting scale. As described above, most standards-based systems have three or four performance standards that create four or five ranges or categories for reporting performance. Information about differences among students *within* any one of those ranges does not register. And those unnoted differences can be very large.

As a result, substantial improvements can go unnoticed while trivially small gains can seem large. For example, let's assume that a state has standards similar to those of the NAEP described above, where a score of 262 corresponds to the basic level and 299 is needed to reach proficient. Now consider a school that starts out with a large number of students at the low end of the basic range, say between 262 and 275. By dint of hard work and careful evaluation of teaching methods, this school raises most of those students to scores just below the proficient cutoff of 299. Now consider a second school that does not manage to create improvements of this size. However, it does manage to nudge some students who are just below the proficient cut up by a very few points, just enough to push them over the standard. The first school has generated considerably more real improvement than the second, but in terms of the critically important percent-proficient statistic—the centerpiece of accountability under NCLB—the first school will appear to have made no gains at all, while the second school will appear to have made substantial progress.

While this example may seem contrived, the problem is real, and many teachers talk openly of the perverse incentives that these distortions create for them. In an accountability system that focuses on standards-based reporting, teachers have an incentive to focus their efforts primarily on students near a cutoff point between standards, because only changes in performance among those students will register. There is even now a common term for these students: "bubble kids." Under NCLB, the incentive is simpler yet: focus on students who can be moved across the proficient cut score, and ignore even the other performance standards because they don't matter for purposes of NCLB accountability.

A final problem inherent in reporting in terms of standards is that such reporting can distort comparisons of trends shown by different groups, such as minority and majority students or students with and without disabilities. For example, a few years ago, a reporter from the *Boston Globe* called me just after that year's results of the state's MCAS assessment had been released. She claimed the results showed that African American students constituted a growing proportion of failing students—that is, those failing to reach the relevant performance standards. Her question to me was this: "Doesn't this mean that the system is failing African American students and that they are falling farther behind?"

To her evident annoyance, I told her that I had no idea and that I would need different data to answer her question. The problem, I explained to her, is that when performance is reported in terms of standards, comparisons of trends in performance between two groups that start out at different levels—such as whites and African Americans in Boston—are almost always misleading. There are two different statistics used for this purpose. One is the statistic she used: the composition of the group failing to (or succeeding in) reaching the standard. You are most likely to encounter this statistic in arguments about equity in college admissions, as in the question, what fraction of the admitted students are from lower-scoring minority groups? The denominator of this fraction is the number of students in the rejected or accepted group. The second statistic, far more common in reports of K–12 test scores, is the percentage of each group reaching (or failing to reach) a standard, such as the percentage of whites or African Americans reaching proficient. In this case, the denominator of the fraction is the number of students in the group in question, such as African Americans. Both of these statistics are problematic, and for the same reason.

Consider a hypothetical comparison between whites and African Americans. Assume that the difference between the means of the two groups is large, that the variability of scores within each group is large, and that most students in each group have scores relatively close to their own group's average. This is precisely what one would typically find.

Now assume something atypical: assume that every single individual, regardless of the group he or she is in, improves by *exactly* the same amount. This would be identical progress by both groups; every single individual makes equal progress, and the entire distribution of scores for African Americans would march upward in lockstep with the distribution of scores for whites. Ideally, we would want a summary of the gains of the two groups in this hypothetical example to show this equal progress. And if you presented the trends in terms of changes in average or median scores for the two groups, you would indeed see identical progress. If you use either of the two types of standards-based statistics, you won't. They will show different changes in the two groups, and the nature of the apparent difference will depend on where the standard lies relative to the two distributions of scores.

Therefore, I told the audibly impatient reporter, the difference between groups that she gave me did not directly measure whether African Americans in Boston schools were falling farther behind whites. That might have been the case, but it was also possible that it was not. With the simple statistics that used to be routinely reported, such as mean scale scores, I could have told her. But differences among groups in terms of standards-based statistics, particularly changes in the percent exceeding the proficient standard, now dominate reporting of the achievement gap. How many readers of a newspaper story showing different increases in the percentages reaching such a standard would realize that they were not necessarily being told whether one group was falling behind or catching up with the other?

Given the weaknesses of standards-based reporting, it is worth returning to the reasons why its proponents so often disparaged norm-referenced reporting. How practical is it to avoid norm-referenced reporting? And is it really true, as some advocates of standards-based reporting argue, that norm-referenced reporting tells you nothing about whether the level of students' performance is acceptable?

Normative data often creep into standard setting. Sometimes this happens during the initial standard-setting process, as when panelists are given impact data. Sometimes it happens after the fact, when policymakers decide that the process has resulted in unreasonable or unacceptable standards. This modest reliance on normative data notwithstanding, standards are sometimes set at levels that normative data suggest are unreasonable. For example, faced with the enormous inconsistencies in the levels at which standards are set across states, some critics argue that all states should use standards as demanding as the proficient standard established by the National Assessment of Educational Progress. But in eighth-grade mathematics, that standard is so high that roughly a third of the students in Japan and Korea, which are among the highest-scoring countries in the world, would fail to reach it.[15] And as we saw in Chapter 5, the gaps between those countries and the United States are very large. To use as a short-term target for all students in the United States a performance level that a third of the students in Japan and Korea could not reach seems at best unrealistic.

In practice, norm-referenced reporting is still used frequently, if sometimes unknowingly, even by its critics. An example would be the widely cited NAEP results that compare states in terms of the percentages of students reaching a given standard, such as proficient. We can find out, for example, that in 2000, 22 percent of fourth-graders in Maryland reached or exceeded the proficient standard. Standards-based, right? But here is the rub: how do you know what to make of this result? Is 22 percent high or low? One way to find out is to compare this percentage to the percentages in other states. NAEP conveniently displays the percentages for all states together, ranked from highest to lowest. (Remember the panty hose chart in Chapter 7?) These charts report performance in terms of *state norms*—that is, by comparison to a distribution of the performance of states, expressed in terms of the percents above proficient. Thus, the NAEP reports rest on both standards and norms. NAEP provides several other forms of state norms, including norms for percentages above other standards and norms based on states' mean scale scores. As noted in Chapter 5, international comparisons such as TIMSS also rest on normative comparisons.

What these examples illustrate is that norm-referenced reporting is hard to avoid because it is informative. And we routinely use norms to evaluate performance expectations. For example, assume that you have to appoint a new coach for a middle-school track team. One applicant comes in brimming with enthusiasm and announces that his target is to have half of the distance runners clocking three-and-a-half-minute miles within a year. What do you do? You send him packing, because he is either utterly incompetent or a liar. (To my knowledge, only one secondary-school student has ever clocked a mile in less than four minutes, and that one time was just barely under four. Even the best adult distance runners in the world don't come close to a three-and-a-half-minute mile.) In other words, you rely on norm-referenced information to tell you that the level of performance he promises is absurd. This example is contrived, but the fact is that we use normative information constantly in all aspects of life—to evaluate the gas mileage of cars, to decide whether a purchase is too expensive, and so on. Testing is no different.

Perhaps in response to this, some states have begun adding normative information to their standards-based reports. A good example is Massachusetts, which uses standards-based reports as its primary method for presenting the results of its MCAS assessment. But simple percentages above the several cut scores are not enough for educators to use to evaluate the performance of their students. Therefore, the Massachusetts Department of Education added normative information to its reports. Some of this consists of normative comparisons of standards-based statistics: comparisons of how your school's percentages above a standard compare with the district and the state as a whole. Massachusetts does the same with percents correct on individual test items. The state provides educators and the public with norm-referenced information to help them make sense of the standards-based performance data.

Given all the problems that arise when student achievement is reported in terms of a few performance standards, what should be done? In a recent article in which he outlined a number of the most serious weaknesses of standards-based reporting, Robert Linn of the University of Colorado suggested that we distinguish the cases in which we do need to make binary, up-or-down decisions based on a test—for example, in setting a passing score on a written driving test or in using tests as a minimum criterion for professional licensure or certification—from those in which we do not need to do so. He suggested that in the latter instance, which includes most achievement testing in elementary and secondary schools, we would do better simply to avoid standards-based reporting.[16] I agree, although, as Linn also noted, we are unlikely to have this option: standards-based reporting is likely to be with us for some time. If so, we need to supplement it with something else that does not share the same weaknesses—and that brings us to traditional scales.

Scales

So let's put performance standards aside and go back to square one. Someone has administered a test to students in your area. Let's say that the test comprises fifty items. What is a useful way to report the results?

The simplest method would be to report a tally for each student: the number of items answered correctly or, if the possible credit varied among items, the total number of points scored. To avoid confounding these tallies with the length of the test, we could convert them to simple percentages: the percentage of items answered correctly or the percentage of possible credit earned. We can call all of these *raw scores*.

This is the kind of test scoring we all grew up with, and it does have some utility. After every exam in my classes today, I present a graph showing the distribution of raw scores. This gives students some valuable norm-referenced information: a comparison of their performance with that of the rest of the class.

But as I noted in Chapter 1, these simple raw scores have very serious limitations. The most important is that if we do not know how difficult the test was, we cannot evaluate how good a given score is. I could write exams hard enough that most students would earn no credit whatever or easy enough that most would get nearly perfect scores, even though their actual knowledge of the course material would be identical in both cases. I have no reason to do either, of course, and in practice I try to construct exams that have roughly the same level of difficulty from one year to the next. But unless I keep my tests virtually identical, I cannot be confident that they are in fact equally difficult. And of course the tests written by different teachers are even less likely to be equally difficult. Therefore, the common convention of assigning a letter grade to a fixed percentage—90 percent of credit gets you an A, or some such—is not useful for large-scale testing programs. It can be serviceable within a single classroom if the teacher has a good grasp of the difficulty of her assignments and tests, but it does not provide the comparability across schools and over time that is important for large-scale assessments.

Faced with this limitation of raw scores, psychometricians have developed a variety of scales as substitutes for raw scores. The scales were designed for different purposes and, unfortunately, can provide somewhat different views of student performance. To clarify this, it is helpful to consider two scales that have nothing to do with testing.

First, let's consider temperature scales. Imagine, for the moment, that one of your friends is considering a move from City A to City B and says: "The temperature drops as much at night in City A as in City B. The difference between the average daily high temperature and the average nightly low is about 9 degrees." You may not know people who actually look such things up, but for purposes of illustration, humor me. Now assume that your friend is an American and that both cities are in the United States, so he means 9 degrees Fahrenheit.

Now suppose that the United States decides to do everyone a favor, follows the lead of the rest of the world, and finally adopts the metric system. What would happen to your friend's conclusion about the similarity of the two cities?

Nothing, of course. The temperature difference between the

daily high and nightly low would be expressed as 5 degrees Celsius rather than 9 degrees Fahrenheit, but it is precisely the same difference in temperature, and the conclusion that the two cities are the same in this respect is unchanged. This may seem obvious (although perhaps not to Nigel Tufnel), but it is not the case with all changes of scale. It is true in this example because the change from Fahrenheit to Celsius is a *linear transformation,* meaning that it is accomplished by multiplying by one constant and adding another. The conversion from Celsius to Fahrenheit requires multiplying by 1.8 (because the degrees are farther apart on the Celsius scale) and adding 32 (because the value of zero is in different places, at the freezing point of water in the case of Celsius, and at a meaningless lower temperature on the Fahrenheit scale). It is called a linear transformation because it is effected by applying a simple linear equation in one variable of the form $y = a + bx$. When a transformation is linear, any two differences that are the same size on one scale (9 degrees Fahrenheit in both cities) will be the same size on the other (5 degrees Celsius in both cities).

Most of the changes in scale we encounter in daily life—from grams to pounds, from dollars to euros, from liters to ounces, from square feet to square yards—are linear transformations, so it is easy to lost sight of the fact that they need not be. Consider the 2004 presidential election.

In recent years, it has become common to refer to states or counties that vote Republican as "red" and to those that vote Democratic as "blue." After the 2004 presidential election, pundits began lecturing us about the great red tide that had left blue voters in small, isolated, and somewhat odd places, like my state of Massachusetts, or California. And the widely known map of how states voted, reproduced in Figure 8.2, seemed to buttress their argument: vast swaths of red (shown in white in the figure) isolated three relatively small areas of blue (in black here).

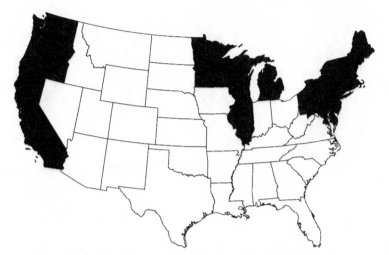

FIG. 8.2.   The 2004 presidential election, with "blue" states in black
and "red" states in white, scaled by geographical area.
Michael Gastner, Cosma Shalizi, and Mark Newman, "Maps
and Cartograms of the 2004 US Presidential Election
Results," *http://www-personal.umich.edu/~mejn/election/*
(accessed December 30, 2006).

They were wrong, and not just because they ascribed persistence to an electoral result that evaporated a mere two years later. Figure 8.2 is fundamentally misleading because it uses the wrong *scale:* it ranks states in order of acreage. Acres, however, don't vote. Montana appears as one of the largest states, but in population it is only a hair larger than the metropolitan area of Albany, New York, which many blue-state residents don't even consider a real metropolitan area.

So what would the map have looked like if the voting were depicted using more reasonable scale that ranks states in order of population? The result, courtesy of two physicists and a statistician at the University of Michigan, is shown in Figure 8.3. This map badly distorts the physical dimensions and locations of the states, but it ranks them properly in order of population.

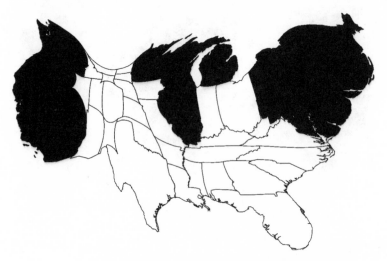

FIG. 8.3. The 2004 presidential election, with "blue" states in black and "red" states in white, scaled by population. Michael Gastner, Cosma Shalizi, and Mark Newman, "Maps and Cartograms of the 2004 US Presidential Election Results, *http://www-personal.umich.edu/~mejn/election/* (accessed December 30, 2006).

Montana is now far smaller than Massachusetts. The blue areas, while still isolated from one another, no longer appear small—and they shouldn't, since their total population is not much different from that of the red area.

This is an example of a *nonlinear transformation*, a change of scale that does not preserve the relationships among the observations—in this case, among the states. New Jersey became a lot larger, Montana became a lot smaller, and Kentucky was not much altered. A comparison made using the first scale—say, that Arizona and New Mexico are about the same—would not be preserved by the transformation to the second map because New Mexico is similar to Arizona in size but has a smaller population.

Unfortunately, many of the scales used in educational testing are nonlinear transformations of each other. For the most part, the choice of scale does not affect rankings—students who score higher on one scale will score higher on another—but it does change *comparisons*. Two groups that show the same improvement over time on one of these scales may not show the same improvement on another.

One common type of scale uses values that are essentially arbitrary. You have encountered a number of scales of this sort in earlier chapters, including the scales used for reporting scores on the SAT, the ACT, the National Assessment of Educational Progress, and TIMSS. That these scales are arbitrary—in one sense of the word—is shown by how different they are. As we know, for example, the SAT scale (within a subject area) runs from 200 to 800, while that of the ACT runs from 1 to 36. There is no substantive reason for this difference; no one would argue that a student who reaches the top score on the SAT knows twenty-two times as much as a student who reaches the maximum score on the ACT. And the ranking of college applicants would not be altered if ACT scoring were switched to match the SAT scale, or the College Board decided to change the SAT scoring to the ACT scale.

Some years ago, a colleague and I submitted a memo to a government agency responsible for a large testing program, and we referred to the scale used in the program as arbitrary. A member of the agency's staff took umbrage and admonished me, saying that the scale was anything but arbitrary, that it was very carefully constructed. She was correct that their scale was carefully constructed, but we were correct that it was arbitrary.

That these scales are arbitrary does not imply that they are casual creations. On the contrary. The construction of these scales entails many steps, but it is a helpful oversimplification to think of it as having two stages. The first of these, which is complex and exacting if done well (as it is with all four of the testing programs I mentioned), results in an interim scale that has technically useful characteristics but that uses a metric that is not fit for public consumption. It is in this first stage that almost all of the complexities of creating a scale are addressed, such as linking the scale to be used for the most recent results with those used in the past. Often, this interim scale approximates the standardized scale described in Chapter 5, with a mean of approximately zero and a standard deviation—a measure of the spread of scores—of approximately one. As noted in Chapter 5, these scales are found handy by statisticians and social scientists, but they do not sit well with the public because they assign students both fractional and negative scores. (Remember, how many parents would understand that their child could answer many questions correctly and nonetheless get a score of zero or, worse, a negative score?) The second stage of scaling, which is simpler and often arbitrary, avoids these problems by transforming the interim scale to make it more palatable. The easiest way to do this is to add an arbitrary number to all scores to obtain a higher mean and then multiply by another arbitrary constant to spread scores out more. In the case of both the SAT and TIMSS, the scale was set to have a mean of 500 and a standard deviation of 100. In 2005, the fourth-grade mathematics results of the National Assessment of Educational Progress had a mean of 237 and a standard deviation of 29. When my colleague and I labeled the scale in question as arbitrary, we were referring only to this second stage; when the agency staffer replied, she was thinking only of the first.

Scales built of arbitrary numbers, no matter how carefully they are constructed, might not seem to be a very helpful way to describe student achievement. But these scales have a number of very important advantages over both raw scores and performance standards.

The most important advantage of these arbitrary-scale scores over raw scores is that they can be made comparable over time and across forms of the test. The College Board could just as easily have set the mean of the SAT at 320 or 40 rather than the 500 they chose, but once they chose 500, a score of 500 means pretty much the same thing regardless of when you take the test, even if your raw score might vary somewhat depending on the items included in each form. A related advantage of these scales over raw scores is that their properties (such as their standard deviations) are known, so if you want more detailed information, say, the score required to get into the top quartile, it can be calculated easily. There are exceptions—for example, the Massachusetts MCAS tests are scaled in an unusual way such that the publicly released scale scores do not provide this sort of information—but they are rare.

You might reply that in many testing programs, performance standards have been made comparable from one year to the next. Indeed, NCLB and many of the state accountability programs that preceded it depend on this: it makes no sense to hold schools accountable for increasing the percentage of students reaching a proficient standard if that standard does not remain consistently demanding. If the test becomes slightly harder or easier as new items are introduced, then the raw score required to reach the standard must change so that the standard itself remains fixed. What is often not apparent unless one reads technical reports is that the key to this consistency is usually scale scores. The results of a test are placed on a scale; the scale scores are then statistically linked to make them comparable across forms or years; and then these linked scale scores are used to make the standards comparable. The performance standards do not offer a means of establishing comparability; they simply get layered on top of the scale that provides this opportunity.

Often the underlying scale is not reported because of the current enthusiasm for standards-based reporting. Not long ago, I had a meeting with the director of a state assessment program in which I argued—to no avail—that he should start reporting scale scores along with performance standards. He replied that it would be too much work for them. I pointed out that he already had a scale in hand; it was used every year to link his standards to the previous year's test. All he had to do was transform it to a more acceptable metric, which is nothing more than simple arithmetic. It says something about the dominance of standards-based reporting that he had never realized this.

Even though they are also in one sense arbitrary, these scale scores have numerous advantages over performance standards. Scales are much more useful than standards for portraying the entire distribution of performance. To take a simple example: suppose you want to track trends in the average performance of a group of students. This can't be done sensibly with standards. And unlike performance standards, scales do not create distortions when one compares trends among different groups of students.

In some respects, the arbitrariness of scale scores is less of a problem than that of performance standards. When performance standards are set, the levels expected of students are arbitrary, and the labels attached to them often carry additional, prior meaning, some of which may be unwarranted. Altering these decisions—selecting a different method that happens to move the standard up or down, or giving a standard a different verbal label—can have a major effect on the way people interpret student performance, even though the performance itself would not have changed. Scale scores lack this baggage. Few people read a report of a new testing program with some prior notion of what a score of 340 means. To take a concrete example: many readers will be familiar with the PSAT (the Preliminary SAT/National Merit Scholarship Qualifying Test), which many high-school sophomores and juniors take for a number of reasons, in part to prepare for taking the SAT a year or so later. The scale used with the PSAT is essentially the SAT scale, but it is divided by 10 so that the two will not be confused—that is, it runs from 20 to 80 rather than 200 to 800.

I have yet to hear anyone express amazement that a student who scored only 70 on the PSAT scored around 700 on the SAT. The numbers used for the two scales have no prior meaning that can clutter up people's understanding of the scores.

That strength is obviously also a weakness: arbitrary numbers with no prior meaning are not very informative. Something has to be done to attach meaning to the numbers. How is a parent to know whether an ACT score of 29 is good news or bad?

One answer is—once again—norms. Often, this normative information is informal and approximate. For example, most parents of college-bound students in states where the SAT dominates hear about the SAT constantly; they read occasional articles about SAT scores in the newspaper; they may have had a chat with their schools' guidance counselors about their own children's scores; and they often know the scores of quite a number of other students. They may also have received sales pitches from test-preparation firms that discuss scores. Through this exposure, they know that a math score of 600 is moderately high.

The NAEP is an interesting example because the agencies responsible for it have wrestled for years with the problem of adding meaning to scale scores and have devised quite a variety of approaches. One, of course, has been to layer performance standards ("achievement levels") on top of the scale. But many of the approaches for giving the NAEP scores meaning rely on normative information. For example, normative data are key to making sense of NAEP's much publicized comparisons among states. How is the commissioner of education in Minnesota to know whether that state's mean scale score of 290 is good or bad? One way is to compare that average with the distribution of state averages, which the NAEP reports provide. The distribution shows that 290 is pretty damned good, at least so far as achievement in the United States is concerned. NAEP also provides, for every state, the proportion of students falling into each of the four performance "bins" created by the achievement levels—a combination of standards-based and norm-referenced reporting.[17]

Often, scale scores are accompanied by a second, explicitly normative scale, most often percentile ranks (PRs). A percentile rank is simply the percentage of scores falling below a given score. For example, to return to the SAT score of 600: parents may think of this as "moderately high," but a look on the Web turns up more precise information: in mathematics in 2005, a score of 600 corresponded to the seventy-fifth percentile—that is, 75 percent of students who took the test obtained scores below 600.[18] Percentile ranks have nothing to do with the percentage of items a student answers correctly; they are simply a way of stating how a student stacks up against others. Many types of admissions tests give students a percentile rank along with a scale score.*

And this is a case where the example of the 2004 election results is relevant: the transformation from scale scores to PRs is not linear. On most tests, a lot of students are piled up with scores near the average, while far fewer have very high or very low scores. We can again use the SAT as an example. A student whose score increases from 450 to 550—from somewhat below average to somewhat above—will show a large increase in percentile rank. Because there are a great many students piled up in that region, he passes a lot of them on the way from 450 to 550. A student who starts at 650, however, and shows the exact same 100-point increase in scale scores, will obtain a much smaller increase in percentile rank because there are far fewer students in the range of 650 to 750. Thus, the two scales portray the two students differently, one suggesting equal improvement and the other suggesting unequal improvement. Which is right? Both are. They just mean different things by "improvement."

---

* Technically, the score itself (in this case, 600) is called the percentile, while the percentage (in this case, 75) is the percentile rank. In practice, however, the term *percentile* is often used for both.

Another category of scales used with some achievement tests is often called *standard scores*. Standard scores differ from the arbitrary scales already noted in that they take exactly the same form from one test to another. They are based on the standardized scale explained in Chapter 5—mean of 0, standard deviation of 1—but are transformed to have different values. One of these scales is called *T-scores*, which have a mean of 50 and a standard deviation of 10. Another, a rather peculiar innovation stemming from the Title I evaluation requirements of the 1970s referenced in Chapter 4, is *normal curve equivalents*, usually labeled simply as NCEs. These are transformed to have a mean of 50 and a standard deviation a bit over 21. Standard scores are often provided with traditional norm-referenced achievement tests but generally are not used with the newer tests designed for specific states. Educators and parents may still encounter them in districts or states that use norm-referenced tests, but the general public rarely does.

A final category of scales are *developmental scales*, which are designed specifically to measure growth in achievement as students progress through school. The hoariest of these is *grade equivalents*, or GEs. These have fallen out of favor over the past several decades, which is a great shame, as they are quite easy to understand and provide an intuitively clear way to think about children's development. A grade equivalent is simply the typical performance—the performance of the median student—at any grade level. It is usually shown in terms of academic years and months (with 10 academic months per school year). Thus a GE of 3.7 is the median performance of students in March of third grade on the test designed for third-graders. GEs tell you whether students are keeping pace with the norm group. Thus, if a third-grader obtains a GE of 4.7, that means that her performance on the third-grade test is well above average—specifically, it is comparable to that which the median student in March of fourth grade would show on the third-grade test. I will use the grade-equivalent scale in Chapter 10 to show how serious the problem of score inflation can be when educators are held accountable for test scores.

As useful as they are, GEs have a number of drawbacks. One is that the rate of growth in a subject area is not constant as children get older. For example, the typical child gains reading skills faster in the primary grades than later on. Therefore, a gain of one GE denotes greater growth in the early grades than in later grades. If you want to know, for example, whether the rate at which students learn math slows down or speeds up when they move to middle school, GEs by their very nature cannot tell you. The average student will gain one GE per year regardless.

The final scale I'll mention, which appears often, is another developmental scale that attempts to avoid this limitation of grade equivalents. Properly, it goes by the cumbersome name *developmental standard score,* but this is often confusingly shortened to developmental score or just scale score. This is an arbitrary numerical scale, seemingly similar to the scales used for the NAEP or SAT, but with a major difference: developmental standard scores are linked across grades in a way that supposedly gives any specific increase in performance the same meaning in every grade. For example, suppose that one student showed a gain from 230 to 250 between third grade and fourth, and a second student increased from 245 to 265 between fourth grade and fifth. If these are developmental standard scores, their identical gains of 20 points would ideally mean that both improved their performance by the same amount. Despite the inconsistent and confusing labeling of these scales, you can often identify them by comparing the numbers across grades. If the numbers are similar across grades, the scale is not a developmental standard score, but if the numbers increase from grade to grade (and the scores are not on a grade-equivalent scale), the chances are good that it is one.

In all fields, scales that have this property—that is, scales on

which any given difference has the same meaning at different levels—are called *interval scales*. Most of the scales we use in daily life
are interval scales. Length is obviously an interval scale—an extra
foot of rope is the same length and will cost you the same at the
hardware store, regardless of whether you have already taken ten
or twenty feet off the spool.

Unfortunately, developmental scale scores cannot be counted
on to be true interval scales. It is rarely feasible to confirm that a
ten-point gain means the same thing in different grade levels, and
it is sometimes clear that it does not. Creating such a scale is not
an entirely practical goal. To create a true interval scale, students
have to be learning the same thing throughout the grade range in
question. If one is comparing, say, reading in grades two and
three, that might be a reasonable assumption, but it is a stretch
when one compares third-grade math to seventh-grade math. Just
how much facility with basic multiplication is equivalent to a
given gain in pre-algebra? A sensible rule of thumb is to treat
these scales as approximate and to be increasingly skeptical as the
grade range they cover grows larger.

Faced with all of these complexities, users often translate scores
into a seemingly simpler but generally completely meaningless
scale: *percentage change in performance*. It's not just lay people who
do this; I have seen it done by brand-name academics as well, although never by a specialist in measurement. For example, at the
2006 annual meeting of the American Educational Research Association, a leading advocate of privatizing American education presented the percent change in scores on the National Assessment
of Educational Progress to argue that there has been little improvement in student performance in recent decades. He was substantively wrong, as we saw in Chapter 5, but for present purposes
the point is that his way of supporting his conclusion, while
commonsensical, was nonsense. The reason: because the average
score on most test-score scales is arbitrary. Consider the SAT

mathematics scale again. When the scale was last revised, it had a mean of 500. Suppose a student's score increased from 500 to 600. That would be an increase of 20 percent. But suppose that, faced with the arbitrary choice, the College Board had instead opted for a mean of 400. Then the student's improvement would have been a 25 percent gain, even though the actual improvement in performance would have been identical.*

The average user of test scores just wants a straightforward way to describe achievement and can be forgiven for being a bit put off by all the complexities described here. What can someone do to make sensible use of these scales without a great deal of fuss?

The cardinal if perhaps unsatisfying rule is *caveat emptor*: be aware of what you are buying, what the test-score scales you are given do and do not tell you about student performance. If given a choice, use the scale that best fits your particular question. If you want to know whether a student is keeping pace with her peers as she moves through the grades, grade equivalents are an appropriate and handy metric. If you want to compare improvements of middle-school kids with improvements by students in the primary grades, they are not.

And be careful not to ascribe more meaning than these reports really have, or to simplify them into something that seems easier to digest. In the case of standards, this means not loosing sight of the fact that performance standards are only an expression of someone's judgment that could as well have been set at a very different level, and that the labels given to them may come freighted with surplus and unwarranted connotations.

---

* This assumes that the standard deviation remains the same. Technically, the problem is that test scores (like Fahrenheit temperature, but unlike length, speed, or any number of other common measures) are not a *ratio scale*, which means that zero on the test score scale does not mean "zero achievement." Zero on most scales is just an arbitrary point. Even on a raw-score scale, where zero means zero items answered correctly, it need not mean "no knowledge of the domain"; it just means no mastery of the particular material on the test. Percentage change is a meaningful metric only in the case of ratio scales.

Chapter 9

Validity

ADMISSIONS OFFICERS use test scores to help them decide which applicants are most likely to succeed in college. Teachers use test scores to help diagnose strengths and weaknesses in students' learning. Seemingly everyone—educators, parents, newspaper reporters, realtors—uses test scores to judge the educational performance of schools, states, and even countries. No Child Left Behind requires that test scores be used to determine which schools warrant sanctions. At the beginning of this book, we drew conclusions about the vocabularies of college students from a hypothetical vocabulary test. In each of these instances, people base a specific inference on a given test score.

To what degree are these conclusions warranted by the test scores used to support them? As I noted at the outset of this book, this is the question of *validity*, which is the single most important criterion for evaluating achievement testing. The importance of validity is widely enough recognized that it finds its way into laws and regulations. For example, the No Child Left Behind Act requires that the assessments required by the law "be used for purposes for which such assessments are valid and reliable."

But what does "validity" actual mean? It seems simple enough; after all, the term is used in common parlance. It turns out, however, that there is more to the story than first meets the eye. Many of the most important current controversies about testing, such as disputes about high-stakes testing, are at their root disagreements about validity, and they cannot be sorted out without a more careful consideration of what validity entails.

This chapter clarifies what we mean by validity, discusses a number of the most fundamental threats to valid inference, and explains some types of evidence we bring to bear to evaluate it. The following chapters apply this notion to three of the most important areas of dispute in American testing today: high-stakes testing, bias, and the assessment of students with special needs.

We use the terms *valid* and *validity* routinely in all manner of contexts. When the cyclist Floyd Landis was accused of using performance-enhancing drugs in his successful bid to win the Tour de France, one of his lawyers stated that "the [drug] test's validity could be one of Landis's defenses."[1] An op-ed column in the *Boston Globe* about the controversy surrounding George W. Bush's use of signing statements ended with the comment that "whether he has been justified [in issuing more signing statements than his predecessors] depends on whether his constitutional arguments are valid."[2] On television, in a CNN segment on headache treatments, one expert said of possible new treatments for migraine that none was yet far enough along in development to permit a valid conclusion about effectiveness.[3]

These three examples seem similar, but there is a subtle distinction among them that is critically important in educational testing. The article about Floyd Landis uses "valid" to describe a test. The other examples use the word to characterize an argument or conclusion.

Properly, the term *validity* is used in educational measurement in the second sense, that is, to describe a specific inference or conclusion based on a test score. Validity is not a characteristic of the test itself. This may seem like splitting hairs, given that we are talking about conclusions that are themselves based on test scores, but it is anything but.

One reason this distinction matters is that a given test score can be used to support a wide range of different conclusions, some of which may be justified and others not. I gave one example in Chapter 6: the "Wall Charts" issued by the Education Department during the Reagan administration. These used average SAT scores as a measure of the relative quality of states' educational programs. Many of us said at the time that the inference about states' educational systems was unwarranted—invalid—because of the many other factors that contribute to differences in states' average scores, including the dramatically different percentages of students choosing to take the test. But this says nothing about the validity of the entirely different inference intended by the designers of the SAT: that students who obtain high scores on this test are more likely to do well in college. By the same token, I noted in Chapter 3 that E. F. Lindquist, one of the most important early developers of standardized achievement tests, argued that these tests, if well designed, could support useful inferences about the relative strengths of students' performance but not about the overall quality of a school program. In his view, which I share, the former inference would be more valid than the latter.

A second and more controversial reason for considering validity to be an attribute of an inference and not of the test itself is that validity depends on the particular use to which a test is put. Of course, different uses may entail different inferences. But the use of the test is important for two other reasons as well.

Some uses of tests actually undermine validity. This is a major point of controversy. In particular, when people are put under sufficient pressure to raise scores on a test, some of them will behave in ways that undermine validity. For example, some teachers will resort to types of test preparation that inflate scores, or even to frank cheating. The following chapter discusses this problem, which has become critically important as the pressures of high-stakes testing have mounted.

And finally, different uses of tests may have different consequences. Partly in response to the work of two of the most important theorists of validity of the past century—Sam Messick of Educational Testing Service (ETS) and Lee Cronbach of Stanford University—it has become common in the profession to consider the *effects* of a testing program to be a part of validity. This concept often goes by the term *consequential validity*. In my experience, this has been a source of unending confusion among people outside the field, and this confusion is hardly surprising. The effects of a testing program can be bad even if the inference based on scores is valid, and vice versa. For example, several jurisdictions, including Chicago and New York City, now retain students in certain grades if they fail to reach a cut score on a single test. These policies have generated vehement debate. One side argues that "social promotion"—promotion to the next grade based on age rather than actual learning—cheats students by allowing them to progress through school without mastering the material they need, while the other argues that retaining students in grade does more harm than good and raises the probability that students will drop out before finishing school. Either side could be right, regardless of the validity of the inferences about achievement—say, proficiency in mathematics and reading—based on the particular scores used for this purpose.

Some years ago, I watched one of the nation's leading experts in measurement testify at a hearing held on Capitol Hill to discuss a proposed system of national tests. The expert explained that such a testing system would have substantial unintended negative effects. She phrased her argument in terms of consequential validity. One of the key politicians at the hearing—a governor very ac-tive in national education policy who supported the idea of national tests—interrupted her to say that he did not understand what she meant by the term. The expert tried to explain. They went back and forth several times, to no avail, as the governor's frustration grew visibly. Given the nature of the hearing, no one in the audience could speak up, so I found myself thinking silently, "Just say, 'Governor, I apologize for slipping into jargon. What I mean is that this program would have some important unintended negative effects.'" She didn't. Instead, she persisted in using the phrase "consequential validity," and eventually the governor gave up, said that he simply did not understand her argument, and told her to move on. One of her most important points had been lost.

Therefore, for the sake of simplicity, I use "validity" to refer only to an inference based on scores. This is not to belittle the importance of the effects of testing. I have spent more of my career investigating the effects of testing than have most of those who insist that their impact is a part of validity. It is simply clearer to use different terms to refer to validity in the classic sense—the quality of the conclusion—and to the effects of testing.

As the NCLB quotation with which I started this chapter suggests, validity is often presented as a dichotomy: a conclusion is either valid or not. Unfortunately, the situation is generally murkier than this. Validity is a continuum, one end of which is anchored by inferences that simply are not justified. At the other end of the spectrum, however, we are rarely fortunate enough to be able to walk away from the table having decided that an inference is valid, pure and simple. Rather, some inferences are better supported than others, but because the evidence bearing on this point is usually limited, we have to hedge our bets.

Before considering the evidence used to evaluate validity, we should start by asking what factors could undermine validity, making our conclusions unjustified. There are many of these, of course, but they fall into three broad categories: failing to measure adequately what ought to be measured, measuring something that shouldn't be measured, and using a test in a manner that undermines validity. I'll leave the third for the next chapter and focus on the first two here.

In the technical literature, a failure to measure what we want measured goes by the cumbersome but useful term *construct underrepresentation*. This harks back to the notion of a test as a sample from a domain. To measure the intended construct well—vocabulary, proficiency in algebra, whatever—we have to sample adequately from the domain implied by that construct. If Zogby had sampled only likely voters over the age of forty-five, for example, that would have been a case of construct underrepresentation: young people vote somewhat differently, so failing to include them in the sample would leave an important part of the construct's domain—the likely voting of younger voters—unmeasured. The construct—the likely behavior of the entire population of voters—would have been underrepresented. As this example illustrates, construct underrepresentation is problematic for validity because it is systematic: something important is left out. If Zogby had sampled a representative group but had polled too few voters, he would have had too much measurement error—a large margin of error—but not construct underrepresentation.

Until the 1980s and 1990s, direct assessments of writing, in which students actually write essays that are scored, were rare in statewide testing programs. Multiple-choice tests of language arts skills were common. Many critics argued, albeit usually without using the actual phrase, that this was a clear case of construct underrepresentation. Certainly, some skills needed for writing can be assessed with multiple-choice items. But some of the essential skills implied by the construct of "proficiency in writing" can be measured only by having students write. As a consequence, direct assessments of writing are now common.

The converse of construct underrepresentation is measuring something unwanted. This goes by the yet uglier term *construct-ir-relevance variance*. The reference here is to the performance of examinees: there is variation in their performance that is irrelevant to the construct intended. This unwanted variance can have any number of sources. The tasks in a test may call for skills unrelated to the construct; they may require unrelated background information that some students lack; irrelevant factors may influence scorers; administrative conditions may affect some students differently than others; and so on. In each of these cases, some students do better or worse because of factors that are unrelated to the construct we think we are measuring.

As this suggests, construct-irrelevance variance can be found in all manner of tests, but it is easiest to illustrate with complex performance assessments. Consider a task called "Density" created by the Council of Chief State School Officers for science assessments in grades five through eight. The purpose of the task, as its name implies, is to assess students' understanding of the concept of density. Students are first asked to do the following in a small group:

1. Use a piece of aluminum foil 15 cm long × 15 cm wide to create a boat that will float in the aquarium.

2. Measure the length and width of the bottom of the boat. Measure the height of the boat. Record this information in Table 1 below.

3. Find the mass of the boat.

4. Add washers to the boat, one at a time, until the boat sinks. In Table 1 record the mass of washers added to the boat to make it sink.

5. Repeat this process, making boats of different shapes and determining how many washers they will hold before sinking.

They are then asked to answer a few questions on their own, for example:

> Suppose that your lab partner creates two boats from two identical pieces of aluminum foil. The volume of Boat 1 is 500 cm³. The volume of Boat 2 is 400 cm³. Which of these boats will be able to support more mass before sinking? Explain your answer.[4]

Whatever its other advantages and disadvantages—the pros and cons of using complex performance tasks of this type for large-scale assessments have been debated for two decades or more—this task clearly provides ample opportunity for construct-irrelevant variance. For example, what happens to a student whose understanding of the concept is fine but who is unable to build the boats well? (The scoring rubric explicitly acknowledges this risk, noting that "the boats can be constructed improperly so that they sink before their density reaches 1 g/ml or tip over.") In other words, differences in students' ability to build little boats out of aluminum foil—an ability entirely irrelevant to the construct the task is intended to measure—will cause variations in student performance. And similarly, what happens to a student whose understanding is fine but who gets paired with students who don't follow directions, are disruptive, or whatever?

Construct-irrelevant variance can also arise from an interaction between the characteristics of a test and those of students taking it. For example, suppose that a test is given only in printed form, using small type. What will happen to the scores of able students with visual disabilities? Their performance will be depressed because of their poor visual ability. This will introduce additional variations in performance that are irrelevant to the construct the test is intended to measure and that would not arise at all if none of the tested students had poor visual acuity. Or suppose that a test of mathematics or science contains some unnecessarily complex language. What will happen to the scores of nonnative speakers of English who have good mastery of mathematics or science but are thrown off by these irrelevant linguistic complexities? These threats to validity will be considered further in Chapters 11 and 12.

No test of a complex domain can be perfect. Some amount of construct underrepresentation and construct-irrelevant variance is inevitable, even in the case of a superb test. This is one reason that most inferences based on test scores cannot be *perfectly* valid. But often they are valid enough to be very useful. So how can one determine how valid an inference is?

Many types of evidence can be brought to bear. In most discussions of the problem, one finds up to four different types of evidence: analysis of the content of the test, statistical analysis of performance on the test, statistical analysis of relationships between scores on the test and other variables, and the responses of students in taking the test. Reliability data, while often not presented as evidence bearing on validity, is also relevant. No one of these types of evidence alone is sufficient to establish that a conclusion is valid, although a single one may be the kiss of death in showing that an inference is *not* valid. As I will explain in Chapter 10, even all of these together are insufficient when high stakes are attached to test scores, but they are the appropriate starting point even then.

In almost anything most readers are likely to encounter, reliability and validity are presented as distinct issues. In technical reports of testing programs, for example, one will typically find separate chapters on each. In fact, however, they are closely related.

Reliability is necessary but not sufficient for validity. Or, to put this differently, one can have a reliable measure without validity, but one cannot have a valid inference without reliability. Remember that reliability is just consistency of measurement. Returning to the example of a bathroom scale, suppose that your scale is highly consistent but consistently wrong. If you step on and off many times, the variation among the repeated measurements will be very small but the average will still be way off—say, fifteen pounds too heavy. This would be a reliable measure, but the inference about your weight would not be valid. Now suppose that there is no bias in the scale—the long-run average of the measurements, if you measured yourself many times in succession, would be about right—but it is highly inconsistent from time to time, let's say, often varying as much as fifteen pounds in either direction. In this case also, your inference about your weight, *if you measured yourself only once,* would not be worth much, despite the lack of bias. That is, its validity would be low because you would often reach the wrong conclusion. You could get a valid inference from this unreliable scale by weighing yourself many times and taking an average, but that is only because the reliability of the average would be much higher than that of a single observation.

So what should one make of the frequently heard complaints about the trade-off between reliability and validity? One hears them often, for example, when people argue about performance assessments versus multiple-choice tests. Proponents of the former often maintain that an excessive concern with reliability leads people to lean toward formats such as multiple choice (and others that permit students to complete many items per hour and that require at most simple scoring) but that this exacts a cost in lower validity. Their argument is that the more reliable tests do not measure some things that they should. In other words, they claim that in pursuit of higher reliability, construct underrepresentation is made worse. To a point, they are correct. It is sometimes the case that to measure certain skills, one needs to use less reliable formats. This is less often true than many think, however; it is often possible to test complex skills with formats such as multiple choice, and performance on complex tasks cannot be counted on to measure the higher-order skills they are often intended to tap. But it is sometimes true, as when one wants to measure writing skills—and for the moment, let's consider this case.

What one has in this case is a difficult trade-off between reliability and construct underrepresentation: to lessen the latter, one inadvertently lessens the former as well. A modest decrement in reliability may be a reasonable price to pay for a substantial improvement in representation of the construct. Beyond a certain point, though, you shoot yourself in the foot: you end up with a test that has the content you want but that produces such unreliable scores that the inferences you need are undermined. There is no optimal answer to this problem; where one draws the line, where the best compromise lies, depends on how the test is to be used. For example, if I were constructing a test that would have a major bearing on decisions about individual students, I would want to keep reliability very high, but I would be willing to be more lenient if the purpose of the test were more descriptive and diagnostic.

A second link between reliability and validity is that both entail a form of consistency. Reliability is the consistency, or *generalizability*, of performance across repeated instances of equivalent measures, such as the times you step on your bathroom scale or the June and November forms of the SAT. But consistency across *alternative* measures of the same construct is a key element of validity. We often can measure the same thing in different ways, and we do not trust these alternative measures if they produce substantially different findings. For example, physicians use two entirely different measures to look for prostate cancer, a physical examination and the prostate-specific antigen blood test, or PSA. Inconsistencies between the results of these two measures have been the source of intense and public debate because to the extent that the two are inconsistent, at least one is wrong, and the validity of inferences about the presence of cancer is suspect until the inconsistencies are better understood. I'll return to this in the following chapter, because consistency between measures is the key to uncovering the sometimes egregious inflation of scores on high-stakes tests.

Leaving aside reliability, the logical place to start in establishing validity is with the content of the test. It is hard to argue that an inference is valid if it is based on a test that includes the wrong content. Results from a casual examination of a test's content are often labeled *face validity*, as in "it seems valid on its face," but people in the business of testing do not consider this real evidence of validity. Rather, they strive for a more systematic evaluation of the content, examining, for example, whether there are obvious gaps in content (construct underrepresentation), whether the balance of emphasis is appropriate, and so on.

Many people go no further than an examination of content, and content-related evidence is emphasized in the documentation of many tests. Unfortunately, this is not sufficient to evaluate validity. It is often difficult even for experts to determine, simply by looking at test items, what knowledge and skills students will bring to bear in trying to answer them. Seemingly minor and sometimes unnoticed details, such as a poor choice of a distractor (a wrong answer in a multiple-choice item) or the accidental use of unnecessarily complex language, can change what an item measures. Moreover, the skills needed to answer an item often depend on students' prior knowledge and training. Consider Figure 9.1, which is similar to figures that commonly appear in assessments of mathematics and science. The graph represents the progress of an individual during a footrace, with time plotted along the bottom axis and distance covered plotted on the vertical axis. The test item might ask the student to identify what is happening at point A (the runner is accelerating) and point B (maintaining a constant speed, her fastest during the period plotted). For a middle-school student who has never seen a graph used in

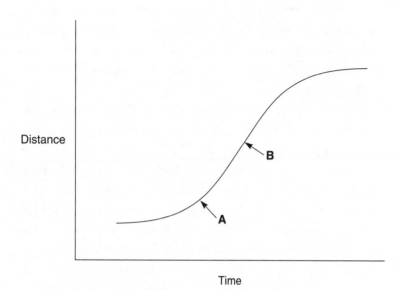

FIG. 9.1. A hypothetical mathematics item.

this way, the problem takes some thought and requires her to translate velocity and acceleration into a representation in coordinate geometry. But this sort of representation often appears in curricula now, and some students will have seen something like it numerous times before encountering it on the test. For those students, the item measures something different: their recall of something previously learned.

Reliance on face validity reached a high point during the wave of enthusiasm for performance assessment, when many reformers and educators assumed that complex tasks necessarily tap higher-order skills better than multiple-choice items do. People were looking for rich, realistic, and engaging tasks to include in tests, so perhaps it was only natural that the tasks themselves, rather than other forms of evidence that I will describe momentarily, became the sine quo non of validity for many people who did not know better. In response, Bill Mehrens, now professor

emeritus at Michigan State University, coined the term "faith validity." And research confirmed that reliance on these types of test
items was indeed a matter of faith: the format of test items does
not always reliably predict the types of skills students will apply in
tackling them.[5]

A second approach to validation is to examine the relationships
between scores on the test and other measures. In some cases, we
can evaluate validity by comparing scores with a criterion, some
gold standard that we trust. You are likely to encounter criterion-
related evidence primarily when tests are used to predict later performance. For example, the conventional way to evaluate the validity of inferences based on college-admissions tests, such as the
ACT and SAT, is to see how strongly scores predict later performance in college. Most often, the criterion is freshman-year
grade-point average, but in some studies it is a longer-term grade-
point average, the probability of graduation within a specified
time interval, or some other measure of performance in college.
Although these are typically called criterion measures, the label is
somewhat misleading, since the measures are hardly beyond question. Grading, for example, is highly subjective and also varies
markedly in severity from discipline to discipline. Grading tends to
be much harsher in mathematics and the physical sciences than in
the humanities. Grading is also vulnerable to bias. One of the
standard ways of evaluating possible bias on these tests is to see
whether students in a given group—say, women or minority students—achieve systematically lower or higher grades than their
test scores predict. But why, in investigating potential bias, should
we assume that the test is suspect but grades are not? It might be
just as reasonable to assume that the test is less biased and use it to
evaluate bias in grading. But these tests are designed to support inferences about performance in college, so whatever one labels it, their ability to predict it is a logical basis for evaluating
them.

Criterion-related evidence is rare in K–12 testing other than college-admissions testing, for the simple reason that we rarely have a gold standard for comparison. If we did, we would often simply use that measure rather than the test we are evaluating. There are some exceptions—for example, when evaluating whether a shorter and less burdensome test does a good job of replicating the results of a trusted but longer and more onerous one. But for the most part, if you look at the technical documentation for a test that is important in your local school district, you will see little or no reference to this form of evidence.

When no criterion is at hand, evaluating validity becomes a more complex task. A common approach is to obtain a variety of different measures of performance, in addition to the one to be evaluated. Then one examines the relationships among all of them, hoping to find that scores on the test in question correlate strongly with theoretically related measures and less strongly with measures that we would expect to be less related. That is, we look for stronger correlations with variables that ought to be more strongly related if the test in question is really measuring what it purports to measure. For example, scores on a new mathematics test ought to correlate more strongly with scores on another mathematics test than with scores on a reading test. Strong correlations between theoretically related measures are called *convergent* evidence of validity; weaker correlations between theoretically unrelated measures are *discriminant* evidence.

The key is to compare different correlations—convergent and discriminant evidence together—not just tests of related content. This is critically important—and it also makes this form of evidence difficult to evaluate—because students who do well in one subject tend to do well in another. As a result, even scores on subjects that we would consider unrelated usually show high correlations with one another. This is illustrated by Table 9.1, which reports the correlations among parts of an old edition of the Iowa

Table 9.1   Correlations among students' scores on tests, Iowa Tests of Basic
Skills, grade 8

	Reading	Language	Work skills	Mathematics
Reading	1.00	—	—	—
Language	0.77	1.00	—	—
Work study skills	0.79	0.80	1.00	—
Mathematics	0.73	0.75	0.83	1.00

Source: A. N. Hieronymous and H. D. Hoover, *Manual for School Administrators, Levels 5–14, ITBS Forms G/H* (Chicago: Riverside Publishing, 1986), Table 6.16.

Tests of Basic Skills. A correlation is a measure of a relationship that ranges in value from −1.0 to +1.0. A value of zero means that there is no relationship at all between the two variables. A value of 1.0 indicates a perfect relationship, which means that values on one variable perfectly predict values on the other, and the two variables are essentially the same.* Height measured in inches and height measured in centimeters would correlate perfectly, with a value of 1.0; they provide exactly the same information, just on different scales.

In the table, all of the ITBS scores are strongly related to one another. To give these values some meaning, consider the correlation of 0.73 between reading and mathematics scores. This indicates that knowing only students' scores on the reading test allows you to predict about half of the variability in their mathematics scores.† Although some students do better in one subject than another, many of the factors that influence their performance—physical health, home environment, some aspects of genetic background, achievement motivation, the quality of their schools, and so on—affect performance in all subjects, so students who score

---

* A positive value means that one variable tends to increase with another—for example, height tends to increase with weight. A negative value indicates that one decreases when the other increases—for example, running speed tends to decrease with weight.

† Specifically, the square of the correlation ($.73^2 = .53$) is the proportion of the variance of one variable predicted by the other. The variance is a specific measure of variability, the square of the standard deviation, explained in Chapter 5.

Table 9.2   Correlations among school averages on tests, Iowa Tests of Basic
Skills, grade 8

	Reading	*Language*	*Work skills*	*Mathematics*
Reading	1.00	—	—	—
Language	0.92	1.00	—	—
Work study skills	0.94	0.92	1.00	—
Mathematics	0.88	0.84	0.91	1.00

Source: A. N. Hieronymous and H. D. Hoover, *Manual for School Administrators, Levels
5–14, ITBS Forms G/H* (Chicago: Riverside Publishing, 1986), Table 6.19.

high in one tend to score high in others as well. When one compares schools' average scores, the correlations are even stronger.
In the same ITBS data, schools' average scores in reading correlated 0.88 with their average scores in mathematics (Table 9.2), indicating that knowing schools' average scores in one of these two
subjects allows one to predict more than three-fourths of the variation in school means in the second subject. As a consequence,
one typically finds only small differences in the correlations between related and unrelated subjects, which makes the use of this
convergent and discriminant evidence difficult.

This form of evidence was essential for evaluating validity in
the case of the portfolio assessments used by both Vermont and
Kentucky in the 1990s. Both states used portfolio assessments
in writing and mathematics but also gave other, standardized
tests. In Vermont, mathematics portfolio scores correlated about
as strongly with a standardized test of writing as with a standardized test of math.[6] In Kentucky, the portfolio assessment of mathematics correlated more strongly with the portfolio assessment of
writing than with anything else.[7] These findings suggest that the
mathematics portfolio assessments were measuring things other
than mathematics—proficiency in writing and differences among
teachers in the way portfolio tasks were generated and revised.

Because few people understand that scores are generally strongly
correlated even across different subject areas, simple correlations

Table 9.3   Correlations between schools' average mathematics scores on
high-stakes and low-stakes tests, nine states and districts

Jurisdiction	Correlation
Florida	0.96
Virginia	0.77
Chicago, IL	0.88
Boston, MA	0.75
Toledo, OH	0.79
Blue Valley, KS	0.53
Columbia, MO	0.82
Fairfield, OH	0.49
Fountain Fort Carson, CO	0.35

Source: J. P. Greene, M. A. Winters, and G. Foster, *Testing High Stakes Tests: Can We Believe the Results of Accountability Tests?* Civic Report 33 (New York: The Manhattan Institute, 2003).

between tests are sometimes erroneously presented as sufficient evidence of validity. In 2003, an unfortunately widely read study purported to show that increases in scores on high-stakes tests provide a basis for valid inferences about improved student performance. The authors wrote: "The report finds that score levels on high stakes tests closely track score levels on other tests, suggesting that high stakes tests provide reliable [*sic*] information on student performance. When a state's high stakes test scores go up, we should have confidence that this represents real improvements in student learning."[8] The authors meant "valid" (inferences justified by the scores) rather than "reliable" (consistent scores). Among the evidence they adduced to support this claim were the correlations shown in Table 9.3. These are correlations between school averages in mathematics on the high-stakes test in each jurisdiction and a lower-stakes test, and they range from 0.35 to 0.96.

Looked at more closely, these correlations provide at least as much reason to doubt the validity of inferences based on high-stakes test as to have confidence in them. The authors present the convergent evidence without the discriminant. The standard of comparison for these correlations is not zero but rather the correlations the high-stakes math tests in question showed with other, theoretically less related measures, which the authors neglected to consider. The correlation between the two math tests was .75 in Boston, but what was the correlation between the high-stakes math test and tests in other subjects? We find a clue in Table 9.2, which similarly provides correlations between school averages, although in a low-stakes context. All but two of the nine correlations in Table 9.3, between math scores on high- and low-stakes tests, are lower than the correlations one finds between theoretically *unrelated* measures in the ITBS data—most by a very large margin. If a school-level correlation of 0.75 between two tests is alone enough to establish validity, one would have to conclude that the ITBS reading test is a valid basis for inferences about mathematics.

A variety of statistical analyses of data from the tests themselves are used routinely to evaluate tests, but much of this work is arcane and is hidden from the view of all but the most determined user of scores. For example, a red flag goes up if members of different groups—say, boys and girls—who have the same score on the test as a whole show markedly different performance on some items. This is a sign of possible bias in those items, which would undermine the validity of inferences for one of the groups. Similarly, one expects that, on average, students with higher scores on the test as a whole will perform better on any individual test item than students with lower scores on the test as a whole. If this is not found, the individual item is measuring something different than the rest of the test.

When efforts began in the 1990s to include more students with disabilities in large-scale testing programs, several studies (including two of my own) looked to see whether these "item-test" correlations were similar for students with disabilities and for other students. If they were not, that would be a sign that the test was not working well for those with disabilities. (In my studies, these correlations were fine, but other problems emerged that called validity into question.)

The least commonly used approach to evaluating validity is to explore how students respond as they tackle individual test items. As I noted earlier, research has indicated that the format of test items is not always a trustworthy indicator of the skills students use in addressing them. In one of the best studies of this problem, researchers had students explain what they were doing—for example, whether they relied on rote application of prior knowledge or employed complex problem-solving skills—as they solved both multiple-choice and performance tasks in science.[9] Because it is so difficult to know what knowledge and skills students actually use in answering test items—and since these can differ from one group of students to another—this type of investigation could add considerably to the evaluation of validity. Unfortunately, it is also an expensive, arduous, and time-consuming method, so it is unlikely to become a routine element of the evaluation of large-scale testing programs.

If you are determined to look, how much of this validity evidence are you likely to find in the readily available information about testing programs? Content-related evidence is almost always presented. How much more you can find depends on the test and how deep you are willing to dig. There is limited public appetite for, say, matrices of correlations showing convergent-discriminant evidence, so you are unlikely to find a comprehensive presentation of the available evidence in a handy location, such as on a state's Web site or in a manual for teachers. But even if you persevere, you are unlikely to find all of what is described here, and you will often find considerably less. The question then becomes: Does the available evidence persuade you that the conclusions you're concerned with are reasonably well supported?

However, these traditional forms of evidence, no matter how complete, cannot address one of the most formidable threats to validity: the risk of inflated scores. We turn to that next.

Chapter 10

Inflated Test Scores

EVERY YEAR, newspaper articles and news releases from education departments around the nation tell us that test scores are up again, often dramatically. Usually, there are some grades or districts that have not made substantial gains, and the gaps in performance between poor and rich and majority and minority often fail to budge. Nevertheless, the main story line is usually positive: performance is getting better, and rapidly.

Unfortunately, this good news is often more apparent than real. Scores on the tests used for accountability have become inflated, badly overstating real gains in student performance. Some of the reported gains are entirely illusory, and others are real but grossly exaggerated. The seriousness of this problem is hard to overstate. When scores are inflated, many of the most important conclusions people base on them will be wrong, and students—and sometimes teachers—will suffer as a result.

This is the dirty secret of high-stakes testing. You may see occasional references to this problem in newspapers, but for the most part, news reports and announcements of scores by states and school districts accept increases in scores at face value. And the problem of inflation is often ignored in the testing profession as well. If you look for an evaluation of validity for a test that concerns you, you are likely to find evidence of the sort discussed in the previous chapter. This evidence is essential, and under low-stakes conditions it may be sufficient, but it will not tell you whether gains produced under pressure are meaningful—in the cumbersome language of the trade, whether inferences about improved learning based on increases in scores are valid.

Not long ago, I was in a meeting called by staff of the *Boston Globe* to discuss the paper's annual reporting of test scores in Massachusetts. Someone raised the problem of inflated scores on high-stakes tests, suggesting that this could distort readers' comparisons of schools. Because I have investigated this issue since the late 1980s, I chimed in to explain. A participant who was then prominent in the state's policy circles and is now the superintendent of a large school district in another state gave a one-sentence, dismissive response: "That's a matter of opinion."

He was wrong: it is not merely opinion. While credible detailed studies of score inflation have been done in only a handful of jurisdictions, the findings of these studies are highly consistent, generally showing large exaggeration of gains in scores on high-stakes tests. A number of studies have compared in less detail the gains in scores on states' tests and the NAEP. These studies show that in many cases—but not all—gains on states' own tests, which are generally the ones used for No Child Left Behind accountability, are much larger than those on the NAEP.[1] These test-specific gains are a sign of inflation. Moreover, a substantial number of studies have documented behaviors by teachers that can cause score inflation. Firms around the nation are eagerly selling materials that make the job of inflating scores easier, and many districts and states are actually purchasing these materials for teachers and students.

When I and others who work on this issue point it out, the re-
actions often range from disbelief to anger. So perhaps it is best to
start on less controversial ground. We see something akin to score
inflation—often called *corruption of measures* in social sciences—in
many other fields as well. It is so common, in fact, that it has the
name Campbell's law in social science: "The more any quantitative social indicator is used for social decision-making, the more
subject it will be to corruption pressures and the more apt it will
be to distort and corrupt the social processes it is intended to
monitor."[2] One can find examples of Campbell's law in the media
from time to time that provide a hint of how score inflation arises
in educational testing.

Frequent travelers are familiar with one example: airline on-
time statistics. Quite some years ago, when the press began giving
considerable attention to these statistics, I and many other travelers began to notice that the on-time rates were improving, but we
did not seem to be arriving at our destinations any faster. On one
long flight that I took often, we were almost always "on time,"
even when we had long waits on the tarmac because there was no
free gate to pull into. The secret was simple: the airline made the
scheduled duration of the flight longer. For example, an article in
the *New York Times* in 2000 reported that "[the scheduled time of]
a flight from Kennedy International Airport to Seattle took 22
minutes and 48 seconds longer than a decade earlier, even though
the time in the air has not changed."[3] Once the scheduled times
had been increased, on-time statistics automatically improved—
but in practical terms "on time" no longer meant the same thing.

For some years, the U.S. Postal Service has had mail sent to
sampled addresses to determine delivery times. In principle, this is
precisely like the political poll and the vocabulary test in Chapter
2: delivery times to the small sample of addresses represent delivery times in the areas from which the samples are drawn. But in
December of 1997, authorities learned that postal employees in

West Virginia had discovered the list of sampled addresses. To make their state's service appear good to higher-ups, the postal employees ensured that those addresses always got good service. They accomplished this by hiring temporary workers to ferret out the test letters so that they could be sped to the sampled addresses. This boosted the state's delivery-time statistics, but of course it left delivery times to the great majority of the state's households unaffected.

The problem of inflation arises in numerous technical fields in which the functioning of a device in complex real situations is simulated by a limited but standardized sample. For example, a variety of benchmark tests over the years have been devised to evaluate the speed of computer chips, and manufacturers use their test results for marketing. This system seems comfortingly objective, but it has two problems: different tests—different samples of performance—can provide disparate results, and manufacturers can game the system by designing chips to do well on the particular tasks sampled in a benchmark test. In fact, some manufacturers were accused of doing precisely this in order to boost their performance ratings to unrealistic levels—that is, to levels that were higher than the chips' performance in a real-world mix of tasks.[4] In one instance, the accusation was reversed: the chip manufacturer AMD accused an industry group of altering a benchmark test to favor Intel chips.[5]

An essentially similar controversy arose about the federal government's diesel emissions tests in 1998. The *New York Times* reported, "The Environmental Protection Agency has discovered that thousands of modern heavy-duty diesel truck engines run cleanly during the agency's mandatory performance tests but give off much more pollution in normal highway use. . . . Officials said the . . . trucks may often give off twice as much pollution as regulations permit."[6] The issue, again, was whether manufacturers deliberately gamed the system, by designing engines to do well on the limited sample of tasks in the government's test, at the cost of poorer performance in actual use. A similar case a few years earlier involving cars had led GM to recall half a million vehicles and pay fines.

Corruption of testing measures affects TV programming as well. "Sweeps weeks" are periods three times a year during which viewing is monitored to help set advertising rates. These measures are taken by sampling both households and weeks of the year, and they are supposed to give advertisers an estimate of the viewership they can expect over longer periods of time. To get the best ratings, producers juice up their programming during sweeps periods, adding whatever sensational material they can to generate a short-term boost in viewership. If they succeed, of course, the measure becomes misleading, because many of the shows will lose viewers once the unusually sensational material ends.[7]

The most disturbing example of a corrupted measure that I have encountered was reported by the *New York Times* in 2005. The School of Medicine and Dentistry at the University of Rochester had surveyed cardiologists around the state. As the *Times* reported, "An overwhelming majority of cardiologists in New York say that, in certain circumstances, they do not operate on patients who might benefit from heart surgery, because they are worried about hurting their rankings on physician scorecards issued by the state."[8] Fully 83 percent of respondents said that the reporting of mortality rates had this effect, and 79 percent admitted that "the knowledge that mortality statistics would be made public" had affected their own decisions about whether to perform surgery.*

---

* These numbers may be off by a modest amount, but not by enough to make the results less appalling. Only 65 percent of the sampled surgeons responded to the survey, which is a marginally acceptable response rate. The risk is that surgeons who did not respond would have given different answers than those who did. But even if all 35 percent who did not respond would have replied to these questions in the negative—an extremely unlikely case—that would still leave more than half saying that publication of mortality measures led to surgeons' declining to do procedures that could have benefited patients.

So it should not be surprising that when the heat is turned up, educators—and students, for that matter—will sometimes behave in ways that inflate test scores. Actually, it would be quite remarkable, given how pervasive the problem is in other areas, if none of them did.

There are two different ways to game the system. Both appear in the examples above, and both come into play in educational testing. The first kind of gaming requires that you distort the measure itself. There are a variety of ways to do this. The simplest is to cheat or lie about the measurement. To return to earlier examples, I could have generated inflated estimates of improvement on our hypothetical vocabulary test simply by changing students' answers after the fact—an expedient that has occurred to more than one teacher, unfortunately. Or in the case of the Zogby poll, pollsters could have bribed the sampled voters to say that they would vote one way or the other, perhaps to generate an illusion of what George H. W. Bush called "the big mo." But as you will see, teachers can generate such distortions without resorting to outright cheating. The airlines' manipulation of on-time statistics may be similar: they did not lie about how long the flights would take, but they created an illusion of improvement by redefining what it means, in practical terms, to be "on time."

The second way of gaming the system is more subtle but perhaps even more important in educational testing: undermining the sample on which the measurement is based. This is illustrated clearly by the vocabulary test in Chapter 2 and the postal-delivery example above. In both cases, the score (the vocabulary test score and the delivery-time statistic) is calculated using a small sample that must represent something much larger—the student's total vocabulary, and delivery times to all addresses in the state. In the postal delivery case, and the vocabulary example in Chapter 2 when I waylaid the students who were to take the vocabulary test and taught them all forty words, this no longer holds true: the measure based on the sample no longer represents the larger whole.

This second form of gaming is important not only because it is a major cause of score inflation, but also because a failure to understand it underlies one of the most common excuses for inappropriate teaching to the test. People will argue, "There is nothing wrong with the items on the test, so what is wrong with focusing our teaching on them?" There was nothing wrong, either, with the addresses sampled by the U.S. Postal Service in West Virginia or the forty words on the vocabulary test. The problem is not bad material on the test; it is that the material on the test is only a small sample of what matters. I'll come back to this in a bit and will provide some concrete examples of test preparation to illustrate the problem.

Inflation of test scores did not become a prominent issue until the late 1980s, but there were hints of it earlier, even before testing became the source of pressure that it is today. People in the field of testing were familiar with a "sawtooth" pattern in scores. In the first years that a district or state used a new test, scores rose rapidly. The increases typically slowed down after a few years. When the jurisdiction replaced this test with another, scores would drop sharply but then would repeat the same rapid initial rise.

There are two possible explanations of this pattern. The charitable interpretation is that students add more knowledge each time a new test is implemented. They gradually master more of the material on the old test, suffer a drop in scores because of the inclusion of new material on the new test, and then raise scores by adding more mastery of the new material to their command of the material on the old test. If this were true, we could be unconcerned with the drop in scores that occurs with the introduction of a new test.

The more skeptical interpretation is substitution: students re-

place mastery of material emphasized by the old test with mastery of material emphasized by the new one, not really reaching a higher level of achievement in the larger domain from which the test samples. You may find one or the other of these explanations more plausible, but the sawtooth pattern in the data cannot tell us which is correct.

The relatively few studies that have addressed this question support the skeptical interpretation: in many cases, mastery of material on the new test simply substitutes for mastery of the old. An important caveat is that the relevant research, while consistent, is quite limited. One reason for this is technical: one needs an appropriate second test to use as a standard of comparison for gains on the high-stakes test, and this is not always available. The larger obstacle, however, is political. Imagine yourself as the superintendent of schools in a state that is experiencing large gains in test scores. I or another researcher contacts you and asks permission to explore the extent to which these score gains, which are enormously important politically, may be exaggerated. This research is a hard sell, and the evaluations don't get done. I've often argued—to little apparent effect—that this is an ethical issue as well as a scientific one: students (and teachers, for that matter) who are subjected without consent to high-stakes testing programs, and the public that pays for them and is asked to have confidence that they will improve students' learning, are entitled to evaluations of the programs' effects.

I encountered political opposition to evaluations of high-stakes testing programs on my first foray into the field, about two decades ago. In the late 1980s, four of us proposed the first systematic, empirical study of this issue, in response to a request for proposals from a state department of education that wanted its new high-stakes testing program evaluated. After we submitted our proposal, I received a call from someone in the department who explained that the state would not allow us to evaluate the validity of score gains. I then obtained permission to conduct the study in a large district, on the condition that we maintain the district's anonymity. We were well on our way—tests had been ordered, classrooms had been sampled, a good bit of time and money had been spent—when I was summoned back for a meeting with the superintendent, who explained that the study could not continue. He said that the study would make the papers, and if a single disgruntled teacher realized that she had been a participant and identified the district, he would be in trouble with his state legislature for engendering controversy about their testing program.

Later, the four of us did obtain permission to conduct the study elsewhere. The price of admission was that we take extraordinary steps to protect the anonymity of the district, so I cannot tell you its name, the state it was in, or even the names of the tests we used. I can tell you, however, that the district was large and that a relatively high proportion of its students were poor and members of minority groups. I can also tell you that although the testing system in this district was considered high-stakes by the standards of the late 1980s, by today's standards it was tame. There were no cash awards to schools for high scores, for example, and no threats to dissolve schools or remove students in response to low scores or a failure to improve them. The pressure arose only from less tangible things, such as publicity and jawboning.

Although dated, the results of this first study are worth some detailed discussion. Other studies show inflation of gains on a high-stakes test, but ours was the only study that checked to see whether performance on a previously used test dropped while scores on a new one rose. And perhaps ironically, it is also useful precisely because it is dated. One will often hear people argue that a testing program is not really "high-stakes" unless it entails tangible and serious rewards or consequences for teachers or students. Our study (and some additional evidence that I will not go into here) suggests that this debate is simply a matter of semantics. If the question is what is needed to put teachers under pressure and induce them to inflate test scores, it is clear that specific and tangible rewards or sanctions are not required.

Before we undertook this study, the district had experienced the typical sawtooth pattern: scores had increased for some years on one test, dropped when the district adopted a replacement, and quickly risen again. In Figure 10.1, the diamond in the upper left represents scores in 1986, the last year that the district used what we labeled the "first district test," which was one of the major nationally normed standardized achievement tests. If the graph included earlier years, you would see that scores on that test had been rising. The squares in the figure represent the new test, labeled "second district test," that the district began using in 1987. You can see that performance dropped when the new test was first used but had returned to the previous high point three years later.

An obvious question is, how different were these two tests? Again, I cannot identify the tests, but I can say that both were traditional, standardized, multiple-choice achievement tests, and both were chosen from among the five tests that then dominated the market. The two tests were quite similar and were intended to represent a similar domain of achievement. They differed only in details.

To understand how large the change in performance was, one needs to consider the scale used on the vertical axis. Performance is displayed in terms of grade equivalents, a scale described in Chapter 8. On the GE scale, the number to the left of the decimal is the grade level, and the number to the right is the number of the month in the ten-month academic year. The data in Figure 10.1 represent mathematics performance in the spring of each year, roughly seven months into the year, so the national median would have been a score of 3.7 (seventh month of the third grade).

With this in hand, you can see that in 1986, the last year the dis-

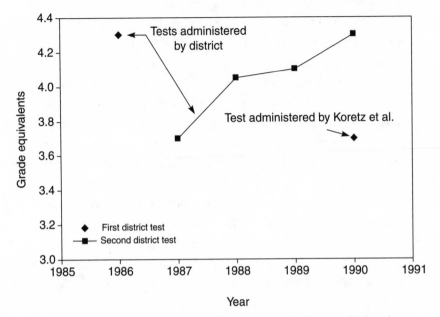

FIG. 10.1. Performance on a moderate-stakes test and an audit test in third-grade
  mathematics. Adapted from D. Koretz, et al., "The Effects of High-
  Stakes Testing: Preliminary Evidence about Generalization across
  Tests," presented at the annual meetings of the American Educational
  Research Association and the National Council on Measurement in
  Education, Chicago, April 1991.

trict used the first test, average performance was at a GE of about
4.3, roughly half an academic year above the national average—
quite good for a district with its demographics. The first year the
new test was administered, scores declined by half an academic
year, dropping the district's mean to the national average. But
scores began to rise again, and a mere three years later the average
was back where it had been on the last year the first test was used.
So in this case, the sawtooth pattern leaves us with a sizable ambiguity: is the district's performance average, or fully half an academic year above average?

  The new element we added—the piece that resulted in our be-

246 Inflated Test Scores

ing rejected for the first study we proposed and tossed out on the second—was additional testing. We administered additional tests to random samples of classrooms two weeks after the district's own testing. The largest group was administered precisely the same test the district had used through 1986. In this case, however, unlike in 1986, students were not prepared by their teachers for this specific test. In fact, neither the teachers nor students knew that this was the test they would be given, although the teachers did know that the district was requiring them to administer an additional test.*

In the sample administered the first district test, which by then had not been used by the district for four years, student scores were on average the same as when the schools first administered the *second* district test in 1987: fully half an academic year lower than in 1986, the last year the district had used the first test. This is shown by the diamond in the lower right of Figure 10.1. Thus, the rise in scores on the second test did not indicate that the district's students had added mastery of that test's material to mastery of the material on the first test. Rather, mastery of the material emphasized by the second test had *replaced* mastery of the content emphasized by the first test. As successive cohorts of students did progressively better on the second test, they lost ground on the first.

I have shown Figure 10.1 to hundreds, perhaps thousands, of people over the years. I often ask: given these findings, which is the more accurate result to give the public? Are the kids in this dis-

---

* A skeptical reader might ask: isn't it possible that the students took these supplementary tests less seriously? That was indeed a risk. We administered a variety of additional tests, one of which was a parallel form of the second district test—that is, a form that used different specific items but was designed to be as similar to the second district test as was feasible. If students were less motivated to do well on the supplementary test, we would have expected a drop in performance between the district's test and this parallel form. The third-graders (shown in the figure) and fifth-grade girls passed that screen; the boys in a few fifth-grade classrooms did not.

trict half an academic year above average, as the district testing program results indicate once the tests have been in place for a few years? Or are they about average, as suggested by the scores on tests for which students have not been specifically prepared—as with our readministration of the first test when it was no longer expected, or with the second test when it was first administered in 1987? A very few have taken the side of the higher scores, and one person, upon hearing the details of the study design, responded simply, "That was mean." But the overwhelming majority of people, when they understand the idea that a test score is a sample from a larger domain, have replied that the lower scores, the scores on tests that were not the specific focus of preparation, are a more realistic representations of students' mastery of the entire domain.

And they are right, even though the public is always given the higher estimate. This study was the first to demonstrate score inflation, analogous to the corruption of West Virginia's measure of mail delivery times. Several studies followed, using different designs and investigating different types of testing programs. They showed similar results.

As the state education department official who killed our first proposed study realized, this research raises the question of validity. Our main focus was the validity of inferences about students' gains in learning, but the results also called into question the validity of the inference that the district's performance was well above average. Inferences of this sort are among the most important in today's educational systems, but you will see no mention of possible score inflation in discussions of the validity of most tests, such as the technical reports of most state testing programs. They will report some of the traditional forms of validity evidence described in the previous chapter, but these are not sufficient to detect inflation of scores.

Given the current high-stakes uses of tests, we can be confident of the validity of inferences about improvement only if we have an additional type of validity evidence: a comparison to a second measure less threatened by the possibility of corruption (often called an *audit test*). The logic of using an audit test is simple: if gains on the tested sample generalize to the domain, they should generalize to other, similar samples from the domain. In this case, the similar sample is the audit test. It could also be a different sample of addresses in West Virginia, or a different sample of voters in a competitor to the Zogby poll.

Given our findings, some defenders of high-stakes testing immediately placed the blame on the type of test used in the district: both tests were entirely made up of multiple-choice items. Therefore, it was important to follow this study by investigating the validity of gains on other types of tests. We had two opportunities to do this in Kentucky, in one instance because of interest shown by the state legislature and in the second because of the efforts of the state's deputy commissioner of education, Ed Reidy, a highly principled man who believed that students are owed serious evaluation of education programs. Kentucky was the ideal place for this type of research: it was a leader in the switch to standards-based assessments and used a variety of formats other than multiple-choice (entirely dropping this format in some years).

The first study in Kentucky examined fourth-grade reading. Kentucky used its own, custom-designed test, called KIRIS (Kentucky Instructional Results Information System), but in authorizing the KIRIS program, the legislature had required that the framework—the document that specified what the test should measure—had to be similar to that of the National Assessment of Educational Progress. Because KIRIS and NAEP were supposed to measure similar aspects of proficiency, NAEP provided an obvious standard of comparison for evaluating gains in KIRIS. If students were truly learning more, and not just acquiring better skills for

Table 10.1   Change in fourth-grade reading performance in Kentucky on the state test (KIRIS) and NAEP, 1992–1994

	KIRIS	NAEP
Change in scale scores	+18.0	−1.0
Change in standard deviations	+ 0.76	−0.03

Source: Adapted from Ronald K. Hambleton et al., Review of the Measurement Quality of the Kentucky Instructional Results Information System, 1991–1994 (Frankfort: Office of Education Accountability, Kentucky General Assembly, June 1995), Table 8.1.

taking this particular test, gains on the KIRIS test should have been mirrored to a substantial degree by improvements on the NAEP.

But in fourth-grade reading, students achieved large gains on the state test that had no echo at all in the performance of the state's students on the NAEP test (Table 10.1). The two tests were reported on different scales, so the scores could not be directly compared. The simplest way to compare them was to standardize them both, converting the change to fractions of a standard deviation (see Chapter 5). The table shows that KIRIS scores increased by about three-fourths of a standard deviation in two years. This is a staggeringly large increase for such a short time, large enough that those familiar with these sorts of data would know that something was amiss. The real check, however, is the comparison with NAEP: at the same time that KIRIS scores increased so dramatically, the state's NAEP scores actually declined trivially.

This one finding was not a fluke. In a subsequent study, a colleague and I investigated a variety of subject and grade levels, and in every case, we found sizable inflation of scores. Some cases were like that of fourth-grade reading: large gains on the state's test, but none whatsoever on an audit test. In other cases, students showed some improvement on the audit test, but far less than on the KIRIS test. For example, in fourth- and eighth-grade math, gains on NAEP tests were roughly one-fourth as large as the gains achieved on the KIRIS tests, which were the tests used for accountability. The situation did not appear any better in high school, where gains in KIRIS scores did not generalize well to the ACT, which is the dominant college-admissions test in Kentucky.*

A similar study explored the so-called Texas miracle, the large rise in scores on the state's high-stakes TAAS test during the 1990s that was accompanied by a rapid narrowing of the performance gap between minority students and non-Hispanic whites. Given how distressingly persistent this gap often is, the narrowing of the difference in Texas was important news. However, it was largely illusory. Texas students did indeed show sizable gains on the NAEP, but these were far smaller than their gains on the state's TAAS test—in some cases, one-fifth as large. And NAEP did not show that the gap between minority and majority students was shrinking markedly.[9] One would expect some difference in trends because the TAAS and NAEP are quite different. Nevertheless, they overlap a good bit and are intended to support somewhat similar inferences, so the large gains in TAAS scores should have been reflected more substantially in the NAEP scores.

Unfortunately, we still know very little about variations in the severity of score inflation. What types of programs are most susceptible? Which types of students or schools tend to produce the most inflated scores? I suspect that all other things being equal, the problem is likely to be worse in the case of historically low-scoring schools, such as many of those that serve predominately poor and minority students. My reasoning is simple: where performance targets are very high relative to current scores and where community supports for achievement are comparatively weak, teachers face a far more difficult task and may be more inclined to

---

* The ACT, unlike the SAT, was designed as an achievement test, and it overlaps sufficiently with KIRIS to make it an appropriate, if not ideal, audit test. Because students self-select to take the ACT, comparisons were based solely on students who took both tests.

cut corners in trying to reach their targets. But the research carried out so far has not been sufficient to test this hypothesis.

Just how do teachers prepare students for the tests for which they are accountable? And which of these methods should be considered "cutting corners," in that they are likely to inflate scores?

Test preparation has been the focus of intense argument for many years, and all sorts of different terms have been used to describe both good and bad forms. For example, some people use "teaching the test" to refer to teaching specific items on the test (clearly bad) and "teaching to the test" to refer to focusing on the skills the test is supposed to represent (presumably good). Others, however, use "teaching to the test" to mean instruction that is inappropriately focused on the details of the test (presumably bad, and likely to inflate scores). I think it's best to ignore all of this and to distinguish instead between seven different types of test preparation:

- Working more effectively
- Teaching more
- Working harder
- Reallocation
- Alignment
- Coaching
- Cheating

The first three are what proponents of high-stakes testing want to see. Clearly, if educators find ways to work more effectively—for example, developing better curricula or teaching methods—students are likely to learn more. Up to a point, if teachers spend more time teaching, achievement is likely to rise, and for this reason the relatively short school year in the United States puts us at a disadvantage compared with other developed nations. The same is true of working harder in school. This can be carried too far, of course. For example, it is not clear that depriving young children of recess, which many schools are now doing in an effort to raise scores, is effective, and in my opinion it is undesirable regardless. Similarly, if students' workload becomes excessive, it may interfere with learning. It may also generate an aversion to learning that could have serious repercussions later in life. But if not carried to excess, these three forms of test preparation can be expected to produce real gains in achievement that would appear not only in the test scores used for accountability but on other tests and outside of school as well.

At the other extreme, cheating is unambiguously bad. Reports of cheating are now commonplace. It can take many forms: providing answers or hints to students during the administration of the test, allowing students to change their answers after the test has been completed, changing the answers for them, providing test questions in advance, and so on. Cheating may or may not be intentional, but regardless, it can produce only score inflation, never real gains in achievement.

What about reallocation, alignment, and coaching? All three can produce either real gains, score inflation, or both.

Reallocation refers to a process that is by now familiar: shifting instructional resources—classroom time, homework, parental nagging, whatever—to better match the content of a specific test. A quarter century of studies confirm that many teachers reallocate instruction in response to tests. And reallocation is not limited to teachers. For example, some studies have found that school administrators reassign teachers to place the most effective ones in the grades in which important tests are given.[10]

Is reallocation good or bad? Does it generate real gains in achievement or score inflation? This depends on two things: what gets more emphasis as a result, *and what gets less*. Clearly, some amount of reallocation is desirable, and indeed it is one of the goals of testing programs. For example, if a ninth-grade math test shows that students do relatively poorly in solving basic algebraic equations, one would want their teachers to put more effort into teaching them this. The rub is that instruction is nearly a zero-sum game, and devoting more resources to topic A entails fewer resources for topic B.

Scores become inflated when topic B—the material that gets less emphasis as a result of reallocation—is also an important part of the domain. As we have seen repeatedly, most achievement tests are a small sample from a large domain of achievement. Therefore, tests necessarily omit significant material—material that is important for the inference that users will base on test scores. When the stakes are low, this is fine: the included material represents the omitted, just as the Zogby poll respondents in Chapter 2 represented you and me—and roughly 122 million others—as well as themselves.

But if teachers respond to a test by deemphasizing material that is important for these inferences but is not given much weight on the particular test, scores will become inflated. Performance will be weaker when students take another test that places emphasis on different parts of the domain. One gets the pattern shown in Figure 10.1, when students were given a test they hadn't prepared for, the test that the district had used until a few years previously. This is score inflation of the sort illustrated by the West Virginia postal service example: the tested sample has become unrepresentative of the domain.

Alignment is a lynchpin of policy in this era of standards-based testing. Tests should be aligned with standards, and instruction should be aligned with both. One rarely hears mention of any disadvantages of alignment. And alignment is seen by many as insurance against score inflation. For example, a principal of a local school that is well known for the high scores achieved by its largely poor and minority students gave a presentation at the Harvard Graduate School of Education a few years ago. At one point, she angrily denounced critics who worry about "teaching to the test." We had no reason to be concerned about teaching to the test in her school, she asserted, because the state's test measures important knowledge and skills. Therefore, if her faculty teaches to the test, students will learn important things. This is, of course, another version of the "tests worth teaching to" argument described in Chapter 4.

This is nonsense, and I have a hunch about what I would find if I were allowed to administer an alternative test to her students. Alignment is just reallocation by another name. Certainly it is better to focus instruction on material that someone deems valuable, rather than frittering time away on unimportant things. But that is not enough. Whether alignment inflates scores depends also on the importance of the material that is deemphasized. And research has shown that standards-based tests are not immune to this problem. These tests too are limited samples from larger domains, and therefore focusing too narrowly on the content of the specific test can inflate scores.

Coaching refers to focusing instruction on small details of the test, many of which have no substantive meaning. For example, if a test happens to use the multiple-choice format for testing certain content, one can teach students tricks that work with that format. One can teach students to write in ways that are tailored to the specific scoring rubrics used with a particular test. There are a wide variety of coaching methods, and they can focus on substantive content as well. For example, one secondary-school mathematics teacher who participated in a study of mine claimed that her state's test always used regular polygons to assess mastery of plane geometry. So, she asked us, why would she bother teaching about irregular polygons? It was a study, not a conversation, so I could not give her the obvious answer: so that your students would learn something about them. Her focus had become the test, not the broader curriculum or the inference about performance that the test was supposed to support.

Coaching need not inflate scores. If the format or content of a test is sufficiently unfamiliar, a modest amount of coaching may even increase the validity of scores. For example, the first time young students are given a test that requires filling in bubbles on an optical scanning sheet, it is worth spending a very short time familiarizing them with this procedure before they start the test.

Most often, however, coaching either wastes time or inflates scores. Inflation occurs when coaching generates gains that are limited to a specific test—or to others that are very similar—and that do not generalize well to other tests of the same domain or to performance in real life.

A good example is training students to use a process of elimination in answering multiple-choice questions—that is, eliminating incorrect answers rather than figuring out the correct one. A *Princeton Review* test-prep manual for the Massachusetts MCAS test urges students to do this because "it's often easier to identify the *wrong* answers than to find the *correct* one." It then provides a contrived example that can be answered by means of a process of elimination "even without knowing a thing about [the topic the item is intended to measure]."[11] This approach might not be possible with an ideally written multiple-choice item; in fact, well-crafted multiple-choice questions often use distractors that will appeal to students because they reflect common misconceptions or errors, and in such cases, eliminating wrong answers may be difficult. However, many multiple-choice items are not ideal, and this technique does often help to raise scores.

What's wrong with this? The performance gains generated depend entirely on using multiple-choice items. All one has to do is to substitute constructed-response items—items that provide no answer choices and require students to write their own answers—and the gains would vanish. And, of course, when students need to apply their knowledge in the real world outside of school, the tasks are unlikely to appear in the form of a multiple-choice item. Thus, coaching students to use the process of elimination inflates scores.

This example shows that inflation from coaching is in one respect unlike inflation from reallocation. Reallocation inflates scores by making performance on the test unrepresentative of the larger domain, but it does not distort performance on the material tested. Delivery times really were shorter to the sampled addresses in West Virginia. In contrast, coaching can exaggerate performance even on the tested material. In the example just given, students who are taught to use the process of elimination as a method for "solving" certain types of equations will know less about those types of equations than their performance on the test indicates.

Coaching that focuses on substantive details of a test can similarly inflate scores by creating performance gains specific to the particular test. For example, consider the teacher who decided to abandon irregular polygons. The real world does not offer adults the courtesy of confronting them only with regular polygons, and neither do some other test authors. The NAEP, for example, has included irregular polygons. So if a test uses only regular polygons to assess knowledge of plane geometry, and if teachers are clever enough to figure this out—on their own or with the help of test-prep materials—the teachers can produce gains in performance that are limited to regular polygons and that will not generalize to some other tests, or to real-world tasks that happen to involve irregular polygons.

The example of irregular polygons may seem far-fetched, but the principle is not. Authors of test-prep materials, and some teachers as well, try hard to identify the recurrent patterns in a given assessment that make coaching feasible. Consider the following example, also from *Princeton Review* test-prep materials for the MCAS: "Whenever you have a right triangle—a triangle with a 90-degree angle—you can use the Pythagorean theorem. The theorem says that the sum of the squares of the legs of the triangle (the sides next to the right angle) will equal the square of the hypotenuse (the side opposite the right angle)." This is followed by a diagram of a right triangle, with the sides labeled *a, b,* and *c,* and the equation $a^2 + b^2 = c^2$.

So far so good. A critic might complain that this is rote and out of context, devoid of any explanation that would make the theorem meaningful, but if the student does successfully memorize what is written, she can apply it to any right triangle on any test and to real-world problems after she leaves school. But then the book continues: "Two of the most common ratios that fit the Pythagorean theorem are 3:4:5 and 5:12:13. Since these are ratios, any multiples of these numbers will also work, such as 6:8:10, and 30:40:50."[12]

Now we have a problem. Here again, the real world does not help us out by presenting us with right triangles with leg lengths in the ratio of 3:4:5 or 5:12:13. Right triangles can show up with leg lengths in any ratio whatever, so long as they conform to the relationship $a^2 + b^2 = c^2$. There is nothing "most common" about these two ratios in the real world. One might as easily encounter, for example, 2:3:3.61. What the authors mean is "most common in the particular test you are going to take." Authors of a different test designed to assess the same standards could use different ratios, and in that case, the performance boost that students got by memorizing these two ratios would be lost. Score inflation again.

The distinctions among the various types of test preparation can be hazy. Consider the following example from Montgomery County, Maryland (where my children went to school), as noted by the *Washington Post* in 2001: "The question on the review sheet for Montgomery County's algebra exam [provided by district officials] reads in part: 'The average amount that each band member must raise is a function of the number of band members, b, with the rule f(b) = 12000/b.' The question on the actual test reads in part: 'The average amount each cheerleader must pay is a function of the number of cheerleaders, n, with the rule f(n) = 420/n.'"[13] Is this an extreme example of coaching, or is it simply cheating? I'd vote for cheating. The district officials provided students with a thinly disguised version of the actual test item. But even if this is better classified as coaching, the upshot is the same: scores will be inflated. If students memorize the solution to the test-prep item, they can "solve" the actual test item with no understanding of basic algebra whatsoever, apart from knowing that an unknown can be represented by any letter. All the real item requires of them is some slightly different arithmetic—the same operations, but with different numbers.

By the same token, the boundary between undesirable and desirable alignment is not always clear. Teachers ought to use performance on tests to guide instruction, for example, by focusing on material on which students do relatively poorly. At what point, though, do they cross the line, robbing Peter to pay Paul?

The acid test is whether the gains in scores produced by test preparation truly represent meaningful gains in student achievement. We should not care very much about a score on a particular test, any more than we would have worried about students' knowledge of the forty specific words on the hypothetical vocabulary test in Chapter 2, or the actual votes cast by the 1,018 voters polled by Zogby on September 10, 2004. What we should be concerned about is the proficiency, the knowledge and skills, that the test score is intended to represent. Gains that are specific to a particular test and that do not generalize to other measures and to performance in the real world are worthless.

Of course, one could simply ignore score inflation, or dismiss it as merely an "opinion." The overwhelming majority of people who use scores do precisely that. The cost, however, is great.

Doing so leads to an illusion of progress and to erroneous judgments about the relative performance of schools. More important, it cheats the students who deserve better and more effective schooling. The alternatives—for educators, policymakers, parents, and others—are more difficult. I will turn to these in the final chapter.

Chapter 11

Adverse Impact and Bias

WHEN I WAS A GRADUATE STUDENT, I took a course on the administration and interpretation of intelligence tests. One requirement of the class was that I practice administering such tests to both children and adults. My adult subjects were friends and spouses and partners of friends, all graduate students or law students at highly competitive universities in the United States.

One of my volunteers was an Israeli graduate student in sociology at an Ivy League university. He was the son of a diplomat and therefore had spent much of his childhood studying English in American schools in Europe. His wife was a native-born American, and they were raising their children to be bilingual in English and Hebrew. All of which is to say that his English was superb, even by the high standards of Israeli academics.

He was also a very smart guy, and for the most part, his performance on the test showed this, despite a very high level of test anxiety caused by the fact that he was taking the test not only in front of me—embarrassing enough—but also within earshot of his wife, who was also a friend of mine. However, his cultural and linguistic background caused him to stumble a number of times.

One question asked what the examinee would do if lost. The Israeli student promptly started by saying, "You would search for . . ." and then became flustered and started repeating the phrase, never completing it. Clearly, anxiety was impeding his search for the phrase he wanted in English. I told him to complete the sentence in Hebrew, and he immediately said that one would search for a "*kever sheikh.*" I did not know what he meant, but once I had taken down his answer, he was able to collect his wits and translate for me: "the tomb of a sheik."

That stopped me in my tracks. Needless to say, this was not one of the answers listed in the manual as warranting even partial credit. I had no idea what he was talking about, and I would offer a wager at long odds that the authors of the test would not have known either. He explained that if lost in the desert, you can search for the tombs of Bedouin sheikhs to help orient yourself, because their openings face toward Mecca. In the environment in which he had grown up, his answer was an intelligent and functional one. On the test, however, as it was supposed to be scored, his answer warranted no credit because the authors of the test had not anticipated the responses of students from that environment and presumably knew nothing about the burial customs of Bedouins. And this was not the only item on the test that caused him difficulties because of language or the culture in which he had grown up.

Under the circumstances, I violated the standardized administrative guidelines and gave him full credit for his answer about Bedouin tombs because it is a sensible one in his native environment—in fact, more sensible than some of the standard full-credit answers. I also made a few other ad hoc adjustments, such as letting him take one numerical portion of the test entirely in Hebrew. In this case, there was no downside to my improvising in this way; no one was going to use the score for any purpose, so I could do as I thought reasonable.

However, suppose I had administered the test under standard

conditions—no material presented in Hebrew, and no ad hoc decisions to allow the examinee to respond in Hebrew—and that I had scored it according to the published, standard rubrics. In that case, the Israeli student's score would have been depressed by his performance on those particular items. The test was designed to support an inference about the student's general intelligence. For purposes of that particular inference, his score would have been misleadingly low, causing us to underestimate his general intelligence.

This is an example of *test bias*. This seems obvious on the surface, but the concept of bias is widely misunderstood, so it is worth explaining here what bias is and is not. There are three common misconceptions about test bias.

First, although people often talk about unbiased (or biased) tests, bias is an attribute of a specific inference, not of a test. Validity, as I explained in Chapter 9, is the extent to which a particular inference is warranted by a given score. Bias refers to a systematic distortion in scores that undermines the validity of a particular inference. In the case of the Israeli graduate student, the distortion arose from cultural and linguistic factors that depressed his score and undermined the validity of the inference about the his general intelligence. Bias can affect an entire group taking a test. For example, in the previous chapter I showed that inflation of scores on a high-stakes test can bias inferences about the proficiency of an entire district's or state's student population. Often, however—as in the case of my Israeli friend—bias affects only certain groups, producing misleading differences in scores between these groups and others.

One inference based on a given test score may be biased while another is not. One example of this, which I described in Chapter 6, was the Wall Charts published by the federal Department of Education early in the Reagan administration. These charts used states' average SAT scores as an indicator of the quality of their schools. For this particular inference, the data were severely biased. In some states, a majority of high school seniors took the test, while in others, only a small number did. In Connecticut, for example, 69 percent of graduating seniors took the SAT, compared with 7 percent in Minnesota. One reason for this disparity was that in some states, most colleges asked for ACT scores rather than SAT scores, so only a small number of students—mostly those applying to highly selective out-of-state schools—had any reason to take the SAT. Therefore, the states in which few students took the test would have had higher average scores than those in which many students took it, even if their educational systems and student populations were identical, simply because the students tested in the former states were a more select group.[1] The bias in this particular inference, however, tells us nothing about whether the inference for which the SAT is designed—prediction of students' performance in college—is biased. I will provide some evidence pertaining to this latter question later in this chapter. (In Chapter 12, I discuss another example of biased and unbiased inferences based on a single score: the two different inferences one might draw from a second-language speaker's scores on a college-admissions test.)

A second common and perhaps more important misconception is that a simple difference in scores between groups implies bias. The Israeli student's score would have been biased not because it was lower than it would have been had he grown up in New England, but because it would have been *misleadingly* low. Similarly, a difference in scores between groups—between poor and rich kids, males and females, blacks and whites, Asian Americans and whites—does not necessarily indicate bias. Bias might contribute to the difference, or it might not. A difference in scores entails bias only if it is misleading (again, for a particular inference).

I will again use the SAT as an example. The large differences in SAT scores among social groups have generated a great deal of debate for many years. For example, SAT scores increase substantially with family income (as reported by test-takers), and mean scores differ markedly among racial and ethnic groups. Are these differences bias? I will provide some data pertaining to racial and ethnic-group differences later, but for the moment, let's consider the relationship with income hypothetically. It is well known that, on average, the schools serving poor children are of lower quality than those serving students from higher-income families. Resources are more limited in schools in low-income areas, for example, and teaching positions are more likely to be filled by inexperienced and uncertified teachers. Now let's assume—hardly a risky assumption—that some of these differences among schools matter and that, as a result, many poor students learn less in school and end up less well prepared for college. If that is true, tests designed to estimate how well prepared students are for college *should* give lower average scores to students from these lower-quality schools, and hence, on average, to low-income children. A valid inference about preparedness for college would *require* that these students obtain lower scores. How much lower the scores should be in order to provide an accurate prediction is an open question. The difference we observe might be either smaller or larger than it should be, in either case constituting bias. Thus a difference in scores between groups is a reason to check for bias but not grounds to assume it.

Possible bias, of course, is not the only reason to be concerned about differences in test scores among groups. These disparities can have important negative effects even if the inferences based on scores are entirely unbiased. Members of lower-scoring groups are more likely to fail to reach the standards required by many elementary and secondary school high-stakes testing programs, less likely to be admitted to many colleges, and less likely to gain employment in some fields.

The negative effects of group differences in test scores are typically labeled *adverse impact,* which is more of a legal term than a technical one. Adverse impact can arise without bias, and conversely, bias can exist even in the absence of any adverse impact. Say, for example, that college-bound high school students who want to become engineers take more mathematics courses in high school than students who want to become English majors, and that the future engineers learn more math as a result. Now say that on the mathematics portion of a college admissions test, both groups had the same average score. In this case, the absence of adverse impact would signal bias—either scores that were misleadingly low for the engineers or too high for the English majors. But most often we are concerned about the possibility that a group has been harmed by testing, and therefore we worry about the possibility that adverse impact, when we find it, is caused or exacerbated by bias.

The final misconception about bias is a confusion between bias and measurement error. Bias and measurement error are fundamentally different, and neither causes the other: a score that is unreliable may be unbiased, and a biased score may be reliable. Remember: reliability is consistency of measurement, and measurement error is simple inconsistency. In Chapter 7, I drew an analogy to a cheap bathroom scale. If the scale is unreliable—if the readings include a lot of measurement error—then there will be a great deal of inconsistency in the readings it provides. But if the scale is only unreliable and not biased, when you step onto it enough times and average the readings, the inconsistency will wash out and the average will be roughly correct. If the scale is biased, however, it will tend to err in the same direction repeatedly, and the long-run average reading will be either to high or too low. I have a humidifier that is reliable but biased: it consistently tells me that the relative humidity in my bedroom is lower than it really is. In fact, within a wide range of humidity, its reliability is perfect: it always reads 25 percent. The general principle is simply that measurement error gradually washes out over repeated measures, while bias does not. When in common speech we label a measure—say, a medical test—"accurate," we generally mean that it is relatively free of both measurement error and bias.

The loss of credit my Israeli student would have experienced on the test, had it been administered and scored in the conventional manner, would have been bias rather than measurement error. It was not a fluke, a random event that might not have happened had I tested him on Wednesday rather than Tuesday. Rather, it was a systematic problem: his performance was depressed by linguistic and cultural factors that would have continued to depress his scores even if I had retested him.

Adverse impact seems more straightforward than test bias. Gauging adverse impact is simply a matter of determining the negative effects a group suffers as a result of test scores—say, a lower rate of acceptance by selective colleges and universities—and if one is concerned only with adverse impact, one need not be troubled with figuring out whether scores are actually misleading. However, there is one poorly understood complexity that arises in cases of adverse impact, which one might call the Berkeley effect.

Berkeley, the oldest campus of the University of California, is one of the most selective public universities in the United States. It has also long been the focus of often bitter arguments about both adverse impact and possible bias in admissions—including, in recent years, the controversy about Proposition 209, the state ballot initiative that banned affirmative action in public institutions in California, and, more recently, charges of discrimination against Asian American applicants. Leaving aside the questions of bias and discrimination, the pattern of adverse impact in admissions—specifically, the highly disproportionate representation of racial and ethnic groups in the newly admitted freshman classes—is dramatic. In 2006, African Americans constituted less than 4 percent of admitted students (excluding the small number who did not identify a racial or ethnic group); Latinos made up 14 percent; whites, 34 percent; and Asian Americans—the highest-scoring of these groups on many standardized tests—46 percent. While Proposition 209 pushed down the percentages for African Americans and Latinos substantially, the pattern of disproportionate representation was striking even in 1997, the last year before Proposition 209 went into effect.[2]

The obvious question is why. Some people suggest that the admissions process, either admissions tests or some other aspect of the process, is particularly biased against high-achieving, non-Asian minority students. I have no privileged information about undergraduate admissions, either at Berkeley or at other similarly selective universities, so I am not able to give a complete answer to this question. However, one part of the answer is clear: this pattern of severely disproportionate representation of groups with different levels of performance can arise without any bias at all. In the absence of affirmative action or bias, disproportionate representation will grow more severe as the selectivity of the university increases. And Berkeley, recall, is a very selective university.

Some years ago, I attended a meeting about adverse impact in college admissions hosted by the Ford Foundation. At one end of the room sat Ward Connerly, the author of Proposition 209 as well as a number of later initiatives to ban affirmative action in other states, and at the time a member of the University of California Board of Regents. At the other end (literally as well as figuratively) sat a number of attorneys with the NAACP Legal Defense Fund and the Mexican American Legal Defense and Educational Fund. I sat in the middle, along with a few other social scientists and some others. Needless to say, it was one of the most interesting meetings I had attended in a long time, although not among the most relaxed.

My task was to explain the relationship between the selectivity of admissions and adverse impact. My conclusion was that the

Berkeley effect should be expected even in the total absence of bias. As admission becomes more selective, low-scoring groups (African Americans and Latinos, for example) will become progressively more severely underrepresented, and by the exact same mechanism, higher-scoring groups (for example, Asian Americans) will become increasingly more substantially overrepresented. This is a mathematical certainty, so long as the distribution of scores conforms even roughly to the bell curve—specifically, so long as there are many students bunched up with scores near their own group's average and progressively fewer with scores further from that average. And this effect is very powerful.

To make this concrete, I presented the group with a series of graphs based on simulated data that I created to mimic a typical difference between African American and white students. I included only these two groups, and to be realistic, I made the African American group smaller, 15 percent of the total pool of applicants. I made other details (the size of the mean difference, the relative size of the standard deviations within each group) realistic as well, but they are not essential, and there is no reason to go into them here. The story line depends on only two things: a substantial difference in average scores, and a distribution of scores that has most students piled up near their group's average.

I simplified the college-admissions process and asked what would happen if colleges used only a simple cut score on an admissions test: if you score anywhere below the cut, you are rejected, and if you score anywhere above the cut, you are accepted. This is not how the process works, or at least not how it should work; admissions staff should avoid a fixed cut score and should look at numerous indicators, not just scores on one test. But this simplification makes it possible to show the problem graphically and concretely.

The results are dramatic. If a system is unselective—everyone is admitted, regardless of scores—there can be no adverse impact, and both groups are represented in the pool of admitted students in proportion to their size in the population: 15 percent African American, and 85 percent white. If a cut score is set at the overall mean—all students with average or above-average scores on a test are admitted, while all other are rejected—the representation of African American students falls sharply, to about 6 percent of admitted students. And a cut score at the mean represents only a modest level of selectivity. To make this concrete, the mean score on the mathematics portion of the SAT for the graduating class of 2006 was 518.[3] Using the mean as the cut score results in severe underrepresentation of African American students, whose representation in the admitted group (6 percent) will be only 40 percent as large as their share of the applicant pool (15 percent).

This result is shown in Figure 11.1, where the vertical dashed line represents the cut score: everyone to the right of the line— with scores above the cut—is admitted, and everyone to the left of the line is rejected. The scores are on a z-score scale (see Chapter 5), with a mean of zero and a standard deviation of one. The cut score—the vertical line—is therefore set at a score of zero. You can see that the group to the right of the line is disproportionately white, compared with the total population of applicants.

What if one makes the system more selective? Consider raising the cut score to one standard deviation above the mean, which corresponds to an SAT mathematics score of 633. This represents a fairly high level of selectivity, although not by the standards of the most selective universities. (According to the *U.S. News and World Report* college rankings, a combined math and verbal score of 1380 places a student at only the twenty-fifth percentile rank among newly enrolled freshmen at Princeton, for example.)[4] With this cut score, almost all African American students would be rejected, and those admitted would constitute only 1 percent of the admitted class (Figure 11.2).

As Figures 11.1 and 11.2 show, the resulting over- and

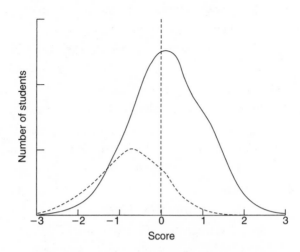

FIG. 11.1. Illustration of adverse impact with a cut score set at the
overall mean; whites represented by solid line, blacks by
dashed line.

underrepresentation of groups is simply a function of the shape
of the distribution of scores, with most students bunched up near
the average of their group. Because of this, as you move the cut
higher, the representation of the lower-scoring group in the admitted pool drops more rapidly than that of the higher-scoring
group.

The figures do not show scores for Asian Americans, but increasing selectivity has the reverse impact on them: it increases
their overrepresentation in the admitted group. The mechanism is
the same: just as the representation of blacks falls relative to
whites because the average score of blacks is lower, the representation of whites drops relative to Asians because the average score
of whites is lower than that of Asians.

The lesson of this exercise is that serious adverse impact need
not indicate bias. There are many other factors that influence admissions at Berkeley, as at all other selective schools, and the mix
of students the university admits reflects more than the Berkeley

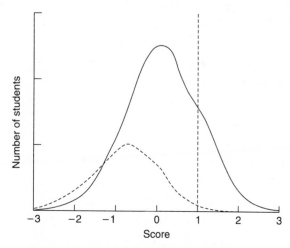

FIG. 11.2. Illustration of adverse impact with a cut score set at one standard deviation above the overall mean; whites represented by solid line, blacks by dashed line.

effect. Moreover, the existence of the Berkeley effect is no reason to dismiss concerns about possible bias. There might indeed be bias for or against any number of groups—for example, legacies (the children of alumni) and athletes, as well as minority-group members—in the admissions process of any college. What the exercise shows, however, is that the severity of adverse impact is not enough to tell us whether bias is present.

Given that even severe adverse impact need not indicate bias, just how can one determine when bias really exists? In some instances—such as the case of my Israeli friend—the existence of bias is fairly clear-cut. Unfortunately, in many cases it is not, and we are sometimes left uncertain whether a difference in performance represents bias or a real difference in proficiency.

The first step in attempting to identify potential bias is to examine the content of the test items, looking for content or even wording that might distort the performance of particular groups. For example, one would not want to use yachting vocabulary in mathematics word problems if a test is going to be administered to poor children in landlocked parts of the Midwest, because failure to know the meaning of *lanyard* could obscure competence in arithmetic. Double negatives would be a risk if a test is going to be administered to non-native speakers of English in whose native language—for example, Russian and Hebrew—a double negative (I don't know nothing) is the appropriate way of expressing a negative (I know nothing). One might also want to avoid language that some students will find offensive even if they find it comprehensible, not only to avoid giving offense but also to avoid a negative reaction that could depress their performance.

Screening of test content for material that could cause offense or generate bias is now a routine part of test development in most high-quality testing programs. It is necessary, but it does not always work. Just as an examination of content is not enough to ensure that a test measures what it is intended to assess, it also is not enough to ensure that items are unbiased, and it can result in rejecting items that in fact will not show bias in practice.

Therefore, we have to turn to empirical evidence: what actually happens when the test is administered? Are there patterns of performance—either overall or for particular groups of students— that suggest bias? Performance is examined not only for the test as a whole, but also on individual test items.

A common way of examining performance on individual test items goes by the cumbersome name of *differential item functioning,* or DIF. DIF refers to group differences in performance on a particular test item among students who are comparable in terms of their overall proficiency. For example, consider gender differences. These differences vary markedly from one test and sample of students to another, but most often, female students outscore male students on test of vocabulary and reading, while males tend to outscore females on tests of mathematics. These differences tend not to be very large, but they appear quite consistently. (The difference in mathematics favoring boys, however, has nearly vanished in the fourth- and eighth-grade mathematics tests of the National Assessment of Educational Progress in recent years.)[5] Suppose we look at performance on a reading test on which girls, on average, outscore boys. We pick an item, and lo and behold, we find that girls performed better on it. This tells us nothing. After all, girls outscore boys on the test, so we would expect them to perform better on a randomly chosen item. But now suppose that we *match* boys and girls on their total scores. We ask: do girls and boys *with the same test score* perform differently on this item? Ideally, the answer would be no. A substantial difference in performance between *matched* boys and girls would constitute DIF.

Screening tests for DIF is now commonplace, in particular, to look for differential performance among racial and ethnic groups and between males and females. And some degree of DIF is commonly found. But while identifying DIF is a step in the right direction, it does not mean we're home free. We still face the task of determining *why* matched students in the two groups perform differently on the item. Bias might cause the matched students to perform differently, but the cause could also be something else, such as differences in instruction. For example, ethnic groups are not uniformly distributed among schools: Asian Americans are concentrated in some regions, Hispanics are concentrated in others, African Americans are concentrated in urban centers and some parts of the South, and so on. In our decentralized educational system, instruction varies from place to place—not only formal curricula and textbooks but also patterns of course taking and tracking. Therefore, DIF can arise from differences in instruction experienced by the average student in various ethnic groups. The same could hold true of social-class differences in performance. Gender differences are a another matter—boys and girls are similarly distributed across regions and, for the most part, schools—but at the high-school level, they may choose different courses, and that too may result in meaningful differences in performance that appear as DIF. If a school discourages smart girls from taking advanced mathematics courses, one would expect DIF showing girls to perform less well on items reflecting content of the advanced courses in which they are underrepresented. This would be grounds for criticizing the school, but it would not constitute bias in the items. They would be correct in showing that girls had learned less of the material emphasized in the courses they had been discouraged from taking.

But in some cases of DIF, bias does seem to be the culprit. For example, a number of studies have found that when students with limited proficiency in English are matched with native speakers whose proficiency in mathematics is similar, those with limited proficiency in English perform less well on linguistically complex test items. This seems clearly to be bias: their performance on these items is depressed not by proficiency in mathematics—what the test is supposed to measure—but by problems comprehending complex forms of English.

Thus, DIF at the level of individual test items is somewhat analogous to adverse impact at the level of an entire test: it is a red flag indicating the need for further investigation, but it does not in itself tell us that we have found bias. To play it safe, test authors often discard items that show very large amounts of DIF, even if they cannot identify its cause. But apart from that, the benefit of DIF is that it allows us to zero in on specific test items that require more examination.

Often, in an attempt to identify possible bias, people examine patterns in scores on entire tests, rather than performance on individual items. This too is less straightforward than it first may seem. A common error—one that is found in the social scientific literature as well as in lay discussions of bias, and that formed the crux of a well-known legal decision about testing for employment screening—is to assume that the size of differences among groups is an indication of bias. That is, if tests show varying differences between groups—say, between males and females or between African Americans and whites—the presumption is that those showing larger differences are likely biased. However, there is no reason to believe that this is true. Just as decisions about content affect the ranking of country means, they can affect the size of differences among groups. For example, years ago I discovered that the size of the gap between African American and white students in mathematics on the National Assessment of Educational Progress varied considerably among the five content areas that the test comprised at the time. The gap was considerably larger, for example, in measurement than in algebra. The size of the difference could be altered simply by changing the relative weights given to these five content areas—just as changing the emphasis on different aspects of mathematics changes the differences between countries on the TIMSS or PISA assessments. But unless you wish to make a very specific inference about mathematics, one that requires a specific relative emphasis on algebra as compared with measurement, for example, there is no reason to conclude that changing the mix in the NAEP would either generate or lessen bias. It would simply give a somewhat different view of mathematics proficiency.

In addition, reliability can cloud comparisons of group differences across different tests. One effect of measurement error is to obscure differences between groups. One can think of true scores as "signal" and measurement error as random "noise." As the ratio of signal to noise drops, it becomes harder to discern the signal through the noise. And thus as a test becomes less reliable, it becomes more difficult to see the relationships between scores and other factors. This problem takes many forms, but one of them is that group differences in scores will appear smaller on unreliable tests than on reliable ones. As one colleague of mine quipped years ago, "The easiest way to shrink group differences in performance is to write lousy, unreliable tests."*

Therefore, to identify bias we need some sort of external comparison, something other than the tests in question to which we can compare test scores. But we do not always have one. I explain one instance in the following chapter: when we try different ways of assessing students with disabilities, we often lack any external criterion—any other, trusted indication of how these students should perform—that help us determine which approaches to assessment provide the most valid (that is least biased) indicators of the proficiency of these students.

One case in which we do have an external standard of comparison is college-admissions tests. The primary inference these tests are designed to support is that students who score higher on the tests will, on average, perform better in college. No test will perfectly predict later performance, so we can expect that many students will do better or worse in college than their test scores predict. That would not constitute bias. The inference would be biased if some group performed *systematically* better or worse in college than their scores predict. In theory, at least, we have a criterion available to us to evaluate bias in this case: we can collect data on students' performance in college, and we can see whether certain groups do systematically better or worse than predicted by their test scores.

We need some measure of students' performance in college to serve as the criterion. One logical option is grades in college courses. Most evaluations of the validity of predictions based on college-admissions tests examine how well scores predict fresh-

---

* Technically, this is the case so long as the statistic used to report the difference is standardized scores. Most of the statistics used to report test-score gaps between groups are standardized—for example, standardized mean differences and correlations.

man grade-point average (FGPA). In these evaluations, bias is usually gauged by over- or underprediction of grades. For example, if there is a bias against a particular group, their scores would underpredict their FGPA—they would do better in college, on average, than their scores predict. The most recent of these validation studies of the SAT examined the FGPA of the 1994 and 1995 entering classes at twenty-three colleges and universities across the nation that varied in terms of location, size, and selectivity and provided estimates of under- and overprediction by race/ethnicity and gender.[6]

The results were not what most people would expect. The study did show a slight bias in the SAT against one group: white women. The mean FGPA attained by white women was slightly higher than predicted by their SAT scores, by about 0.10 grade point (on a scale on which an A+ is 4.3, an A is 4.0, an A− is 3.7, a B+ is 3.3, and so on). Predictions for minority women were very close to the actual mean FGPAs attained by those groups. The largest biases—although still very small—were in favor of minority men. African American and Latino men attained average FGPAs about 0.15 of a grade point lower than predicted by their scores. White and Asian American males obtained grades about 0.05 of a point lower than predicted.*

What should one make of the findings of this study and others similar to it? There are quite a number of reasons to take them with a grain of salt. I stressed in Chapter 9 that a criterion should be a trusted measure, and there are ample grounds not to place too much trust in college grades. To begin, grades are typically quite unreliable. Studies correlating scores with college grades

---

* To some degree, these slight biases may stem from the statistical method employed rather than the substantive characteristics of the SAT. These studies impose a single linear regression prediction model on groups with substantially different mean scores. This approach will tend to generate underprediction for high-scoring groups and overprediction for low-scoring groups.

pose several analytical problems: we lack grades for students who were rejected or who were accepted but decided not to enroll, and the range of test scores among enrolled students is often severely restricted. Perhaps most important, we have no reason to trust that college grades are themselves free of bias. For example, let's say that we are concerned about the possibility that admissions tests are biased against minority students. Why would we assume that the grades students receive—most often assigned by professors or teaching assistants who know the students' race or ethnicity—are less likely to be biased than scores on a test that is scored, for the most part, without that information?

Another complication is that there are many reasons why students do well or poorly in college, some of which have nothing to do with the academic achievement and reasoning skills that admissions tests measure. For example, some students from disadvantaged backgrounds may not have learned study skills appropriate for the level of demand imposed in college classes. Years ago, Uri Triesman, then a professor of mathematics at Berkeley, explored why non-Asian minority students had a high failure rate in his freshman calculus class. One of the factors he identified was that far fewer of these students realized the benefits of forming study groups. He successfully reduced the failure rate with a variety of initiatives, one of which was setting up study groups for the entire class.

Once again, the solution lies in being more specific about the inference based on scores. One question is whether college-admissions tests provide biased indicators of the likely success of non-Asian minority students in colleges as they now exist. This study suggests that the SAT is not biased for this purpose. An entirely different question is whether the SAT and other admissions tests provide an unbiased estimate of the potential of these students to succeed if colleges were to provide additional supports of various sorts, such as the one that Triesman introduced in his class at

Berkeley years ago. The study cited here does not answer this second question—for minority students or for any others.

All in all, just how common and severe a problem is test bias, in the sense that the term is used in measurement? How often are there systematic distortions in the inferences based on test scores? A theme throughout much of this chapter is that people often assume bias when they should not. Neither a large score difference between groups nor severe adverse impact necessarily indicates bias, and careful test authors now routinely use both screening of content and statistical analyses to lessen the potential for bias. In some instances in which many people assume bias—for example, in the prediction of college performance by admissions tests—the evidence does not show it.

None of this, however, is to suggest that the problem of bias, and potential bias, is minor. I would like to end with four cautions.

First, the fact that large score differences between social groups need not indicate bias does not imply that they never do. The appropriate response is to treat these score differences as a reason to check for bias.

Second, our information about bias is often incomplete. Bias, like validity, is somewhat elusive. Techniques for identifying it are limited, and evaluations of potential bias are often imperfect. And a lack of bias for one group—or for one inference—need not imply a lack of bias for another. The evaluation of potential bias, like other aspects of validation, is an ongoing process.

Third, while in some contexts bias may be less widespread than many observers assume, in other cases, it is more common. The most important example of this was discussed in Chapter 10: score inflation. Most people who use the scores from high-stakes tests—educators, policymakers, writers, parents, realtors—believe that they are unbiased indicators of improved learning. The evidence to date suggests otherwise: the research shows not only that scores can be biased but also that the size of that bias is often huge. For example, the bias shown in Table 10.1, which arose in the space of only two years, was nearly the typical size of the total black-white gap in scores. Whether that bias affects some groups more than others remains largely unknown.

And finally, there are some contexts in which potential bias is particularly pervasive and difficult to address. Perhaps the most important example is the assessment of students with special needs, to which I turn in the following chapter.

Chapter 12

Testing Students with Special Needs

FEW ISSUES IN MEASUREMENT raise such intense emotions as the assessment of students with special needs: those with disabilities or with limited proficiency in English.* Both groups are large, and the latter group is growing rapidly. A major thrust of state and federal policies since the 1990s has been to increase the participation of these students in large-scale testing programs and to ensure that, to the extent feasible, they are assessed in the same way as other students. Federal law imposes substantial requirements on states in terms of how they test students in both groups.

---

* One note on terminology, to avoid giving offense: it is politically correct now to shun the old term "limited English proficient" (LEP) in favor of "English language learner" (ELL) in describing students who are not native speakers of English and who have not attained full fluency in English. For various reasons—for example, because it defines a group by a deficit, what students lack or cannot do—many find LEP disparaging, and using ELL avoids that problem. However, for most questions of measurement, LEP describes what is relevant: the fact that some students have a level of proficiency in English that is limited enough to interfere with assessing them appropriately and thus to undermine the validity of conclusions about their knowledge and skills. In contrast, for present purposes, "English language learner" is a red herring: we will not be concerned here with the question of which of these students are learning English. Hence, for the sake of accuracy, I will use "limited English proficient" as a purely descriptive term, with no disparagement intended.

These goals are laudable, but the difficulties inherent in testing these groups appropriately are daunting. In 1997, I served on a study panel of the National Research Council (NRC), a research arm of the National Academy of Sciences, the National Academy of Engineering, and the Institute of Medicine, that issued a report discussing how to incorporate students with disabilities into standards-based education reform. While supporting the goal of including these students in regular assessments, the panel wrote: "The meaningful participation of students with disabilities in large-scale assessments and compliance with the legal rights of individuals with disabilities in some instances require steps that are beyond current knowledge and technology."[1] Despite an increase in research since that time, this conclusion remains true today, and to some degree it applies to students with limited English proficiency as well. Worse, some of the quandaries we face in assessing these students are not entirely tractable, at least at the present. We can't expect that, in the near term, more research and technical improvements will solve all of them. And to the extent that we *do* know how to test these children well, some aspects of current policy seem to be wide of the mark.

Because the story I tell here is discouraging, I should make clear that I strongly support efforts to include students with special needs in the general curriculum and, to the extent that it is both practical and sensible, to include them in general-education assessments. My concern with the education of students with disabilities goes back a long way; fresh out of college, I taught emotionally disturbed children, and that led me to graduate study of atypical child development.

I also have firsthand experience being less than fully proficient in a second language. When I was young, between my stint as a special education teacher and my graduate studies, I lived briefly on a kibbutz in northern Israel, at the bottom of the mountain where Saul was vanquished by the Philistines—a kibbutz that was hit by a missile fired by Hezbollah as I was writing this chapter. I worked hard to learn Hebrew, and in some ways, I became fluent. In daily activities, I often thought in Hebrew, and I dreamed in Hebrew some of the time.

My proficiency, however, had serious limits. I was, to use the analogous acronym, LHP: limited Hebrew proficient. Switching into Hebrew made me, well, boring. I had too limited a vocabulary to discuss most interesting or complex ideas, or even to understand others when they discussed them. In those days, the buses had speakers broadcasting the Voice of Israel. When the news came on, the driver would turn up the volume, and the passengers would fall quiet. When the announcer started discussing something that Henry Kissinger had said, I understood that he was discussing what Kissinger had said. I just could not figure out *what* Kissinger had said. And I had almost no sense of humor, because a good bit of humor requires play on words. To this day, decades later, I recall the first joke I understood in Hebrew. It was a simple and bad joke, but even so, I didn't get it the first time around. And, of course, I was prone to embarrassing mistakes, such as the time that I inadvertently tried to bribe an Uzi-toting guard because I confused the similar-sounding verbs for "photograph" and "pay." Or the time, some years later, when for the same reason I explained to an incredulous cousin of my wife's that I was a symphony conductor for the U.S. Congress.

We should move forward with the inclusion of students with special needs in large-scale testing programs, but we should do so with our eyes open, cognizant of the gaps that remain in our understanding and of the deficiencies in our methods for testing them.

⬭ Students with Disabilities

Deciding just who should be counted as disabled is no simple matter. At what point, for example, does a vision problem, an orthopedic problem, a difficulty concentrating, or emotional distress cross the boundary from being a bother to being a disability? A recent survey of the prevalence of mental illness (the National Comorbidity Survey Replication) sparked an intense academic and public debate about the dividing line between normal states and mental illness—for example, between severe unhappiness and clinical depression.[2] Much the same problem arises with other disabilities. But when the issue is testing students with disabilities, the problem goes far beyond disagreements about the severity required for initial diagnosis.

In most of what is written about the education of students with disabilities, information on the prevalence of disabilities reflects a legal criterion: eligibility for services under Part B of the Individuals with Disabilities Education Act (IDEA).* People most often use the term *identification* to refer to a determination that a student has a disability for purposes of the law, and *classification* to refer to the label given to the student's disability. In recent years, roughly 11 percent of students ages six to seventeen nationwide have been served under Part B. However, this percentage varies strikingly from state to state. In the 1999–2000 school year, the lowest reported prevalence was in Colorado (about 9 percent), while the highest, almost 16 percent, was in Rhode Island (see Table 12.1). The other states were strung out along the full range between them.

The differences in prevalence rates reported by the states be-

---

* IDEA is the principal federal statute pertaining to education of the disabled, the current incarnation of the pathbreaking Education for All Handicapped Children Act of 1975, which many people knew by its Public Law designation, P.L. 94-142. P.L. 94-142 was the first federal statute establishing the rights of students with disabilities to an appropriate public education. It was the source, for example, of the familiar requirement that these students be educated in the least restrictive environment practical. Part B of the statute is the primary grant program funding services for students with disabilities—the principal focus of the frequent and well-publicized debates in Congress about the adequacy of federal funding for the education of the disabled.

Table 12.1   Percentage of students ages 6–17 served under IDEA Part B, states
and U.S. (50 states and D.C.), selected disability categories, 1999–
2000

	Lowest state	Highest state	U.S. total
All disabilities	9.1 (CO)	15.6 (RI)	11.3
Specific learning disability	3.0 (KY)	9.1 (RI)	5.7
Speech/language	1.0 (IA)	3.9 (WV)	2.3
Mental retardation	0.3 (NJ)	3.0 (WV)	1.1
Emotional disturbance	0.1 (AR)	1.9 (VT)	0.9
Visual disabilities	0.02 (IA, NJ)	0.08 (TN, UT)	0.05

Source: To Assure the Free Appropriate Public Education of All Children with Disabilities,
23rd Annual Report to Congress on the Implementation of the Individuals with Disabilities Education Act (Washington, DC: U.S. Department of Education, 2001), Table
AA10, *http://www.ed.gov/about/reports/annual/osep/2001/appendix-a-pt1.pdf* (accessed
7/20/06).

come far larger, and are simply not credible, when one looks at
individual categories of disability. The reported prevalence of specific learning disabilities varied threefold, from 3 percent in Kentucky to 9 percent in Rhode Island. The difference between the
highest and lowest reported prevalence of mental retardation was
a factor of 10.*

For the most part, these dramatic state-to-state variations do
not reflect real differences in the prevalence of disabilities. Rather,
they arise primarily from differences in state and local policies pertaining to identification and classification. Research has shown
that the practices of educators add yet more inconsistency, so
even under the strictures of a specific state's policies, one often

---

* The terms *incidence* and *prevalence* are often confused in popular use. Incidence is the
number of new cases of a condition occurring the in the population during a specified period of time. Prevalence is the number of cases present at a given time. Thus, the incidence
rate can be far higher than the prevalence rate if conditions are short-lived. The prevalence
of head colds among my students during the first week of October last year was very low.
The incidence rate over the course of the semester was quite high. The identification rates
shown here are prevalence rates: the proportion of students in the stated age group who
have a given disability condition on a given date.

finds dramatic variations from location to location that for the most part seem to lack any substantive justification. For example, for several years I served on a committee advising the New York State Education Department on educating students with disabilities. A frequent topic was the anomalously high and seemingly unwarranted prevalence rates reported by some downstate suburban districts—rates that were considerably higher than any in Table 12.1.

Inconsistencies in *identification* rates are clearly important because, under federal law, identification gives students legal rights that other students do not share—of particular relevance here, certain rights with respect to testing, but also rights to services that are often intensely controversial because of their expense. In contrast, many people in the field of special education argue that the inconsistencies in *classification* are unimportant. One reason is that many students have more than one disability, and the choice of the primary disability may be arbitrary. Their more important argument is that the services delivered to a student should be based on each individual's functional impediments to learning, not the broad classification into which the child's disability places him. Two students classified as having different primary disabilities may need the same services, and two others with the same classification may require different services.

I have little quarrel with this argument when it is applied to instruction and other educational services, but it is unrealistic when applied to testing. It might be ideal to fully individualize testing without regard to classification, but often we cannot. Categories of disability are important for purposes of testing, and the often wild inconsistencies in classification pose a serious impediment to improving our methods for testing students with disabilities.

Federal statutes—in particular, IDEA and No Child Left Behind, but also several other statutes—impose numerous requirements for testing students with disabilities.[3] IDEA mandates that states must establish performance goals for students with disabilities that are as consistent as is feasible with those for other students. States must include students with disabilities in general state- and districtwide testing programs used to assess other students, "with appropriate accommodations, where necessary." States must also implement "alternate assessments" for the relatively small number of students who are unable to participate in the general education assessments because of severe disabilities.[4] Many of the decisions about the education and testing of each child must be made by IEP (individualized educational program) teams comprising the parents, educators, other relevant professionals, and, when appropriate, the student. States typically provide guidelines to IEP teams for using assessment accommodations, sometimes explicitly prohibiting some of them, but the decisions are made by the IEP team.

NCLB explicitly accepts the framework provided by IDEA and builds on it. It requires that 95 percent of students with disabilities be tested, that their performance be reported separately when they are numerous enough to allow sufficiently reliable results, and that schools be held accountable for their progress. NCLB also calls for "reasonable adaptations and accommodations for students with disabilities."[5] As we will see, the regulations implementing NCLB's provisions for testing students with disabilities are draconian.

The key to one of the most difficult problems arising from testing students with disabilities is the need for "appropriate accommodations" and "reasonable adaptations and accommodations," language that is echoed in the regulations of many states. These terms are used inconsistently, but I will follow the most common convention and use "accommodation" to refer to changes in testing that do not include direct alterations of the tested content and that are intended not to change what is measured by the test. These can include changes in the presentation of the test (such as providing a braille version to a blind student), in the setting or other aspects of administration (allowing a student to take the test in a room with no other students or with more frequent breaks), or in the allowed mode of response (for example, allowing a student with an orthopedic handicap to dictate rather than write her answers).

The requirement of "appropriate accommodations" seems innocuous enough; after all, one would hardly want inappropriate ones. But what would make changes in testing "appropriate" and "reasonable"? This turns out to be an extraordinarily difficult question, one of the most vexing in the field of measurement today. To address it, one has to start with the purpose of accommodations.

Even though accommodations are a deliberate violation of standardization, they share its primary goal: to improve the validity of conclusions based on test scores. Usually, we standardize assessments to remove misleading sources of variations in scores. For example, if I allowed my students to look at notes when taking a test and you did not, our students' scores would not be comparable. My students' scores would be boosted by my more lenient rules, independent of their actual level of achievement. Therefore, in most instances a comparison based on a standardized test provides a stronger basis for comparison than one that has not been standardized.

When students have certain disabilities, however, their scores on a test administered in a standard manner may be misleadingly low. The clearest example is students with visual disabilities. If a student cannot read text easily, her score on a test presented in standard printed form obviously will be lower than her proficiency would warrant. Accommodations are intended to offset impediments such as this in order to level the playing field—to make a score obtained from a student with a disability more comparable to the same score obtained by another student tested under standard conditions. In the case of a student with a severe visual disability, that would require presenting the test in some form other than standard print—in large type, in braille, or orally.

The metaphor for accommodations that I suggested to the NRC panel I referenced earlier was a corrective lens. Let's say that you want to evaluate a student's proficiency in algebra, so you administer a standardized algebra test. Think of the test as a vertical ruler. Students with greater proficiency should obtain higher scores, placing them higher up on the ruler. The test will provide an estimate of where each student's height marker should be. This estimate will be fuzzy because of measurement error, although for most students, the fuzziness will extend equally in both directions, and if you tested them repeatedly and took an average, you would gradually zero in on the right estimate. But what happens to a student who has a visual disability and can read the test materials only very slowly and with great strain? Your estimate of proficiency for him will not only be fuzzy but will also be biased downward, lower than his actual proficiency warrants. If you tested him repeatedly, you could reduce the fuzziness but you would zero in on the wrong score.

The ideal accommodations would function like a corrective lens, offsetting the disability-related impediments to performance and raising your estimate of the student's proficiency to the level it should be. This would make the scores obtained by students with disabilities *comparable in meaning* to the scores obtained by other students. Let's say that two students, one with a severe visual disability who was given no accommodation and another with no disability at all, both got a score of 30 (out of a maximum of 36) on the mathematics portion of the ACT college-admissions test. Without more information, the admissions officer receiving these two scores would infer that the two students showed comparable mastery of the mathematics content and skills measured by the test. This would be wrong: without accommodations, the two scores of 30 do not have a comparable meaning. Ideally, with accommodations they would.

Thus the purpose of accommodations is not to help students score better but *to help them score as well as their actual proficiency warrants,* and not higher. In other words, their purpose is to improve validity, not to increase scores. However, this distinction is not always recognized. Some years ago, the special education director of a state that I will not name told me that all students, not just students with disabilities, should be offered accommodations. Fearing (correctly) that I knew the answer, I asked her why. "They would do better," she replied. That's a bit like saying that kids who don't want to go to school one day should have a chance to dip their fever thermometers into hot water before handing them to their parents.

The greatest problem in assessing students with disabilities well is that we often don't know which accommodations will offset the bias caused by the disability without giving the student an unfair advantage. Worse, there are instances in which the design of fully adequate accommodations may not even be feasible. To illustrate this, I'll use two cases. In the case of visual disabilities, which are very rare, we have a pretty good, although not perfect, idea of the accommodations we should provide. Learning disabilities, which are far more common, present much more formidable difficulties.

Several years ago, I had a student who had a rare and serious visual impairment, congenital achromatopsia. In people with normal eyes, vision under bright light is the function of cone photoreceptors, while vision under low-light conditions is handled by rod photoreceptors. People with achromatopsia lack normal cone vision and therefore must rely on rod photoreceptors under all lighting conditions. The consequences are poor visual acuity, an inability to adapt to bright lighting (rods saturate at relatively low levels of light), and varying degrees of color blindness. My student's condition was sufficiently serious that she was identified as legally blind, although she was not totally without sight.

Following her suggestions, I was able to provide a few accommodations to help her function well in class. I lowered the lighting, reserved her a seat that placed her with her back to the window and the best possible view of the screen on which I displayed slides, and gave her printed materials in much larger type. I tried to avoid writing or drawing on the board because she was unable to read what I wrote, but when I had to, a teaching assistant copied what I wrote and provided it to her. With these few accommodations, she was able to follow classes well.

My exams, however, which are standardized, were a problem for her. I present tests in printed form, and students type their answers directly onto computers in a brightly lit lab. She could not easily read the standard type, particularly in the bright light, and the font on the computer screen was too small for her to read. Under these standard conditions, her performance on the test would have been misleadingly low.

In response, we gave her the exam in an adjacent room with greatly reduced lighting. We provided a computer with a larger screen and software that allowed her to change the size of the typeface. The exam questions were loaded onto the computer so that she could read them using whatever size typeface was best for her. These were all violations of standardization, but in this case, the effect was unquestionably to make her score (a very high score, in the end) a more accurate portrayal of her actual mastery of the course content.

This story's happy ending, however, should not leave us sanguine about the general case. There were a number of reasons why we were able to accommodate this student effectively, and in most other cases, at least one of them does not obtain. We were helped by the level of resources I could bring to bear, which few public schools can match. There were other reasons for our success, however, that had nothing to do with resources and that are more important for the big picture. The student's disability had four characteristics that facilitated designing appropriate accommodations.

First, the student's disability—both the fact that she had a disability and *which specific disability she had*—was unambiguous. Second, her disability, while rare, was well understood, and its consequences for performance on a test administered under standard conditions seemed clear. Her symptoms fit the standard description of the syndrome to a tee, and her disability classification alone was sufficient to indicate several appropriate accommodations, such as large type and lowered illumination. This is no different from what often happens in medicine. You see a doctor because of symptoms, and the diagnosis is usually the key to effective treatment.

Third—and I cannot overstate the importance of this point—the impediment this student faced, her lack of visual acuity, was *unrelated to the content and skills the test was designed to measure*. In the ugly jargon of the trade, she faced "construct-irrelevant" barriers to performing well on the test. Therefore, the effects of the disability on her performance on the standard test were clearly bias: if given the exam in standard form, her score would imply a lower level of mastery than she had actually attained. If we could find an accommodation that would do nothing but offset this impediment, validity would be increased.

And that points to the fourth and final factor working in our favor: it seemed reasonably clear how to design practical accommodations to ameliorate the bias without biasing her scores in the other direction. For example, there was no reason to expect that lowering the lights or increasing the type size would have given her any unfair advantage.

Yet even in the case of visual disabilities, which are much easier to address with accommodations than some other disabilities, we may do less well than I did with this student, either under- or over-compensating for the disability. Some years ago, a blind student pointed out to researchers from the Educational Testing Service that simply presenting the text in braille may not fully level the playing field for certain types of tests. It is not uncommon for students to return to the text of a test item, particularly if it is long or complex, to extract specific information. For example, a complex mathematics task might require that you return to the prompt repeatedly for numerical data or to extract information from a graphic. This takes additional time for students who read braille, this one student claimed, because they cannot skim quickly and must go over the entire item or a large part of it more slowly to re-locate the information. The student maintained that this places them at a disadvantage, particularly if they do not receive additional time.[6]

I do not read braille and can't attest to the importance of this student's concern, but the problem of skimming does affect a good many students with disabilities or with limited proficiency in English, and it is a good example of the kinds of subtleties entailed in designing effective accommodations. Although this may not be obvious, fluent readers of English generally do not read letter by letter and instead often apprehend parts of words or entire words at a glance. (In fact, it is not practical to read English fluently letter by letter because pronunciation even of strings of letters varies from word to word; for example, contrast the last four letters of *through* with *enough*.) One indication of this is that rather than being stymied by incorrectly spelled words, as they would be if reading letter by letter, fluent readers can often easily understand them by substituting the correct letters quickly and sometimes without being aware of it. For example, the text in Figure 12.1 has been circulating on the Internet since at least 2003. Most of you who are native speakers of English will find this passage

Aoccdrnig to a rscheearch at Cmabrigde Uinervtisy, it deosn't mttaer in waht oredr the ltteers in a wrod are, the olny iprmoetnt tihng is taht the frist and lsat ltteer be at the rghit pclae. The rset can be a toatl mses and you can sitll raed it wouthit porbelm. Tihs is bcuseae the huamn mnid deos not raed ervey lteter by istlef, but the wrod as a wlohe.

FIG. 12.1. Text with letters scrambled in each word.

According to a research at Cambridge University, it doesn't matter in what order the letters in a word are, the only important thing is that the first and last letter be at the right place. The rest can be a total mess and you can still read it without problem. This is because the human mind does not read every letter by itself, but the word as a whole.

FIG. 12.2. Flipped but corrected text.

trivially easy to read, despite the scrambling of letters. There is much disagreement about whether it is the first and last letters of the misspelled words that enable us to do this, as the passage claims. But it is nonetheless clear that fluent native readers can apprehend entire words and very quickly compensate for errors in the text.[7]

Now, to simulate artificially what some nonfluent readers confront, look at Figure 12.2, which has all of the errors in this text corrected but has the text flipped horizontally. If you are like me, you found this correct but reversed text very difficult to read and were able to read it only very slowly. Those of you who have learned a language that uses an alphabet other than the Latin one used in English may have experienced a bit of déjà vu when you tried to read this; reading it is similar to the task of reading a truly unfamiliar orthography. The *letters* are only moderately difficult to recognize when reversed, but virtually none of the reversed *words* is recognizable at a glance, so we are reduced to reading the text letter by letter and then assembling the letters into words. This is analogous to the process used by many beginning readers and some older children with reading difficulties. It also may be analogous to the search process described to ETS by the student using braille.

An obvious response would be to allow additional time for students who have to read braille. Additional time is the most common accommodation offered in systems that administer tests with time limits. But how much time should be allowed? Offering too much additional time may run the risk of overcompensating—creating an unfair advantage—rather than merely leveling the playing field. In one recent case, a student sitting for a state bar examination, which is normally administered in eighteen hours over three days, requested and received nearly five times that amount of time spread over roughly two weeks. Is five times the normal amount enough to offset the effects of disability without conferring unfair advantage? Ten times?

A study two decades ago of the SAT and GRE scores of students with disabilities showed that this is not an abstract concern:

> Except for those from hearing-impaired students, SAT scores from . . . [administrations with accommodations] have a strong tendency to over-predict the college performance of students with disabilities. [That is, they score higher on the test than their subsequent performance in college would suggest is accurate.] This effect is strongest for relatively high-scoring learning disabled students. . . . One possible explanation . . . is . . . the policy of extending unlimited time to persons taking special test administrations. . . . There is some indication that gain occurs for students whose disability necessitates the extra time . . . but there is also an indication that more capable students are taking longer amounts of time.[8]

Notwithstanding the difficulties in getting accommodations exactly right for students with visual disabilities, this type of disability is still one of the easiest to accommodate. It is often far more difficult to choose accommodations that will create a reasonably unbiased estimate of proficiency. First, it is often unclear what specific disabilities students have, as evidenced by the chaotic patterns in classifications from state to state and among districts and schools within many states. And even when the disability is clear, the impediments it causes may not be.

The most fundamental difficulty, however, is that in some instances, the impediments caused by the disability are directly relevant to the knowledge and skills the test is intended to measure. In these cases, offsetting those barriers with accommodations can create an unfair advantage, potentially biasing scores in the other direction. This is not merely a difficult technical problem; in some instances, it may not be entirely feasible to create the reasonable accommodations called for by statute. The same may sometimes be true in testing students with limited proficiency in English as well. This is the primary reason for the pessimism with which I opened this chapter.

The problem of construct-relevant disabilities is perhaps clearest in the case of specific learning disabilities, which make up the largest classification of disabilities and account for roughly half of all students receiving services under IDEA. The most common learning disability, dyslexia, interferes with students' ability to read. "Reading" can mean several things, but for this purpose let's use a simple definition: the ability to decode and infer the meaning of printed text as commonly presented (for example, in books or newspapers). Dyslexia interferes with the processes entailed in decoding, such as differentiation of phonemes, but not the higher-order cognitive processes involved in reading, such as drawing inferences from text.

Now, to make this example as extreme as possible, consider tests of reading, which are mandated by NCLB and were ubiquitous beforehand anyway. These pose a truly vexing problem: we can't separate the impediments caused by the disability from the construct we are trying to measure. Absent accommodations, my student with achromatopsia would have done poorly on my test because she is unable to read small type, but that inability was entirely irrelevant to the constructs I was trying to measure with my test. This is not the case when a dyslexic student takes a reading test. His dyslexia impedes his ability to read the test well, but his reading proficiency is precisely what we are trying to gauge by testing him. There may be aspects of the task of reading that he performs better than his score indicates—for example, his weak decoding may obscure a solid ability to draw inferences from passages of text—but his overall proficiency in reading is poor, nonetheless, because he cannot decode well. And there is no obvious way to use accommodations appropriately. You could read the test to him or present it on tape, thus circumventing the dyslexia, but this would fundamentally change what the test measures. It would no longer measure "the ability to decode and infer the meaning of printed text as commonly presented." It would measure something else, perhaps "the ability to understand and draw inferences from oral speech." If you were an employer looking to fill a position that required substantial reading, which score would you consider a more valid basis for evaluating this student: the score obtained under standard conditions, where the student had to read the text, or the score obtained with this accommodation, which required only that the student comprehend oral speech?

You might venture that this example is too extreme, but in fact, educators and policymakers are now arguing about how best to administer reading tests to dyslexic students, and in any event, the problem is not limited to reading tests. The example used by the NRC panel mentioned earlier to illustrate this problem was mathematics tests. Many contemporary tests of mathematics strive to include realistic problems of the sort that students would encounter outside of school. Many of these tests entail a good bit of reading; some also require that students write explanations of

38. The planning committee at Lane Middle School is planning a pizza party for its 127 eighth-grade students. They got this menu from The Pizza Palace.

The planning committee took a survey of a random sample of 26 eighth-grade students by asking, "What kind of pizza do you want?" This is what they found.

The Pizza Palace

FREE DELIVERY

PIZZA IS OUR SPECIALTY

	Medium (Serves 4)	Large (Serves 6)
Cheese	$9.00	$11.00
Sausage	$9.75	$12.00
Pepperoni	$9.75	$12.00
Vegetarian	$9.50	$11.75

Favorite Kind of Pizza				
Kind of pizza	Cheese	Sausage	Pepperoni	Vegetarian
Number of students	7	3	9	7

The committee has a budget of $300 for the pizza. What kinds and sizes of pizzas could the committee order so that each of the 127 students can have his or her favorite kind of pizza?

a. Explain how you used the results of the survey to decide which pizzas to order.

b. Show or describe the calculations needed to be sure that there will be enough pizza for the 127 students.

c. Show or describe the calculations needed to be sure that the cost of the pizzas totals $300 or less.

You do not need to find the cheapest way to buy enough pizza. You only need to make sure that the total cost is $300 or less.

FIG. 12.3. An eighth-grade mathematics item requiring substantial reading and writing. From the 2000 Massachusetts MCAS assessment.

their answers. An example of such an item, taken from a middle-school mathematics test, is shown in Figure 12.3.

Clearly, the more reading and writing a math test requires, the more likely it is that the scores of dyslexic students will be adversely affected by their disabilities. But is this adverse effect a bias that should be offset by accommodations, or is it in fact a realistic indicator of lower proficiency? The answer, the NRC panel explained, is that it depends on the *specific inference* you base on the scores—that is, it depends on what you mean by "proficiency in mathematics." On the one hand, if you were using scores to estimate skills such as computational facility, the performance of dyslexic students on math tests that require substantial reading clearly would be biased downward, because their difficulties in reading would make it hard for them to demonstrate their computational skills. On the other hand, if you were using scores to estimate how well students can apply such skills to real-world problems of the sort they may encounter later, including mathematics problems embedded in text, the scores would be less biased. If one designed an accommodation that fully offset these students' reading difficulties, they would obtain misleadingly high scores, because their ability to apply math skills to real-world problems presented in text would be overestimated. Those on the NRC panel saw this as yet another example of the trade-offs involved in testing: they saw good reasons to include such realistic tasks in mathematics tests, but they recognized that the cost would be to make them problematic for some students with disabilities.

This problem was at the core of a disabilities-related case decided by the Supreme Court in 1979. A woman was denied admission to a training program in nursing because of a severe hearing disability. The reason given for her rejection was that she was unable to understand speech without lip reading and that this made it impossible for her perform adequately in the training program or to care safely for patients. She sued under Section 504 of the Rehabilitation Act of 1973, another federal statute that protects the rights of the disabled and that affects public K–12 education as well. The Supreme Court held for the school, arguing that the disability undermined the plaintiff's qualifications to function as a nurse. Had she been "otherwise qualified" (the statute's language) despite her disability, she would have prevailed.[9] In the jargon of testing, had the consequences of her disability been irrelevant to the construct (her functioning as a nurse), she would have had a better case, but in fact they were directly relevant to it.

The prevalence data noted in Table 12.1 make it clear that the cases in which the appropriate accommodations are ambiguous are numerous, and the clear-cut cases are the rare exception. In the 1999–2000 school year, for example, students with visual disabilities constituted less than half of one percent of students with disabilities and five hundredths of one percent (5 students per 10,000) of the school-age population. Students classified as having orthopedic impairments—another group for whom accommodations are reasonably clear—numbered 14 per 10,000 students. The big numbers are found for the groups that pose much more difficult problems—in particular, students with learning disabilities.

So image yourself as a member of an IEP team responsible for selecting appropriate assessment accommodations for a student with a disability. Let's assume that you have a student with a disability that that is problematic for testing, such as a learning disability. Where could you find guidance based on solid research evidence for determining how this child should be tested?

A logical first step would be to turn to your state's guidelines for assessing students. I don't know how often IEP teams do this, although data on the assignment of accommodations by practicing educators suggest that many don't pay the guidelines much heed. Indeed, under current law there is an incentive to ignore any restrictions implied by state guidelines because there are serious potential costs for failing to provide sufficient accommodations to improve scores (such as failing to make adequate yearly progress under NCLB) and few risks in providing excessive ones. Nonetheless, let's suppose you and your teammates carefully review the guidelines.

In many instances, you would still not have your answer. Although some states have produced carefully written and informative guidelines, they are insufficient to identify the appropriate accommodations for many students. For one thing, such guidelines are markedly inconsistent from state to state, and there are even cases in which one state explicitly permits an accommodation that another explicitly prohibits.[10] These conflicting guidelines can't all be right, so even if you follow your particular state's guidelines, you might happen to be in a state whose advice is wrong. Moreover, state guidelines are usually too general to solve your problem. For example, many warn IEP teams not to use accommodations that change the meaning of the test score or undermine validity, but they don't generally explain what that means in practice—for example, by outlining which specific accommodations would meet this goal for students with specific disabilities.

You might become ambitious and decide to explore the relevant research on your own. As someone who has carried out a bit of that work, I can assure you that you would be disappointed. There is not a great deal of it, some of it is not very good, and it leaves many of the most important questions unanswered. Indeed, the weak state of the research literature is one of the reasons that states' guidelines are not more useful than they are.

There are several reasons why the research is so unsatisfactory. One is simply that until recently, not many people toiled in this vineyard. Another is that it can be politically difficult to conduct certain types of high-quality work in this area. For example, late in the 1990s, I was twice able to obtain permission from a state superintendent to conduct true experimental tests of the effects of accommodations. For this purpose, true experiments, with subjects randomly assigned to treatments, are the gold standard, and only a handful of experiments have been conducted to evaluate accommodations. Both of my studies were undermined by midlevel managers in the state's education agency, well after work had started. The second time, I confronted one of the managers and insisted on an explanation. The study, he explained, was simply politically too risky.

Research in this field confronts three additional problems that are more fundamental. One is the chaotic classification of students' disabilities. Whatever the arguments against using classifications in choosing services for students, it is unarguable that they are important for assessment. It would be nonsensical, for example, to offer to a student with orthopedic limitations the accommodations I provided to my visually disabled student. As noted in the National Research Council study cited earlier:

> To design an accommodation that will increase the validity . . . of scores for students with disabilities, one must first identify the nature and severity of the distortions the accommodation will offset. These distortions depend on the disability. . . . Because disability classifications tell us who may have underlying functional characteristics that are linked to potential score distortions, ambiguities or inconsistencies in classifying students with disabilities have serious implications for assessments. . . . If classification of a disability is incorrect or imprecise, determining whether the accommodations selected are valid will be difficult.[11]

Let's say you want to determine the effectiveness of a new medication for multiple-drug-resistant tuberculosis, or MDR. Obviously, you would have to start with people who have MDR, and you would have to examine the effects of the medication on the symptoms caused by MDR. Similarly, if we want to examine how effectively a large-type presentation of a test works for students with visual disabilities, we have to start with students who have visual disabilities. Because the diagnostic criteria for most disabilities are so unclear and the resulting classifications so dramatically inconsistent, it is difficult to obtain reasonable samples and to generalize to similarly disabled students in the general population.

Another difficulty is that we rarely have a *criterion*—that is, a measure that we can trust enough to use it as a standard for evaluating the effects of various accommodations. Let's say, for example, that we want to find out how well two amounts of extra time—half again the normal time, and twice the normal time— offset the bias arising from a specific disability. So we administer the test three ways to three groups of similar students with this disability: one group has the standard amount of time, another has half again as much, and a third group has twice as much time. We find that the first group gets the lowest scores and the third gets the highest. Which of the three sets of scores is the most accurate? With what would you compare them to find out? For most K–12 testing, we lack a trustworthy standard with which to compare them.[*]

Finally, there is the particularly vexing problem of disabilities that create impediments related to the construct measured by the test—as, for example, when we need to gauge the achievement of students with dyslexia. This is at least as much a logical problem as a technical one, and in these cases we face a fundamental ambiguity in our interpretation of scores. Given this logical problem, it seems unlikely that research will point to a way to obtain scores from these students that are fully comparable to scores from other students. A more realistic if less satisfying goal would be to improve what we learn about these students, even if the information we glean is not entirely comparable to that about others. Consider again the problem of assessing students with dyslexia in mathematics when the assessment intentionally embeds mathematical skills in "real-world" contexts that entail reading and writing. It might be feasible to develop an assessment and a system of accommodations that would allow conclusions such as "this student has strong computational skills but is largely unable to apply them to problems involving text." This would be a very useful inference, but it would not allow us to say "a score of 143 from this student with disabilities indicates the same level of proficiency in mathematics—as we have defined it, to include applications to written problems—as the same score obtained by other students."

---

[*] An exception is college admissions tests. These are designed to predict performance in college, so we can use this performance—for example, freshman-year grades—as the criterion. This was done in an ETS study cited earlier (see page 295).

We face yet one more issue in assessing certain students with disabilities: deciding how to test very low performing students. Not all students with disabilities score poorly, of course, but over-all, students with disabilities are disproportionately represented at the low end of the distribution.

How should very low performing students, whether disabled or not, be tested? If the only concern is accurate measurement—and that is a very big "if," because testing has many goals—the answer is clear. The hypothetical vocabulary test in Chapter 2 provided a first hint. A test that is far too difficult provides very little informa-tion about the level of an examinee's performance. Confronted with a vocabulary test comprising words such as *siliculose,* most of us would have gotten all or virtually all items wrong. This would have given us a "floor effect": a bunch of scores piled up at or near the lowest possible score. Such an outcome would have told us that none of us knows the meaning of siliculose, but it would have given us no information about where we each fall on the continuum of vocabulary skills.

There are two different principles in play in this case. The first is simply that an achievement test ought to measure the content that students are actually studying or expected to study. If the mathematics lessons of a middle-school student with a severe cognitive disability are focused on number concepts and very ba-sic arithmetic, it will not be useful to give him a test in which he has to solve linear equations. Instead, we have to test such stu-dents differently from others, for example, by giving them a test designed for earlier grades. This principle may seem obvious, but it is often—increasingly often, as we shall see momentarily—ignored.

Second, even within a given domain of content, the difficulty of a test should be matched to the student's level of performance. The reason is reliability. All other things being equal, making a test either too hard or too easy for a person increases the amount of error and decreases reliability. In Chapter 7, I explained the standard error of measurement, the range of uncertainty that surrounds any test score. In practice, there is no single standard error. Rather, there are many: the margin of error for students for whom the test is appropriately difficult is smaller than those for higher- and lower-scoring students. This one reason that some tests, most notably the Graduate Record Examination taken by applicants to most graduate schools, are administered by computer. The GRE is a *computer-adaptive test* (often abbreviated CAT), in which the performance of students on early items leads to their being assigned either easier or more difficult items to better match their performance level. The result is a higher level of reliability because students are not wasting time on items that are too easy or difficult for them. When the mismatch between a student's proficiency and the difficulty of a test is severe—as is the case for some students with disabilities in many current assessment systems—the unreliability of scores becomes very large.

In fairness to the policymakers who have recently made what I consider bad decisions about testing low-performing students—including some with disabilities—determining how to test these students does pose a substantial dilemma. Optimal measurement is not the only concern. When a test is used for accountability, designing it to be psychometrically appropriate for low-scoring students may reduce incentives to raise those students' achievement. Given that many students with disabilities have traditionally been presented with an insufficiently demanding curriculum that severely limits their options for later education and work, this is a serious concern. Compounding this concern is the fact that achievement is a continuum. If one makes special allowances for students who are very far below average, what about those who perform a bit better? At what point is it no longer reasonable to hold students to a lower standard? These are not easy questions to answer.

Nonetheless, the decisions made under NLCB about assessing low-achieving students, while still evolving and gradually becoming less stringent, are draconian. The story, as it has emerged in a series of regulations and notices of proposed rulemaking (NPRMs), is baroque and requires that one distinguish among "alternate assessments," "alternate standards," and "modified standards." As noted earlier, IDEA requires that students too severely disabled to take a regular test, even with accommodations, be given an "alternate assessment." The law does not specify how many such children there are, but the general expectation is that there are few. A number that is commonly bandied about is 2 percent of all students, although I have not been able to ascertain where that number comes from.

The initial NPRM labeled lower standards "alternate standards" and allowed districts and states to apply these to only one half of one percent of students. The NPRM explicitly stated that "alternate standards" are distinct from the "alternate assessment" required by IDEA and that some students could take the latter while still be held to grade-level standards. The rationale capping the use of alternate standards at one half of one percent was originally also explicit: mildly retarded students should be held to grade-level standards. Only students with more severe cognitive disabilities than that—moderately, severely, and profoundly retarded students—would be eligible for lowered standards. The NPRM specifically identified these as students performing more than three standard deviations below the mean. Any students in excess of the one-half percent cap assessed with alternate standards would be automatically labeled "not proficient" for purposes of accountability (that is, for determining adequate yearly progress), thus putting the district at greater risk of sanctions. The final version of these regulations, published in December 2003, made a number of major changes. The cap was raised to 1 percent to allow for geographic variability in the prevalence of cognitive disabilities. The references to mental retardation and students more than three standard deviations below the mean were eliminated, in part because it was feared that this would result in excessive reliance on IQ tests to classify students. However, this appears to have been a matter of terminology, and the regulations retained the requirement that students with mild cognitive disabilities be assessed using regular standards.[12]

Just how draconian are these requirements? One way to put them into perspective is to consider what the lowest-scoring students held accountable to the regular standards are studying. Eighth-grade students with mild cognitive disabilities in a well-designed educational program could be expected to be reading at a fourth- or fifth-grade level and to have progressed in mathematics to the point of performing simple arithmetic. Yet under the provisions of NCLB, within twelve years such students must be achieving at the proficient standard, which the statute defines as a "level of high achievement" for the grade in which the student is studying.[13] No more simple arithmetic; now we are talking about prealgebra skills and application of arithmetic to reasonably complex problems, such as the eighth-grade mathematics item shown in Figure 12.3.

Normative information makes it even clearer how severe these requirements are. Let's say that states adopt proficiency standards comparable in difficulty to those in the National Assessment of Educational Progress, which many education reformers insist they should. As I noted in Chapter 4, roughly one-third of students in Japan and Korea would fail to reach NAEP's proficient standard if they were administered that assessment. Thus, the implementing regulations for NCLB imply that at the end of the twelve-year period specified by the statute, mildly retarded students in the United States should outscore roughly a third of the students in two of the highest-scoring countries ever to participate in international assessments of mathematics.

This might be called the Little Engine That Could approach to variations in student performance, an extreme form of the myth of the vanishing variance I noted in Chapter 6.[14] To expect mildly retarded students to outperform the entire bottom third of students in the highest-scoring countries in the world, and to expect this to happen in twelve years, no less, is remarkably naive. I have no doubt that the motivation for this mandate is good, an attempt to force schools to attend more to the achievement of students with disabilities. This stands in contrast to earlier federal requirements that focused primarily on procedural issues, such as the appropriate classroom placements for students. Nonetheless, as a former special education teacher, I consider the extremity of the requirements unfair to teachers and cruel to students, because it forces them to take tests on which they cannot be successful and to be labeled as failures even if they are working well relative to their capabilities.

I'll offer one example to make this concrete. During my time as a special education teacher, one of my jobs was to teach remedial reading. It was beyond a doubt the most difficult teaching I have ever undertaken, and I don't think I was very good at it. I had students in the fifth grade who were reading at the second-grade level. In very approximate terms, they were acquiring reading skills at perhaps one-third the average rate. Now suppose I had managed to *double* the rate at which they gained these skills, which would have been a noteworthy success for both me and my students. The students would have gone from being far behind grade level to modestly behind, and they and I, under the new rules, would have been failures.

Two years after the publication of these regulations, the U.S. Department of Education published another NPRM that would make the requirements somewhat less stringent; these were finalized in April of 2007.[15] The revised regulations acknowledged that there are other students beyond the 1 percent whose disabilities make it impractical to expect them to reach grade-level proficiency even with the best instruction, and it allows states to apply "modified achievement standards" in testing a maximum of an additional 2 percent of students. These modified standards would reflect "reduced breadth or depth of *grade level content*" (emphasis added).[16] How this would work in practice is a puzzle. In subjects in which the curriculum is cumulative, such as reading and basic math, most low-achieving students will fail to keep pace with their agemates and will eventually end up studying below-grade material.

The specifics of the regulations, however, are far less important than the fundamental dilemma that they highlight: the difficulty of deciding how best to test low-achieving students. On the one hand, I and many others consider the current drive to improve the performance of low-scoring students essential and long overdue. This requires that higher standards be imposed for these students. At the same time, even if we were to succeed in this respect, we will still confront a very wide distribution of performance. The dilemma is to find a way to meet the goal of confronting unwanted variations in performance while still being realistic about the variations that will persist.

Students with Limited English Proficiency

The issues that arise in testing students with limited proficiency in English are in some ways strikingly similar to those we face in assessing students with disabilities. But there are a number of important differences as well.

My own experience living in Israel and having limited Hebrew proficiency can illustrate this, although one has to go beyond my embarrassing gaffes and boring speech. Another limitation of my proficiency, more relevant to this discussion, was that I would have performed very poorly on Hebrew-language tests. I understood this at the time, because I was thinking about doing graduate work in Israel and knew full well that I did not have the mastery of the language needed for serious study. But my language limitations became even clearer to me recently, when I gave a series of seminars in Jerusalem on testing issues and had occasion to review several forms of the PET, the Hebrew-language college admissions test that is analogous in many ways to the SAT. Had I taken the PET back then without any accommodations, I would have ended up with an appallingly low score. There would have been many items that I would not have been able to read at all, and many others that I could have read only with a great deal of additional time.

With this background, let's suppose I had taken the PET and then applied to an Israeli university. What should the admissions officers have concluded about me based on my dismal score?

If they had inferred that I lacked the mathematical and other cognitive skills needed for university-level study, they would have been wrong. If this were the intended inference, then the score I would have obtained without accommodations would have been biased, and badly so. Suppose that the admissions officers wanted an answer to a similar question: whether, with additional time and language study, I could be a competent student in a Hebrew-language university program. In this case as well, my score would have been downwardly biased, giving them much too bleak an answer.

Now suppose they wanted to answer a third question: whether I was *at that time, and with the proficiency I had then,* likely to be successful in Hebrew-language university study. In that case, my low score would have been right on the money: I would have been a weak student indeed.

What is the distinction between the first two questions, for which my score would have been biased, and the third, for which it would not have been? The issue is the same as that which arises in testing students with disabilities: whether the impediment—

stemming from a disability or from limited proficiency in the language of testing is relevant to the question the score is used to answer. Using the PET without accommodations to evaluate my math skills would have been analogous to my administering my exam without accommodations to the student with achromatopsia. The reasons for my doing poorly on the PET and her doing poorly on my exam would not have been relevant to the inference that is based on the test scores, and therefore the scores would have been biased. Using the PET without accommodations to evaluate whether I had *at that time* the capability to do well in Hebrew-language university study is more nearly analogous to assessing a dyslexic student in reading. For answering those questions, my limited proficiency in Hebrew and the student's dyslexia are relevant to what we are trying to measure.

Now suppose that I had taken the PET in English (they do have translated forms) or with some other accommodations to offset my limited proficiency in Hebrew. (I don't think any other accommodations would have sufficed, but for the sake of discussion, suppose that some would.) Then, my accommodated score would have provided a better answer to the first question: I had the cognitive skills needed for university study, even though my Hebrew was primitive. But by the same token, my accommodated score would have provided an *upwardly* biased score for purposes of the third question—that is, it would have provided far too optimistic a prediction of how I would have fared in the university that year.

This example makes it clear that there are several important similarities in testing students with disabilities and students with limited proficiency in English. One is that there is not always one "right" way to assess these students. How they should best be tested—whether translations should be used, whether accommodations should be offered, and so on—depends on the inferences the scores will be used to support. And we must be much more specific about the intended inferences than we often are. It is not enough to refer to "mathematics proficiency" or "readiness for university study."

Also, in testing both groups, we confront impediments that are both irrelevant and relevant to the constructs we are trying to measure. When these barriers are irrelevant—as was the case for my student with achromatopsia—we can try to offset them with accommodations. When the impediments are relevant to what we are trying to measure—as in the case of a reading test administered to a dyslexic student—we face a logical problem, not a merely technical one, and accommodations are unlikely to solve it fully.

There are a few other important similarities between these two groups of students. One is that the research exploring how best to test them is still limited. In recent years, a number of people have been studying both the effects of accommodations for LEP students and aspects of test design that might lessen the construct-irrelevant barriers they face. For example, by avoiding unnecessary complexity of language in mathematics tests, such as the use of the passive voice, complex tenses, rarely used words, or excessively idiomatic phrases, one might be able to lessen the difficulties LEP students face. This research, however, is still sparse.

An anecdote from one of my classes underscores the problem of idiomatic speech. One year, more than half of the students in an advanced methods course I teach were foreign students. By any reasonable definition, they were all quite fluent in English; after all, they were successfully pursuing graduate studies at Harvard with no special support. One day, in the middle of class, I saw a student from Chile lean over and whisper something to the student next to her, who was from Brazil but was also fluent in Spanish. She in turn leaned to the student next to her, who was from Venezuela, and whispered something. The Venezuelan student (who, as it happens, has since studied the effects of linguistic complexity of mathematics test items on the performance of LEP students) leaned across two native speakers to whisper something to a student from Mexico. At that point, I decided it was time to stop the class, and I asked the first student what the problem was. She gave me with a very puzzled look and said, "What does it *mean* when you say that something 'is small potatoes'?" I had not even realized that I had used the idiom. No competent test author would use that phrase in a mathematics test item, but we do routinely use more subtle complexities of language that as native speakers we do not even perceive. For example, we face the problem of *polysemy*—the multiple, unrelated meanings many words have. Native speakers easily shift among them and realize, for example, that "cutting a price" means "reducing a price," not cutting as with a knife. Second-language speakers find this much more difficult, as they often know only the more common meanings of a word.

And one final similarity: LEP students, like students with disabilities, are a heterogeneous group in that they speak literally hundreds of native languages from many fundamentally different language groups. For example, even though German is a far more inflected language than English, its tense structures are quite similar, and I found them easy to learn. In contrast, Hebrew has fewer tenses but a variety of other verb "constructions" that have no parallel in English. And Chinese uses no tenses at all. It is likely that the difficulties LEP students face in taking English examinations may differ depending on the structure of their native language. For example, there is some research that shows that substituting words with Latinate roots for words with Germanic roots makes test items easier for native speakers of Spanish—hardly a surprising finding—but this would not likely be of much help for a native speaker of Korean, which shares no roots with either language. However, research investigating the effects of these differences on test performance is barely in its infancy.

There are important differences between the two groups of

students as well. One is that the problem of construct-relevant barriers to performance on tests affects all LEP students on many tests, while it is a serious problem only for a subset of students with disabilities. A second difference is that while many disabilities are persistent, the difficulties faced by some LEP students—the ones who really are English language learners—will decrease over time. They may never disappear entirely, and we don't know a great deal about how quickly some of them lessen, but it is clear that most students who have been in the United States for some years fare much better than they did as newcomers.

We face truly daunting obstacles in attempting to test students with disabilities and students with limited proficiency in English. In some cases, test scores can support only limited conclusions about proficiency—more limited than we would like—and in others, we simply cannot, at this time, obtain good scores. Yet these difficulties are not a reason to throw in the towel. If we use tests carefully, remaining aware of the limitations inherent in testing these groups, we can obtain useful information about the students' performance, even if that information is somewhat more limited and ambiguous than we would like. And similarly, if we are sufficiently careful, testing can foster substantial educational benefits for these students. At the same time, ignoring or downplaying the unavoidable problems in testing these students will result in misleading information and will run the risk of harming precisely the students we aim to help.

Chapter 13

Sensible Uses of Tests

YOU CAN NOW UNDERSTAND the student I mentioned in Chapter 1—the one who said in class that she was "so damned frustrated" by the steady loss, day by day, of simple and straightforward answers about testing. You may recall my response to her: that the purpose of learning about these initially discouraging issues was to cobble together a more reasonable understanding of testing, one that would allow her and her fellow students to use tests more productively. I maintained that without an understanding of the core principles and concepts of testing, one cannot fully make sense of the information tests provide or reach sensible resolutions of the many intense debates about testing in our schools.

The risk of misunderstanding test scores should be clear enough by now, but how can one apply the principles described in this book to interpret scores well and to make better decisions about using tests? There is no single recipe, of course, because tests have many different uses and are employed in many different contexts. Nonetheless, there are some general guidelines we can follow.

Let's start with what an end-user of test scores—a parent, a writer, an educator, a taxpayer—can do to interpret scores sensibly and thus get the most useful information from them and avoid serious misunderstandings. A test, even a very good one, is always just a test: a valuable source of information, but still only a limited and particular view of student performance. With that in mind, what factors that might threaten the specific inference you need? How can you address them in a way that gives you a conclusion you can trust?

The list of threats to the conclusions commonly based on test scores—threats to validity—is long. Some of the big ones:

- There is measurement error, to start, which creates a band of uncertainty around each student's score.

- When we are concerned with aggregates, such as the average score or percent proficient in a school, there is sampling error as well, which causes meaningless fluctuations in scores from one group of students to another and from one year to the next. This is a particularly serious problem for small groups—for example, when tracking the performance of small schools or, even more problematic, the performance of groups of students within a school.

- The results we rely on are sometimes specific to a given test. Different choices of content, different methods of scoring, different item formats, even different mathematical methods for scaling a test can produce somewhat different patterns of scores.

- Different ways of reporting performance do not always paint the same picture. This is a particular concern in the light of the current reliance on standards-based reporting, which is one of the worst ways to report performance on tests and is sometimes simply misleading.

- Potential bias should always be a concern, especially when assessing certain groups of students, such as those with disabilities or limited proficiency in English.
- The current ubiquitous and intense pressure to raise scores creates the potential for seriously inflated scores.

How can one avoid being tripped up by such a long list of potential problems? First, be careful about the inference one draws. Second, look for additional information. Let's consider some specific cases.

In Chapter 5, I discussed international comparisons of test scores, which have become a tremendously powerful influence on the public debate and on policy, not only in the United States but also in many other nations around the world. What seems to interest people the most is the horse race, the ranking of countries in terms of their students' performance. These rankings are often expressed in terms of an "international mean." Most often, the conclusions based on the data are somewhat vague, referring only in general terms to proficiency or performance in an entire subject area, such as mathematics. Take this description from the *New York Times* of results from the Trends in International Mathematics and Science Study: "Eighth-grade students in the United States scored better in both mathematics and science last year than in 1999, but still lagged their peers in a number of other industrial countries."[1] Or this description of an earlier round of TIMSS, from a U.S. Department of Education Web site: "In 1999, U.S. eighth-graders exceeded the international average of 38 nations in mathematics and science."[2] Note that these descriptions refer only to proficiency in mathematics, not to any specific mix of mathematical content or skills. There is nothing in these statements to imply, for example, that the much greater representation of algebra in this assessment than in the other main international assessment, PISA, was either appropriate or undesirable. What threats to these inferences are most important?

To start, the notion of an "international mean" is useless. The average can vary markedly from survey to survey, depending on the mix of nations participating in the survey. As I pointed out in Chapter 5, the United States was above the national mean in one part of a TIMSS report and below it in another part of the *same* report—because the two sections made use of different samples of nations. Thus the first step is to ignore statements about nations' performance relative to "the international mean" and concentrate instead on specific comparisons that are likely to be the most informative. For example, it may be useful to contrast the performance of American students to that of students in the high-scoring countries of East Asia, or to compare students in our country with those in more similar countries, such as England and Australia. However, that is only a first step. Once that is done, how can we put ourselves on safe ground?

In the case of international comparisons, sampling error is one of the easiest threats to tackle. The surveys used to compare student performance across countries—most notably, the TIMSS and PISA surveys—address sampling error carefully. If we just want to compare averages, we can put sampling error aside so long as the differences among the means are large enough to be statistically significant, and the reports tell us which ones are.

Another concern is more threatening: results that are specific to the one test you happen to be using. I showed in Chapter 5 that the PISA and TIMSS tests rank countries quite differently, and even changes in the emphasis given to the content areas included in either one of the tests will change the rankings to a modest degree. It is therefore prudent to ignore small differences, which are the least likely to be consistent across different tests or even different weightings of content areas within a single test. The fact that a difference is statistically significant is not protection enough, because the calculation of statistical significance does not take into account variations in results across tests.* You are a lot safer concluding that the United States lags behind Japan than inferring that our students perform better than those in Slovenia. The difference between the United States and Slovenia was statistically significant in the 2003 TIMSS, but it was one-sixth the size of the gap between the United States and Japan.

You are safer, but still not entirely safe. Occasionally, even large differences turn out not to be consistent from one test to another. In the 2003 TIMSS assessment of eighth-grade mathematics, Norway scored far below the United States. The difference was by any reasonable standard very large, about two-thirds as large as the gap between the United States and Japan. Yet in the PISA assessment of the same year, Norway outscored the United States, not by a very large amount, but by enough that the difference was statistically significant. Several factors could have contributed to this striking disparity in the results, including differences in test content, age level (the PISA students were about two years older), and the construction of the sample (TIMSS sampled by grade in school, while PISA sampled by age). But regardless, the many people who treat either one of these assessments as the definitive answer, the "correct" summary of the relative achievement of nations in "mathematics" (without any qualifier about the mix of content implied by "mathematics"), would be on very thin ice.

---

* A note here for the technically oriented reader: in most statistical reports, statistical significance takes only sampling error into account. In some of the most sophisticated assessments—the National Assessment of Education Progress was a pioneer in this respect—the calculation of statistical significance takes into account both sampling and measurement error. However, measurement error arises from fluctuations in performance across alternative tests of the *same* design, such as alternative forms of the SAT. Our concern here is different: variations in performance across tests of *different* designs, such as differences between the TIMSS and PISA tests.

And this points out one of the best ways to avoid misusing test data: don't treat any single test as providing the "right," authoritative answer. Ever. When possible, use more than one source of information about achievement—results from additional tests, or information from other sources entirely. With data from several sources—PISA, several iterations of TIMSS, and a few earlier international studies—we can see that there is little doubt: the United States always scores far below Japan, even though it does not always score above Norway.

When additional data are unavailable—unfortunately, an all too common situation today—you have to turn back to approach number one: be careful about your conclusion. Hedge your bets. Consider the information from the single test as just one snapshot of performance, necessarily incomplete and probably modestly different from that which you would obtain if you had another, also reasonable measure. This is true even when your test is a very good one. A more accurate way to phrase the conclusion above offered by the *New York Times* would have been: "Eighth-grade students in the United States scored better in mathematics in 1999, as mathematics was measured by the TIMSS test." This would not help most readers of the *Times*—they would have no idea what the caveat means—but that is the qualification that you should keep in mind.

With additional data or without, you should hedge your bets in another way as well: by avoiding spurious precision. Take the gap between the United States and Japan. It always appears, and it is always large, but it is not always exactly the same size. It is safe to conclude that "in eighth-grade mathematics, the average score in Japan is generally far above that in the United States, typically by nearly a full standard deviation." It is not safe to conclude that "the mean difference in eighth-grade mathematics between the United States and Japan is 0.83 standard deviation" (the 2003

TIMSS result). The latter, more specific estimate is justified only if you want to burden yourself with a more specific and less interesting inference: "the mean difference in eighth-grade mathematics between the United States and Japan, *specifically on TIMSS in 2003,* was estimated to be 0.83 standard deviation, with a margin of error of . . ."

Consider an example that is more controversial than interpreting international comparisons: making sense of the results of the state-mandated tests now used to hold teachers—and often students—accountable. Sharp increases in scores are widespread, and they are almost always presented as straightforward and trustworthy indicators that students' achievement has improved apace. But is that inference warranted?

Sampling error is more of a concern in this case than in interpreting international surveys. Statewide results reflect the performance of many students, so sampling error is not a major threat to them. However, many of the inferences that matter are about smaller groups: students within one grade level in a single school or, more extreme, the subgroups of students whose performance must be reported separately under the requirements of No Child Left Behind, such as the students with limited English proficiency within a given grade in a single school. These results often rest on a small number of observations. Figure 7.3 in Chapter 7 shows that even if subgroups are not reported separately, the performance of small schools is highly unstable, and the performance of subgroups is typically far more erratic. So you should pay little attention to year-to-year changes for small groups, even for entire schools, and instead look for trends over several years. Unfortunately, you are unlikely to see data presented this way in the papers, or even on the Web sites of most state education departments. The burden will usually fall to you.

As important as the problem of sampling error is, however, it is not the elephant in the room. The most serious threat to the validity of inferences from high-stakes tests is the risk of score inflation. Granted, there is not a great deal of research addressing this problem. Nevertheless, the research we do have shows that scores on high-stakes tests can quickly become inflated, often by a very large amount. The best advice based on research available now is that you should not take improvements in scores on high-stakes tests at face value. They may be a sign of real gains by students, but they cannot be trusted until they are confirmed by other data. These might be data from other achievement tests (for example, the NAEP, or a second, lower-stakes test administered by the district or state) or from different sources, such as college admissions tests and rates of assignment to remedial classes at the postsecondary level. Be especially wary of huge and very rapid gains, which are increasingly common.

This is just another case of relying on more than a single measure of achievement, but with a twist. In the case of international assessments, we need to be careful about alternative tests providing somewhat different views of performance at any one time. In the case of state tests, the analogue to the risk of differences between the PISA and TIMSS tests is the risk that, if a state hired two vendors to write new tests, the two tests might rank students, schools, or districts somewhat differently. The problem of score inflation is different. Even if two tests *initially* provide similar results, they may not continue to do so once the effects of high stakes are felt.

This is precisely what happened in Kentucky in the 1990s. When the state introduced its high-stakes high school test, the state's Department of Education showed that there was a moderately high degree of consistency between the results of that test and the those of the ACT, which is the primary college-admissions test used in Kentucky, and assured parents that "it is not overly presumptuous to assume that increased learning that leads to improvement on one is likely to lead to improvement on the other."[3] Not overly presumptuous, perhaps, but certainly overly optimistic. In actual fact, there was no consistency in the *change over time* shown by the two tests: mathematics scores on the state test rose very rapidly, while scores on the ACT mathematics test did not improve at all.

Let's say you are interested in learning how much student achievement has improved overall in your state or, more specifically yet, whether any progress has been made in narrowing the performance gap between racial and ethnic groups. You look up the data—or simply encounter it in the morning paper—and discover that everything is presented in terms of the percentage of students reaching or exceeding some performance standard, most likely the "proficient" standard. In Chapter 8, I sketched out a number of reasons why this is a flawed way of reporting performance—it obscures a great deal of information, exaggerates the importance of other information, and distorts comparisons of trends in performance between higher- and lower-scoring groups of students. Let's leave aside for the moment the previous problem, which is that the percentages labeled proficient may be severely exaggerated. What can you do to avoid the problems inherent in standards-based reporting?

One option is to hunt for an alternative form of reporting, one that is more informative and less likely to distort the trends that interest you. Many states have more reasonable scales but don't report them—or give them little emphasis—because of both the requirements of NCLB and the widespread, if misplaced, enthusiasm for standards-based reporting. In fact, many states need these better scales; they are what their psychometricians use to place the standards at comparable levels of difficulty from one year to the next, as the specific test forms are changed. So with a bit of digging, you may be able to get scale scores that would provide you with a better comparison of trends among groups. And if you are ambitious and are willing to do a little hand calculation, you may even be able to get the standard deviations of those scales, which would let you put all of the differences and changes that interest you into fractions of a standard deviation, thus making them roughly comparable to all sorts of other data. The state or local education agency may even have calculations of that sort or be willing to provide them.

But say that there are no scale scores to be found, or at least none that anyone wants to give you. What then? Absent some mathematical techniques that are too complex to present here, there is nothing you can do to undo the distortions that standards-based reporting can create. Nonetheless, you can still avoid the other major pitfall of standards-based reporting: interpreting standards to mean more than they do.

Keep in mind what performance standards are—and are not. They are just cut scores on a continuum of performance. Newspapers and press releases from education departments will often present the findings as if they portray a few qualitatively distinct groups, such as students who are "proficient" and students who are not. But there are only trivial differences between students just above and just below a standard, and there can be huge differences among students who fall between two of the standards and who are therefore assigned the same label. Moreover, the process of setting standards, while arcane and seemingly "scientific," is not a way of revealing some underlying truth about categories of student achievement. The methods used are just a very complicated way of using judgment to decide which score is high enough to warrant the label "proficient."

To help yourself avoid overinterpreting performance standards, you could try relabeling them for yourself. Rather than calling them below basic, basic, proficient, and advanced—labels that carry a lot of unwarranted freight—try thinking of them as four merely arbitrary levels of performance, say, level 1, level 2, level 3, and level 4. Proponents of standards-based reporting might say that this suggestion is over the top and that the standards are in some way tied to descriptions of what kids actually can do. There is some truth to that claim, but the uncomfortable fact is that the various methods used to set the performance standards can be strikingly inconsistent. Some of the students who are "proficient" when one method is used will not be proficient when another is tried, even if the definitions of proficient are identical. Moreover, most of the methods employed are quite far removed from examining actual work by real students. There is no reason to expect that if you and your friends lined up 100 students in order, ranging from the lowest-performing to the highest, and examined their work, you would end up placing a "proficient" cut anywhere near where your state education department placed it by using the bookmark method, the modified Angoff method, or any other. I think you are more likely to be misled by taking the descriptions of standards at face value than by treating the standards as arbitrary classifications.

Finally, what can you do about the ubiquitous attempts to use scores as a simple indicator of school effectiveness or quality? Try the Nancy Reagan approach: "Just say no." There are three distinct reasons why scores on one test, taken by themselves, are not enough to tell you which schools are good and which bad. The first is that even a very good achievement test is necessarily incomplete and will leave many aspects of school quality unmeasured. Some hard-core advocates of high-stakes testing disparage this argument as "anti-testing," but it is a simple statement of fact, one that has been recognized within the testing profession for generations.

The second reason not to assume that higher scores necessarily identify better schools is that, in the current climate, there can be very large differences among schools in the amount of score inflation. Some schools take more shortcuts than others in the race to raise scores, and the papers are full of implausible stories about schools that have made huge improvements in a short time.

The third and perhaps most important reason scores cannot tell you whether a school is good or bad is that schools are not the only influence on test scores. Other factors, such as the educational attainment and educational goals of parents, have a great impact on students' performance. Separating the impact of school quality from the powerful effects of the many out-of-school influences on achievement is a very difficult task, and it can't be done with the data typically available to school systems. The result: one can safely assume neither that the schools with the largest score gains are in fact improving the most rapidly nor that those with the highest scores are the best.

So how should you use scores to help you evaluate a school? Start by reminding yourself that scores describe some of what students can do, but they don't describe all they can do, and *they don't explain why they can or cannot do it.* Use scores as a starting point, and look for other evidence of school quality—ideally not just other aspects of student achievement but also the quality of instruction and other activities within the school. And go look for yourself. If students score well on math tests but appear bored to tears in math class, take their high scores with a grain of salt, because an aversion to mathematics will cost them later in life, even if their eighth-grade scores are good.

This list is only illustrative. You may want to use scores for an entirely different purpose, one for which the most important risks of misinterpretation are somewhat different from those above. For example, many teachers want diagnostic information about the relative strengths and weaknesses of their students' performance. (Am I more successfully teaching them to compute than to apply mathematics to problems?) When I was in school, a primary function of testing was to provide information of this sort, and for obvious reasons many teachers still want it, even if the political world is much more interested in simple summary judgments of students' overall level of performance. This use of test score raises a different problem: are the differences in performance between different parts of the test sufficiently reliable that they can be used as a basis for changing instruction?

The task of interpreting test scores well is a bit like playing jazz. The key to improvisation is knowing the chord changes. The principles explained in the previous chapters are the chord changes, and you need to do the improvisation, thinking carefully about the threats to the inferences you want to make and about how best to keep yourself on safe ground.

These principles have also have implications for those who control or would like to influence the design of testing programs in their schools. The first piece of advice I would offer those making decisions about testing is to avoid unrealistic expectations. This might be called the Rolling Stones principle: "You can't always get what you want . . . and if you try sometime, you find you get what you need." Unrealistic expectations about testing are everywhere. They seem to rest on an inconsistent, even paradoxical view of the complexities of measurement and of the advice offered by people like me. On the one hand, the complexities of testing are widely discounted, and the complications raised by experts are often derided as being too arcane to matter. But on the other hand, there seems to be a widespread faith in the wizardry of psychometrics, a tacit belief that no matter what policymakers and educators want a test to do, we can somehow figure out how to make it work.

One widespread unreasonable expectation is that a test created for one purpose will do just fine for many others. But a single test cannot serve all masters. Remember: a test is a small sample of a large domain. Charged with the task of creating one of these samples, people in my field should design the test to best serve the most important goals of those requesting it. Test design and construction entail a long series of trade-offs and compromises. Invariably, serving one master well means serving others more poorly. A test optimized to provide information about groups, for example, is not optimal for providing scores for individual students. That is why the National Assessment of Educational Progress cannot provide scores for individuals. A test that is constructed of a small number of large, complex tasks in an effort to assess students' proficiency in solving complex problems will be poorly suited to identifying narrow, specific skills that the students have nor have not successfully mastered. I could give many other examples.

Decision makers should determine what goals are most important for a test and then accept the fact that the result will cost them in terms of other goals. This unwelcome advice is widely ignored, and the consequences can be substantial. Consider the NCLB requirement that nearly all students, regardless of their level of performance, be assessed using the same tests. Whatever the political virtues of this requirement, it is bad measurement: we know that one cost of designing a test so that it does a good job of measuring the performance of high achievers is that it will do a poorer job with low achievers, and vice versa. To obtain valid and reliable information about what students are learning, we need to focus tests on their levels of performance and on the content that they are actually studying.

Further examples of unrealistic expectations are those spelled out in laws and regulations for testing students with special needs—those with disabilities or limited proficiency in English. These regulations hold that we should provide such students with "appropriate accommodations," and often the expectation is that, with these accommodations, the students' scores students will be comparable in meaning to those obtained by others. But there are limits to our ability to make the scores obtained by some students with special needs truly comparable. In part this reflects a dearth of research and development, but sometimes the problems are logical, not technical. In those cases, there are limitations on the inferences we can safely draw about the students, with or without testing accommodations. This is not a reason to exclude these students from testing, and it is certainly not an argument against further research to help us assess them better. The students and their teachers would be better served, however, if we frankly acknowledged the limitations of what we can do, interpreted the students' scores appropriately, and tailored our educational responses accordingly.

In some instances, the performance targets used in large-scale testing programs are also unrealistic. The notion that we can figure out what "proficient" students should be able to do and then require schools to get them there has its appeal, but as previous chapters have showed, the way that this is now done can be a house of cards. If we are going to continue to use tests to set performance goals for teachers and schools, we need to find better ways of doing so, approaches that reflect realistic and practical expectations for improvement. To do that, we must use empirical data to set targets, not vague ideals made up of whole cloth. These data might include historical data about rates of change, evaluations of exemplary programs, or data about exemplary schools. And in setting goals, we need to recognize that wide variations in performance are a human universal, something that our educational system would have to address even if we had the political will and the means to reduce the glaring social inequities that plague our educational system and our society.

A related bit of advice: just as I advise users of test scores not to rely on performance standards for interpreting student performance, I urge those in control of testing programs not to force users to do so. "Percent above proficient" is an arbitrary number. It obscures a great deal of information, and trends in this percentage can be seriously misleading. If it is important to set some standards to reflect expectations, then do so, but don't deprive users of the data from other forms of reporting that are more informative and less prone to distortions. Report standards alongside data in more useful forms, such as scale scores and percentiles.

A final, and politically unpalatable, piece of advice: we need to be more realistic about using tests as a part of educational accountability systems. Systems that simply pressure teachers to raise scores on one test (or one set of tests in a few subjects) are not likely to work as advertised, particularly if the increases demanded are large and inexorable. They are likely instead to produce substantial inflation of scores and a variety of undesirable changes in instruction, such as an excessive focus on old tests, an inappropriate narrowing of instruction, and a reliance on teaching test-taking tricks.

I strongly support the goal of improved accountability in public education. I saw the need for it when I was myself an elementary school and junior high school teacher, many years ago. I certainly saw it as the parent of two children in school. Nothing in more than a quarter century of education research has led me to change my mind on this point. And it seems clear that student achievement must be one of the most important things for which educators and school systems should be accountable. However, we need an effective system of accountability, one that maximizes real gains and minimizes bogus gains and other negative side effects. We need a system analogous to an FDA-approved drug: both effective and safe. All that we have seen so far tells us that the simple test-based accountability systems we use now do not meet this standard.

While this caution about simple test-based accountability is viewed in today's education policy world as extreme, it is anything but. Both the gaming of the system that we have seen in numerous studies and the resulting bias in the measure used for account-ability—in this case, score inflation—are predicted by economic theory. We have seen these problems arise in any number of other fields, areas as diverse as health care, environmental regulation, job training programs, and crime statistics. In fact, as noted in Chapter 10, the distortion that arises when one measure is used for accountability is so common that it has come to be known as Campbell's law, after an expert in program evaluation who wrote about it more than three decades ago.[4] There is no reason to expect test-based accountability education to be exempt from Campbell's law, and the research evidence indicates that it is not.

Advocates of current test-based accountability systems often counter by arguing, "So what if the gains are distorted? What matters is that students learn more, and if we get that, we can live with some distortion." Hypothetically, yes, we could live with it if we knew that students were in fact learning more and if the distortions were small enough that they did not seriously mis-lead people and cause them to make incorrect decisions. But in fact, we don't really know how much—or whether—the real learning of students has changed as a result of these programs. Because so many people consider test-based accountability sys-tems to be self-evaluating—they assume that if scores are increas-ing, we can trust that kids are learning more—there is a disturbing lack of good evaluations of these systems, even after more than three decades of high-stakes testing. And as I noted in Chapter 10, such evidence as there is does not leave me sanguine. What we do know is that score inflation can be enormous, more than large enough to seriously mislead people. Moreover, we usually cannot distinguish between real and bogus gains. As a result, we don't know which schools to reward, punish, or emulate. This allows the adults in the game to declare success, leaving only the stu-dents behind.

In all, educational testing is much like a powerful medication. If used carefully, it can be immensely informative, and it can be a very powerful tool for changing education for the better. Used indiscriminately, it poses a risk of various and severe side effects. Unlike powerful medications, however, tests are used with little independent oversight. Let the buyer beware.

Notes

Acknowledgments

Index

Notes

1. If Only It Were So Simple

1. J. Hassell, "Bush Hints at Compromise on Standardized Test Plan," *Seattle Times,* March 15, 2001.
2. Stephen P. Klein et al., *What Do Test Scores in Texas Tell Us?* Issue Paper IP-202 (Santa Monica, CA: Rand, 2000).

2. What *Is* a Test?

1. F. J. Fowler, "How Unclear Terms Affect Survey Data," *Public Opinion Quarterly* 56, no. 2 (1992): 218–231.
2. H. J.Parry and H. M. Crossley, "Validity of Responses to Survey Questions," *Public Opinion Quarterly* 14, no. 1 (1950): 16–80.
3. Andrew Biemiller, "Oral Comprehension Sets the Ceiling on Reading Comprehension," *American Educator* 27 (Spring 2001): 23.
4. Massachusetts Department of Education, *2005 MCAS Technical Report* (Malden, MA: Massachusetts Department of Education, 2006).
5. "Test Scores Move Little in Math, Reading: Improvement Appears Slight since No Child Left Behind," *Washington Post,* October 20, 2005, p. A03.

3. What We Measure

1. E. F. Lindquist, "Preliminary Considerations in Objective Test Construction," in E. F. Lindquist, ed., *Educational Measurement* (Washington, DC: American Council on Education, 1951).
2. H. D. Hoover et al., *Iowa Tests of Basic Skills, Interpretive Guide for School Administrators* (Chicago: Riverside Publishing, 2003).
3. Lindquist, "Preliminary Considerations in Objective Test Construction," 142.
4. Hoover et al., *Iowa Tests of Basic Skills, Interpretive Guide.*

4. The Evolution of American Testing

1. H. D. Hoover et al., *The Iowa Tests of Basic Skills Interpretative Guide for School Administrators, Forms K and L, Levels 5–14* (Chicago: Riverside Publishing, 1994).
2. For the full rankings, along with a table showing which differences are sta-

tistically significant and thus trustworthy, see I. V. S. Mullis et al., *TIMSS 2003 International Mathematics Report* (Chestnut Hill, MA: International Study Center, Boston College, 2004), 34, 38. Available at *http:// timss.bc.edu/timss2003i/intl_reports.html*.

3. "Standardized Tests: What Are We Trying to Measure?" *Talk of the Nation*, National Public Radio, March 21, 2002. *www.npr.org/templates/story/ story.php?storyId=1140228* (May 24, 2006).

4. See, for example, Mullis et al., *TIMSS 2003 International Mathematics Report*, Exhibit D.2, 412.

5. This impact of NAEP and Title I were first remarked upon two decades ago; see P. W. Airasian, "State Mandated Testing and Educational Reform: Context and Consequences," *American Journal of Education* 95 (1987): 393–412, and E. Roeber, "A History of Large-scale Testing Activities at the State Level," paper presented at the Indiana Governor's Symposium on ISTEP, Madison, IN, February 1988.

6. See R. M. Jaeger, "The Final Hurdle: Minimum Competency Achievement Testing," in G. R. Austin and H. Garber, eds., *The Rise and Fall of National Test Scores* (New York: Academic Press, 1982).

7. National Commission on Excellence in Education, *A Nation at Risk* (Washington, DC: U.S. Department of Education, 1983).

8. J. J. Cannell, "Nationally Normed Elementary Achievement Testing in America's Public Schools: How All 50 States Are above the National Average," *Educational Measurement: Issues and Practice* 7, no. 2 (1988): 5–9.

9. Individuals with Disabilities Education Act Amendments of 1997, 20 U.S.C. §1412(a)(17). No Child Left Behind Act of 2001, 20 U.S.C. 6311 et seq.

10. See, for example, R. L. Linn, "Assessments and Accountability," *Educational Researcher* 29, no. 2 (2000): 4–16.

5. What Test Scores Tell Us about American Kids

1. National Commission on Excellence in Education, *A Nation at Risk* (Washington, DC: U.S. Department of Education, April 1983). Available at *www.ed.gov/pubs/NatAtRisk/index.html* (accessed 8/9/05).

2. Paul E. Peterson, "A Ticket to Nowhere," *Education Next* (Spring 2003): 39–46. Quotation is from pp. 39–40.

3. National Center for Education Statistics, *The Condition of Education, 2006* (Washington, DC: U.S. Department of Education, 2006), Appendix 1, Table 7-1.

4. National Center for Education Statistics, *NAEP 2004 Trends in Academic Progress: Three Decades of Performance in Reading and Mathematics, Findings in Brief* (Washington, DC: U.S. Department of Education, 2005), 8.

5. Archived information, *Policy Brief: What the TIMSS Means for Systemic School Improvement*, November, 1998. Available at *www.ed.gov/pubs/ TIMSSBrief/student.html* (accessed 6/2/2002).

6. L. S. Grønmo, and R. V. Olsen, "TIMSS versus PISA: The Case of Pure and Applied Mathematics," paper presented at the Second IEA International Research Conference, Washington, DC, November 8–11, 2006.

7. See, for example, I. V. Mullis et al., *TIMSS 1999 International Mathematics Report* (Chestnut Hill, MA: International Study Center, Boston College, 2000), chap. 3.

8. Ibid., Exhibits 1.1 and 1.4.

9. These results can be found in I. V. S. Mullis et al., *TIMSS 2003 International Mathematics Report* (Chestnut Hill, MA: International Study Center, Boston College, 2004), 34.

10. Ibid., Exhibits 1.1 and 1.2.

11. Organisation for Economic Co-operation and Development Directorate of Education, *Learning for Tomorrow's World: First Results from PISA 2003* (Paris: OECD, 2004).

12. Warwick B. Elley, *"How in the World do Children Read?"* The Hague: International Association for the Evaluation of Educational Achievement, 1992.

6. What Influences Test Scores

1. J. S. Braswell et al., *The Nation's Report Card: Mathematics 2000* (Washington, DC: National Center for Education Statistics, 2001), 153.

2. Personal communication, February 1996.

3. W. H. Schmidt, "High-School Course-Taking: Its Relationship to Achievement," *Journal of Curriculum Studies* 15, no. 3 (1983): 311–332.

4. For example, see P. Kaufman and K. A. Rasinski, *National Education Longitudinal Study of 1988: Quality of the Responses of Eighth-Grade Students in NELS:88* (Washington, DC: U.S. Department of Education, National Center for Education Statistics, 1991).

5. N. Caplan, M. H. Choy, and J. K. Whitmore, "Indochinese Refugee Families and Academic Achievement," *Scientific American* (February 1992): 36–42; N. Caplan, M. H. Choy, and J. K. Whitmore, *Children of the Boat People: A Study of Educational Success* (Ann Arbor: University of Michigan Press, 1991).

6. B. Hart and T. R. Risley, *Meaningful Differences in the Everyday Experience of Young American Children* (Baltimore: P. H. Brooks, 1995).

7. For a discussion of this evidence, see D. Koretz, "What Happened to Test Scores, and Why?" *Educational Measurement: Issues and Practice* 11, no. 4 (Winter 1992): 7–11. More extensive discussion can be found in D. Koretz,

Educational Achievement: Explanations and Implications of Recent Trends (Washington, DC: Congressional Budget Office, August 1987).

8. Koretz, *Educational Achievement*.

7. Error and Reliability

1. No Child Left Behind Act, 20 USC 6311(b)(3)(C).

2. Massachusetts Department of Education, *Guide to the MCAS for Parents/ Guardians* (Malden, MA: Massachusetts Department of Education, n.d.), 9.

3. R. K. Hambleton et al., *Review of the Measurement Quality of the Kentucky Instructional Results Information System, 1991–1994* (Frankfort: Office of Education Accountability, Kentucky General Assembly, June 1995).

4. College Entrance Examination Board, *SAT Program Handbook 2004–2005* (New York: CEEB, 2005), 38–40.

5. College Entrance Examination Board, *Test Characteristics of the SAT: Reliability, Difficulty Levels, Completion Rates*. Available at: *www.collegeboard .com/prod_downloads/highered/ra/sat/sat-test-characteristics.pdf* (accessed 7/24/07).

6. H. D. Hoover et al., *Iowa Tests of Basic Skills, Interpretive Guide for School Administrators* (Chicago: Riverside Publishing, 2003).

7. Massachusetts Department of Education, *2003 MCAS Technical Report* (Malden, MA: Massachusetts Department of Education, 2003), 67.

8. *Washington Assessment of Student Learning, Washington Alternate Assessment System (WAAS), 2001 Technical Report* (Itasca, IL: Riverside Publishing Company, n.d.).

9. T. J. Kane, and D. O. Staiger, "The Promise and Pitfalls of Using Imprecise School Accountability Measures," *Journal of Economic Perspectives* 16, no. 4 (2002): 91–114.

10. American Educational Research Association, American Psychological Association, and National Council on Measurement in Education, *Standards for Educational and Psychological Testing* (Washington, DC: American Educational Research Association, 1999), see Standard 13.7.

8. Reporting Performance

1. *This Is Spinal Tap*, directed by Rob Reiner (1984).

2. M. Sacchetti, "Teachers' Math Skills Are Targeted," *Boston Globe*, January 2, 2007, B1, B3.

3. M. Perie, W. Grigg, and G. Dion, National Center for Education Statistics, *The Nation's Report Card: Mathematics 2005*, NCES 2006-453 (Washington, DC: U.S. Government Printing Office, 2005). See p. 16.

4. There are many methods for setting standards. The details are difficult to keep straight and are superfluous for purposes of this chapter. For those interested in pursuing this, I recommend as a starting point a very clear introduction written by Ronald Hambleton, "Setting Performance Standards on Achievement Tests: Meeting the Requirements of Title I," in L. Hansche et al., *Handbook for the Development of Performance Standards: Meeting the Requirements of Title I* (Washington, DC: Council of Chief State School Officers, 1998). Available at: *www.ccsso.org/content/pdfs/hansche.pdf.*

5. James S. Braswell et al., U.S. Department of Education, *The Nation's Report Card: Mathematics 2000* (Washington, DC: Office of Educational Research and Improvement, 2001), Figure 1.3.

6. W. J. Popham, *Criterion-Referenced Measurement* (Engelwood Cliffs, NJ: Prentice-Hall, 1978); Hambleton, "Setting Performance Standards on Achievement Tests," in Hansche, ed., *Handbook for the Development of Performance Standards, 87–115.*

7. R. M. Jaeger, "certification of Student Competence," in R. L. Linn, ed., *Educational Measurement,* 3rd ed. (New York: American Council on Education/Macmillan, 1989), 485–514.

8. For example, see R. L. Linn, "Performance Standards: Utility for Different Uses of Assessments," *Education Policy Analysis Archives* 11, no. 3 (2003); available at: *http://epaa.asu.edu/epaa/v11n31/* (accessed 6/30/06; journal available only in electronic form, and articles have no page numbers within issues); and L. A. Shepard, "Implications for Standard Setting of the National Academy of Education Evaluation of the National Assessment of Educational Progress Achievement Levels," in *Proceeding of the Joint Conference on Standard Setting for Large-Scale Assessments,* vol. 2 (Washington, DC: National Assessment Governing Board and National Center for Education Statistics, 1994), 143–160.

9. R. M. Hauser, C. F. Edley Jr., J. A. Koenig, and S. W. Elliott, eds., *Measuring Literacy: Performance Levels for Adults, Interim Report* (Washington, DC: National Academies Press, 2005), Tables 5-5b and 5-5c.

10. For data on state standards, see L. Olson, "Defying Predictions, State Trends Prove Mixed on Schools Making NCLB Targets," *Education Week,* September 7, 2005, and associated tables; these are available at: *www.edweek.org/ew/articles/2005/09/07/02ayp.h25.html?qs=_defying_predictions_.* (accessed 1/5/07). For data on states' percentages proficient on NAEP, see Perie, Grigg, and Dion, *The Nation's Report Card.*

11. H. I. Braun and Jiahe Qian, "An Enhanced Method for Mapping State Standards onto the NAEP Scale," in N. J. Dorans, M. Pommerich, and

P. W. Holland, ed., *Linking and Aligning Scores and Scales* (New York: Springer-Verlag, 2007), 313–338.

12. H. D. Hoover, "Some Common Misconceptions about Tests and Testing," *Educational Measurement: Issues and Practice* 22, no. 1 (2003): 5–13.

13. E. H. Haertel and D. E. Wiley, "Response to the OEA Panel Report, 'Review of the Measurement Quality of the Kentucky Instructional Results Information System, 1991–1994,'" unpublished paper prepared for the Kentucky Department of Education and Advanced Systems in Measurement and Evaluation, 1995.

14. See, for example, R. M. Hauser et al., eds., *Measuring Literacy: Performance Levels for Adults* (Washington, DC: National Academies Press, 2005).

15. R. L. Linn, "Assessments and Accountability," *Educational Researcher* 29, no. 2 (2000): 4–16.

16. Linn, "Performance Standards: Utility for Different Uses of Assessments."

17. See, for example, Perie, Grigg, and Dion, *The Nation's Report Card*, 14.

18. College Board, *2005 College-Bound Seniors* (New York: College Board, 2005).

9. Validity

1. J. Macur, "Testing Is Just First Step in Case against Landis," *New York Times*, August 5, 2006.

2. C. Bradley and E. Posner, "Signing Statements: It's a President's Right," *Boston Globe*, August 3, 2006, A11.

3. *House Call with Sanjay Gupta: A Look at What Causes Headaches*, September 25, 2004. From *http://transcripts.cnn.com/TRANSCRIPTS/0409/25/hcsg.00 .html* (accessed 8/21/06).

4. This task can be found at *http://pals.sri.com/tasks/5–8/ME127/* (accessed 1/10/07).

5. For example, see L. S. Hamilton, E. M. Nussbaum, and R. E. Snow, "Interview Procedures for Validating Science Assessments," *Applied Measurement in Education* 10 (1997): 181–200.

6. D. Koretz et al., "The Vermont Portfolio Assessment Program: Findings and Implications," *Educational Measurement: Issues and Practice* 13, no. 3 (1994): 5–16.

7. R. K. Hambleton et al., *Review of the Measurement Quality of the Kentucky Instructional Results Information System, 1991–1994* (Frankfort: Office of Education Accountability, Kentucky General Assembly, June 1995.

8. J. P. Greene, M. A. Winters, and G. Foster, *Testing High Stakes Tests: Can We Believe the Results of Accountability Tests?* Civic Report 33, Executive Summary (New York: The Manhattan Institute, 2003).

9. Hamilton, Nussbaum, and Snow, "Interview Procedures for Validating Science Assessments."

10. Inflated Test Scores

1. See, for example, R. L. Linn and S. B. Dunbar, "The Nation's Report Card Goes Home: Good News and Bad about Trends in Achievement," *Phi Delta Kappan* 72, no. 2 (October 1990): 127–133; B. Fuller et al., *Is the No Child Left Behind Act Working? The Reliability of How States Track Achievement* (Berkeley: University of California, Policy Analysis for California Education, 2006).

2. Donald T. Campbell, "Assessing the Impact of Planned Social Change," in G. M. Lyons, ed., *Social Research and Public Policies: The Dartmouth/OECD Conference* (Hanover, NH: Public Affairs Center, Dartmouth College, 1975), 35.

3. L. Zuckerman, "Airline Math, an Early Arrival Doesn't Mean You Won't Be Late," *New York Times*, December 26, 2000.

4. See, for example, A. Hickman et al., "Did Sun Cheat?" *PC Magazine*, January 6, 1997; and P. H. Lewis, "How Fast Is Your System? That Depends on the Test," *New York Times*, September 10, 1998, E1.

5. J. Markoff, "Chip Maker Takes Issue with a Test for Speed," *New York Times*, August 27, 2002, C3.

6. J. H. Cushman, "Makers of Diesel Truck Engines Are under Pollution Inquiry," *New York Times*, February 11, 1998.

7. P. Farhi, "Television's 'Sweeps' Stakes: Season of the Sensational Called a Context Out of Control," *Washington Post*, November 17, 1996, A01.

8. M. Santora, "Cardiologists Say Rankings Sway Choices on Surgery," *New York Times*, January 11, 2005.

9. S. P. Klein et al., *What Do Test Scores in Texas Tell Us?* Issue Paper IP-202 (Santa Monica, CA: Rand, 2000). Available at: *www/rand.org/publications/IP/IP202/*.

10. For a good overview of some of the most important research on teachers' and principals' responses to testing, see B. Stecher, "Consequences of Large-Scale, High-Stakes Testing on School and Classroom Practice," in L. Hamilton et al., *Test-Based Accountability: A Guide for Practitioners and Policymakers*, (Santa Monica, CA: Rand, 2002). Available at: *www.rand.org/publications/MR/MR1554/MR1554.ch4.pdf.*

11. J. Rubinstein, *Princeton Review: Cracking the MCAS Grade 10 Mathematics* (New York: Random House, 2000), 15.

12. J. Rubinstein, *Princeton Review: Cracking the MCAS Grade 10 Mathematics*, p. 31.

13. V. Strauss, "Review Tests Go Too Far, Critics Say," *Washington Post*, July 10, 2001, A09.

11. Adverse Impact and Bias

1. These data and evidence of the strong relationship between the percent taking the test and state mean scores can be found in E. B. Page and H. Feifs, "SAT Scores and American States: Seeking for Useful Meaning," *Journal of Educational Measurement* 22, no. 4 (1985): 305–312.

2. See *www.ucop.edu/news/factsheets/2006/fall_2006_admissions_table_c.pdf* (accessed 2/6/07).

3. College Board, *2006 College-Bound Seniors* (New York: College Entrance Examination Board, 2006).

4. See *www.usnews.com/usnews/edu/college/rankings/brief/t1natudoc_brief.php* (accessed 3/23/07).

5. For a review of gender differences in performance on many tests, see Warren W. Willingham and Nancy S. Cole, *Gender and Fair Assessment* (Mahwah, NJ: Lawrence Erlbaum, 1997). The most recent NAEP results can be found in National Center for Education Statistics, *The Nation's Report Card: Mathematics 2005* (Washington, DC: U.S. Department of Education, 2005).

6. See B. Bridgeman, L. McCamley-Jenkins, and N. Ervin, *Prediction of Freshman Grade-Point Average from the Revised and Recentered SAT I: Reasoning Test*, College Board Research Report No. 2000-1, ETS RR No. 00-1 (New York: College Entrance Examination Board, 2000).

12. Testing Students with Special Needs

1. National Research Council, Committee on Goals 2000 and the Inclusion of Students with Disabilities, *Educating One and All: Students with Disabilities and Standards-Based Reform* (Washington, DC: National Academy Press, 1997), 103.

2. R. C. Kessler et al., "Prevalence, Severity, and Comorbidity of Twelve-Month DSM-IV Disorders in the National Comorbidity Survey Replication (NCS-R)," *Archives of General Psychology* 63, no. 6 (2005): 617–627.

3. 29 U.S.C. §§794 et seq.; also, the Americans with Disabilities Act (42 U.S.C. §§121011 et seq.) and the Goals 2000: Educate America Act (20 U.S.C. §§5801 et seq.).

4. 20 U.S.C. § 1412(a)(17).

5. 20 U.S.C. 6311 (b)(3)(C).

6. M. Rogosta and B. Kaplan, "Views of Disabled Students," in W. W. Willingham et al., eds., *Testing Handicapped People* (Boston: Allyn and Bacon, 1988), 57–70.

7. For an interesting discussion of this example and related research, see *www.mrc-cbu.cam.ac.uk/personal/matt.davis/Cmabrigde/*.

8. W. W. Willingham et al., *Testing Handicapped People* (Boston: Allyn and Bacon, 1988), 129.

9. *Southeastern Community College v. Davis*, 442 U.S. 397 (1979). For a discussion of the case, see *http://caselaw.lp.findlaw.com/scripts/getcase.pl?court=US&vol=442&invol=397* (accessed 7/21/06).

10. M. L. Thurlow et al., *2001 State Policies on Assessment Participation and Accommodations*, Synthesis Report 46 (Minneapolis: University of Minnesota, National Center on Educational Outcomes, 2002). Available at *http://education.umn.edu/NCEO/OnlinePubs/Synthesis46.html* (accessed 10/21/07).

11. National Research Council, *Educating One and All*, 177–178.

12. For the notice of proposed rulemaking, see *Federal Register*, March 30, 2003, 13796ff. For the final implementing regulations, see *Federal Register*, December 9, 2003, 68698ff. The explanation for the excision of references to students performing three standard deviations below the mean can be found on p. 68704.

13. 20 U.S.C. §6311(b)(1)(D)(ii)(II).

14. W. Piper, *The Little Engine That Could* (New York: Platt and Munk, 1930).

15. See *Federal Register*, April 7, 2007, 17748ff.

16. Ibid., 17748.

13. Sensible Uses of Tests

1. K. W. Arenson, "Math and Science Tests Find 4th and 8th Graders in U.S. Still Lag Many Peers," *New York Times*, December 15, 2004. Available at: *www.nytimes.com/2004/12/15/education/15math.html?ex=1175227200&en=c9be2729f4b06bcd&ei=5070* (accessed 3/27/07).

2. National Center for Education Statistics, "International Comparisons in Education, Trends in International Mathematics and Science Study: Mathematics and Science Achievement of Eighth-Graders in 1999." Available at: *http://nces.ed.gov/timss/results99_1.asp* (accessed 3/27/07).

3. Kentucky Department of Education, *KIRIS Accountability Cycle 2 Technical Manual* (Frankfort: Kentucky Department of Education, 1997), 14–17.

4. D. T. Campbell, "Assessing the Impact of Planned Social Change," in G. M. Lyons, ed., *Social Research and Public Policies* (Hanover, NH: Public Affairs Center, Dartmouth College, 1975), 3–45.

Acknowledgments

One evening some years ago, several students who had taken one of my courses in educational measurement attended a lecture given by one of the nation's most important education policy-makers. The students were angered by his presentation, less because many of his claims about educational testing were dead wrong than because he presented them with so much certainty and self-assurance nonetheless. I encounter this sort of reaction from students fairly often. One of these three, however, was unusually upset and wrote me a long and irate e-mail about it late that night. She ended by telling me that I needed to write a book that would help lay people understand educational testing. I had been thinking about this for some time, and her note was the tipping point. So to begin, I want to thank the many former students who have urged me to write this book—especially Marina Lang, who sent me the e-mail that night, and Chris Olson Lanier, a former acquisitions editor who shared her expertise and got me moving.

I owe thanks to many others for help with this effort. I want to express my gratitude to the Carnegie Corporation of New York, and especially to Dan Fallon, chair of the foundation's Education Division, for helping to support this work. I am indebted to my editor at Harvard University Press, Elizabeth Knoll, who lived up to her considerable reputation, always offering helpful and insightful guidance and providing needed criticism with remarkable tact. Like most academics, I usually dislike having anyone fiddle with my text, but I eagerly awaited the packages with Elizabeth's comments. I am indebted to my wife, Doreen Koretz, for encouraging me to write the book and then suffering the consequences with good humor and her usual patience. I thank the many colleagues and friends without whose enthusiasm for the goals of this book it would have been much harder to persevere. And finally, as someone who has taught at almost all levels from fourth grade through graduate school and who takes teaching very seriously, I want to thank the many colleagues who have taught me so much. There are far too many to mention them all, but there are two I must single out: H. D. Hoover, professor emeritus at the University of Iowa, and Robert Linn, professor emeritus at the University of Colorado, eminent scholars and good friends who have been unfailingly generous in sharing their expertise over many years.

Index